JUST THE FACTS ABOUT ABOUT WASHINGTON, D.C.

ALBERT E. KENNEDY

A & N BOOKS, LLC

Printed in the U.S.A. by
Signature Book Printing, Inc.
8041 Cessna Avenue
Gaithersburg, MD 20879
301-258-8353

To order *Just The Facts About Washington, D.C.* directly
from the author, please visit our website at
www.home.earthlink.net/~abekennedy or write to A & N
Books, LLC, P.O. Box 1094, La Plata, MD 20646-1094.

ISBN 978-0-578-05779-8

PREFACE

As long time Washington-area residents who appreciate the endless selection of things to see and do, my wife, Nancy, and I visit and revisit the many monuments, memorials, and museums within a short drive from our doorstep.

Always on the lookout for information about the places we visit, we noticed two similarities about the written sources of information. First, most of the sources required the reading of several pages of text before finding a single interesting fact, and second, no one source consolidated the many facts under one cover.

Just The Facts About Washington, D.C. is intended to provide the reader with facts without the fluff. However, more specifically, it is intended to educate the families, teachers, students, and amateur history buffs about the lives of the people who are celebrated through the monuments, memorials, and exhibits at the museums.

So enjoy your trip through history!!!!!!!!!!

ABOUT THE AUTHOR

As a Vietnam-era veteran, Albert "Abe" Kennedy retired as a chief master sergeant from the United States Air Force after 22 years of service. He earned a Bachelor of Arts degree in business from Kansas-Newman University and a Master of Arts degree in business from Central Michigan University. He also earned an Associates of Arts degree in paralegal studies from the Community College of the Air Force and a teaching certification in social studies through the College of Notre Dame of Maryland.

Much of his spare time is spent reading about and visiting places of interest to find that elusive fact about the history of the United States and the lives of the men and women who contributed to this history.

DEDICATIONS

Dedicated to Nancy♥♥ – My wonderful and loving wife, terrific travel companion, editor, and invaluable contributor to this book.

And a special dedication to all of our men and women in the United States military who have served, protected, and sacrificed for our country. Thank you.

TABLE OF CONTENTS

FACTS ABOUT THE NATIONAL ARCHIVES 97

FACTS ABOUT THE FORD'S THEATRE.................105

FACTS ABOUT THE PETERSEN HOUSE.......................115

FACTS ABOUT THE UNITED STATES HOLOCAUST MEMORIAL MUSEUM 118

FACTS ABOUT ARLINGTON NATIONAL CEMETERY

FACTS ABOUT THE KENNEDY GRAVESITES AT ARLINGTON NATIONAL CEMETERY

FACTS ABOUT THE TOMB OF THE UNKNOWNS AT ARLINGTON NATIONAL CEMETERY

FACTS ABOUT THE MEMORIAL AMPHITHEATER AT ARLINGTON NATIONAL CEMETERY

FACTS ABOUT THE CITY OF WASHINGTON, D.C.

During the past two centuries, several generations of Americans have witnessed dramatic changes to a city located on a site previously occupied by the Manahoac, Monacan, and Piscataway Indian tribes. Its new citizens described the early city as a "howling and malarious wilderness in the woods." Not only has Washington, D.C. grown to become one of the most powerful seats of government, it has also become a center for culture; offering visitors from around the world a wide range of attractions and an almost unlimited source of entertainment. However, before you start your amazing journey through the many attractions offered by this city on the Potomac, take a few minutes to learn about how a little patch of wilderness evolved into a city that many citizens and visitors believe symbolizes a nation dedicated to democracy....Our Nation's Capital.

SELECTING THE SITE FOR THE CAPITAL OF THE UNITED STATES AND THE CITY'S EVOLUTION

1. The Residence Act of July 16, 1790, directed the federal government to establish a permanent capital city for the federal government before the year 1800.

2. The Residence Act also authorized the President of the United States, who was then George Washington (1789-1797), the power to select the permanent seat of government.

3. President Washington was authorized to choose a site for the nation's capital city on land that stretched from the east bank of the Potomac River between the mouth of the Eastern Branch to a site nearly 70 miles northwest on the east bank of the Connogocheague Creek (now Conococheague) near Hagerstown, Maryland.

4. Other areas seriously considered for the permanent site of the nation's capital were near Germantown, Pennsylvania, and the cities of Baltimore, Maryland, Philadelphia, Pennsylvania, and New York City, New York.

5. The selection of the permanent site of the federal government resulted from a compromise between the southern and northern states. Representatives from the northern states wanted the seat of government at a site further north, the southern states wanted it further south. As a compromise, one that garnered the support of the northern states for a seat of government further south was the federal government's offer to accept the $21,500,000 in war debts accumulated by both the northern and southern states during the Revolutionary War.

View of Washington, D.C.

6. In 1788, Maryland ceded approximately 69 square miles of land and in 1789, Virginia ceded an additional 31 square miles to the federal government for the site of the U.S. Capital.

7. The original landmass of Washington, D.C. totaled approximately ten-miles-square or 100 square miles.

8. Because the land offered by Virginia was retroceded (returned) to Virginia in 1846, all of the land on which the capital now stands rests on soil that was formerly a part of Maryland.

9. President Washington appointed city commissioners to administer the city.

10. The site of the new *National City* was initially referred to as *Federal City*. A term often credited to George Washington.

11. On September 9, 1791, the new city was officially renamed *Washington*, in honor of the first President of the United States, George Washington (1789-1797).

12. Its designation as the *District of Columbia* (D.C.) honors the memory of Christopher Columbus.

13. On March 30, 1791, nineteen landowners transferred land to the federal government for the site of the nation's capital. (The names of these men are on a monument in the Ellipse south of the White House.) It was agreed that the landowners would receive half the city lots platted on their former holdings, as well as $66.67 an acre for as much land as was needed by the government for public buildings and public improvements. The government would retain half the lots and all the land designed for streets. The government intended to use the sale of the lots to fund the construction of the city. George Washington purchased six lots. Two of these lots were purchased for $606.97 in 1799, and are located across from the Union Station Plaza. A plaque near the Senate Gate Fountain, as photographed above, describes the purchase.

14. President Washington commissioned Pierre Charles L'Enfant to survey and plan the city. However, because of L'Enfant's disagreements with the city's commissioners, he was dismissed in 1792 without fully completing his assignments.

15. President Washington then chose Andrew Ellicott from Maryland, and his assistant, Benjamin Banneker, to survey the land destined to become Washington, D.C. Fortunately, L'Enfant had his plans engraved in 1791, and had briefed President Washington on their contents.

16. Benjamin Banneker was a self-educated freed Negro and a prominent astronomer and mathematician.

17. On April 15, 1791, surveyor Andrew Ellicott installed the first of 40 stones that marked the boundaries of the new city. The sandstone markers, rising approximately two feet off the ground, were placed at one-mile intervals around the city during 1791 and 1792. They formed the diamond–shaped territory of the nation's capital – 14 on Virginia land and 26 on Maryland land. Of the original 40 stones, 38 remain embedded at their original locations.

18. Each marker was inscribed with the magnetic compass reading, and the words Jurisdiction of the United States, the name of the state where it was located, either Virginia or Maryland, the mile number, and the year it was placed at the location.

3

19. The four corner stones that were installed to mark the boundaries of the city of Washington, D.C. still exist. The north cornerstone is located just off East-West Highway near Silver Spring, Maryland, with the east cornerstone being located just off the intersection of Eastern and Southern Avenues near Seat Pleasant, Maryland. The west cornerstone is off Arizona Avenue, near Falls Church, Virginia, and the southern cornerstone, the first cornerstone to be laid, is located at the southern tip of Jones Point, Virginia, near what is now the Wilson Bridge.

20. On December 1, 1800, the federal capital was transferred from Philadelphia, Pennsylvania, to Washington, D.C.

21. At the time of the 1800 census, the population of Washington, D.C. included 10,066 whites, 793 free Negroes, and 3,244 slaves.

UNIQUE FACTS ABOUT WASHINGTON, D.C.

1. Temperatures in Washington, D.C. average 27 degrees Fahrenheit during January and 88 degrees in July.

2. Washington, D.C. receives an average of 40 inches of precipitation over the course of the year.

View of Washington, D.C. from Arlington Cemetery

3. Washington, D.C. is divided into four parts - Southeast, Southwest, Northeast, and Northwest. These four parts meet at the U.S. Capitol Building.

4. The District flower is the American Beauty Rose.

5. The District bird is the Wood Thrush.

6. The District tree is the Scarlet Oak.

7. The motto of Washington, D.C. is "*Justitia Omnibus* - Justice for all."

8. At 409 feet, the highest natural point in Washington, D.C. is at Fort Reno National Park in the Tenleytown neighborhood of northwest Washington. The fort was one of the locations attacked by Confederate General Jubal Early in July 1864. After the Civil War, the area was used as a *Freetown* for former slaves.

9. Since 1938, the flag of Washington, D.C. has consisted of three red stars above two horizontal red stripes on a white field. This pattern, designed by Charles Dunn, is based on the coat-of-arms used by the family of George Washington.

Flag of Washington, D.C.

10. In 1802, President Thomas Jefferson (1801-1809) appointed Robert Brent as the first mayor of Washington, D.C.

11. In 1850, Washington, D.C. became the first large city to abolish slave trading. Slavery was outlawed in Washington, D.C. in April 1862.

12. In the early 1870s, the Board of Public Works, headed by Alexander R. Shepherd, oversaw the creation of 120 miles of sewers, 150 miles of road improvements, 280 miles of sidewalks, 30 miles of water mains, 39 miles of gas lines, 3.5 million cubic yards of excavation, and the planting of more than 60,000 trees.

13. In 1895, the first underground trolley system was constructed in Washington, D.C. This limited trolley evolved into the current extensive Metro system that speeds workers and visitors to all points within Washington, D.C.

14. In 1950, the population of Washington, D.C. peaked at just over 800,000 people. During the past few years the population of the city has averaged between 550,000 and 600,000 citizens.

15. It was not until the presidential election of 1964 that the citizens of Washington, D.C. could vote in presidential elections. The 23rd Amendment to the U.S. Constitution, which was ratified on March 29, 1961, granted this voting right.

FACTS ABOUT THE CAPITOL BUILDING

President George Washington (1789-1797) accepted the challenge of overseeing the construction of the U.S. Capitol Building. To accomplish his goal, a site had to be selected, money appropriated, designers hired, diagrams approved, conflicts resolved, and work completed. However, even with all the encountered problems, the efforts of the president, the members of Congress, and the countless ordinary Americans who participated in the planning and construction of the Capitol Building, saw their ideas and labor evolve into a symbol of democracy that is immediately recognized by visitors to Washington, D.C. – The U.S. Capitol Building.

THE CONGRESS OF THE UNITED STATES

1. There are three branches of the United States government. The legislative branch makes the laws (Congress), the executive branch carries out the laws (headed by the president), and the judicial branch (Supreme Court) interprets the laws to determine if they are lawful according to the U.S. Constitution.

2. The Congress of the United States was created by Article I of the United States Constitution.

3. Two houses of government form Congress. These houses are the Senate and the House of Representatives.

4. The Senate consists of 100 senators – two from each of the 50 states.

5. To qualify as a senator, a candidate must be at least 30 years of age, a U.S. citizen for at least nine years, and a resident of the state he/she is elected to serve.

6. U.S. Senators are elected for a period of six years. One-third of the senators are elected/re-elected every two years.

7. There are 435 members of the House of Representatives.

8. Each state of the United States has at least one representative in the House of Representatives. Elected for two-year terms.

9. State representation in the House of Representatives is proportional to its population. More representatives are elected to represent the more densely populated states and fewer representatives are elected to represent the states with smaller populations. Members of Congress represent districts within their states.

10. To qualify as a member of the House of Representatives, a candidate must be at least 25 years of age, a U.S. citizen for at least seven years, and a resident of the state he/she serves.

THE LOCATIONS AND EVOLUTION OF THE CAPITOL BUILDING

1. Before 1791, the federal government had no permanent site. The early sessions of Congresses met in eight different cities: Philadelphia, Pennsylvania; Baltimore, Maryland; Lancaster, Pennsylvania; York, Pennsylvania; Princeton, New Jersey; Annapolis, Maryland; Trenton, New Jersey; and New York City, New York.

2. Between 1789 and 1790, Congress convened in Federal Hall in New York City, New York.

3. Between 1790 and 1800, Congress convened in Congress Hall in Philadelphia, Pennsylvania.

4. The same three commissioners appointed by George Washington to oversee the construction of Washington, D.C. also oversaw the construction of the Capitol Building.

5. Pierre Charles L'Enfant was initially tasked with designing the Capitol Building, but he was fired when he chose not to accept the authority of the D.C. Building Commission and to provide the Commission with any designs or drawings. He claimed the plans were in his head and the commission should trust him.

6. After L'Enfant was fired, Secretary of State Thomas Jefferson suggested that a $500 prize and a city lot be awarded for the best Capitol Building plan.

7. On April 5, 1793, the D.C. Building Commission accepted the plan proposed by Dr. William Thorton from the 18 submitted plans. Thorton was from the British West Indies.

8. Benjamin Henry Latrobe was appointed the first architect responsible for supervising the construction of the Capitol Building.

9. In August 1793 workman started digging the foundation. On September 18, 1793, President George Washington (1789-1797) dedicated the first cornerstone for the Capitol Building in the southeast corner of the building.

10. No surviving records have revealed where the first cornerstone was placed, and the cornerstone has never been rediscovered. The most recent unsuccessful search for the cornerstone was in 1998.

11. Most of the original Capitol Building was constructed primarily out of sandstone from the quarries at Aquia, Virginia. The sandstone was replaced with marble and granite as the Capitol Building expanded.

12. On November 22, 1800, the first session of Congress in the new Capitol Building was convened. It consisted of 32 members of the Senate and 106 members of the House of Representatives.

U. S. Capitol Building

13. The Capitol Building is located on Capitol Hill at the east end of the National Mall.

14. The Capitol Building on Capitol Hill is located on what was formerly known as *Jenkins' Hill* or *Jenkins' Heights*.

15. The plateau on which the Capitol Building is located is 88 feet above the level of the Potomac River.

16. The boundaries of the Capitol grounds are Independence Avenue on the south and Constitution Avenue on the north. First Street on the northeast/southeast forms the eastern boundary and First Street on the northwest/southwest forms the western boundary.

17. In 1801, the United States Supreme Court and the courts of the District of Columbia occupied the Capitol Building.

18. In 1814, a covered one-story walkway connected the chambers of the House of Representatives and Senate.

19. On August 24, 1814, the British Army burned the Capitol Building.

20. If it had not been for the rain during a very bad thunderstorm soon after the torch was set to the Capitol Building, the building would have sustained considerably more damage. Some historians believe the storm was actually a hurricane.

21. After the burning of the Capitol Building by the British Army, Congress met in a brick building on the site of the present day U.S. Supreme Court. The structure was referred to as the *Old Brick Capitol.*

22. On December 6, 1819, five years after the British attack, Congress reoccupied the Capitol Building for a second time.

23. The Capitol Building is the centerpiece of the Capitol Complex, which includes six principal Congressional office buildings and three Library of Congress buildings constructed on Capitol Hill during the 19th and 20th centuries.

24. The cornerstones of the new wings to the Capitol Building, which currently house the Senate and the House of Representatives, were dedicated during ceremonies on July 4, 1851. The House of Representatives occupied its chamber in 1857 and the Senate in 1859.

25. In 1959, President Dwight Eisenhower (1953-1961) dedicated the fourth and final cornerstone of the Capitol Building.

THE DESIGN AND SIZE OF THE CAPITOL BUILDING

1. Through a series of eight major construction projects, the exterior of the Capitol Building has been expanded from a single small building, housing both the Senate and House of Representatives, to its current size. Viewing the Capitol Building from the National Mall, the below shaded blocks show the construction of the original building (1st Wing) and five of the seven additions to the exterior as they occurred.

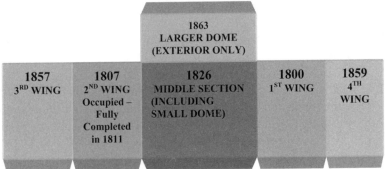

Stages of Construction – U.S. Capitol Building

2. Between 1884 and 1891, the sixth addition to the Capitol Building, which consisted of adding marble terraces to the north, west, and south sides of the Capitol, was completed.

3. Between 1959 and 1963, the seventh addition saw the construction of the largest modification to the Capitol Building since the exterior of the Capitol dome was finished in 1863. During the four-year project the old east front of the Capitol Building was torn down and duplicated in marble. The construction also extended the front of the Capitol Building by 32 feet.

4. In addition to the major projects described above, there have been several other projects to strengthen, renovate, and preserve the Capitol Building.

5. The exterior of the larger dome was completed in December 1863. The interior of the dome was completed in January 1866.

6. Excluding the visitor center, the Capitol Building contains 540 rooms, 658 windows, and 850 doorways on five levels.

7. The design of the Capitol Building is 19th century neoclassical architecture derived from ancient Greek and Roman designs.

8. The Capitol Building covers 175,170 square feet of the grounds, or approximately four acres.

9. The floors within the Capitol Building cover approximately 16-1/2 acres.

10. The length of the Capitol Building from north to south is 751 feet.

11. The greatest width of the Capitol Building, including approaches, is 350 feet.

12. The height of the Capitol Building from the baseline to the top of the statue of Freedom is 288 feet.

13. Twenty-four columns grace the west face (National Mall side) of the Capitol Building. Each column was crafted from Potomac freestone, which is 240 feet long by 3 feet in diameter.

14. There are pediments over the entrance to the central section of the Capitol Building and the entrances to the House of Representatives and Senate (East Front). A pediment is a form of classical architecture in a triangular space forming the gable of a pitched room with carved figures in the interior. These allegorical figures, representing a symbolic portrayal of an idea or principle, were raised by crane onto their positions.

15. The primary entrances to the Capitol Building for the members of Congress, their staff, and visitors who have business at the Capitol are through three porticos. A portico is a colonnaded (columned) porch found on Classical and Neoclassical buildings, usually with a pediment above. The pediments over the entrances to the Capitol Building are titled and symbolize the following:

   • Central Portico - The original pediment was completed in 1828. Titled *The Genius of America*, it is 12 feet high by 60 feet wide. The central figure represents America, with the figure on her right representing Hope and on her left representing Justice.

The implication is that America may hope for success so long as she cultivates justice. This is the entrance that was used by most visitors to the Capitol Building prior to the construction of the visitor center.

- In 1959-1960, the Central Portico was replaced with the marble reproduction that is seen today.

- Senate Portico - Completed in 1863, the 12-foot-high by 60-foot-wide pediment is titled *The Progress of Civilization.* The central figure represents America. The figures on her right represent the confrontation between American pioneers and the American Indians. The figures on her left represent the advantages of liberty and civilization.

- House of Representatives Portico - Completed in 1916, the 12-foot-high by 60-foot-wide pediment is titled *The Apotheosis of Democracy.* The central figure represents Armed Peace and its protection of Industry on the left and Agriculture on the right. The waves on each side of the portico represent the Atlantic Ocean and Pacific Ocean.

16. Beneath the porticos are doors that lead to the Rotunda, House of Representatives, and the Senate. The doors symbolize the following:

- Rotunda - Columbus Doors. Completed in 1858, the doors reflect on the life and accomplishments of Christopher Columbus.

- House of Representatives - American Revolutionary War Doors. Completed in 1905, the 8-foot-wide by 15-foot-high doors reflect on the events of the American Revolutionary War.

- Senate - George Washington and the Revolutionary War Doors. Completed in 1868, the 7-foot-wide by 14-foot-high doors reflect on the life of Washington as a farmer, soldier, and President of the United States. The marble figures over the door symbolize Justice and History.

THE CAPITOL VISITOR CENTER

1. Construction on the visitor center began in August 2002 and was dedicated on December 2, 2008 at a cost of $621 million. This date marked the 145th anniversary of the completion of the Capitol Dome — December 2, 1863. The original plaster model for the Statue of Freedom greets visitors at the entrance to the Exhibition Hall.

Visitor Center showing Plaster Model of Statue of Freedom

2. Facts about the Visitor Center include:

   - Size - 580,000 square-feet, three-story, underground complex.
   - The floor of the atrium is 35 feet below ground.
   - 20,000 square-feet Great Hall – Bill H.R. 3315 changed the name to Emancipation Hall, in honor of the 400 to 600 slaves and freed slaves who contributed to the construction of the Capitol Building.
   - 16,500 square-feet Exhibition Hall, which can comfortably hold 4,000 visitors.

Head of the Statue of Freedom

   - There are six skylights, two of which measure 20 feet by 70 feet.
   - The shape and orientation of the visitor center encompasses 170,000 square feet of space for the House and Senate.
   - Twenty-four statues of notable citizens are displayed in the visitor center. The statues represent the diversity of the United States.
   - The Wall of Aspirations is a 186-foot-long marble wall that has encased, in special display cases, historic documents from the Library of Congress and the National Archives.
   - Computers provide short backgrounds about the Capitol Building and the governing bodies it houses.
   - Six alcoves house artifacts, documents, images and videos to tell the story of Congress and the establishment of American democracy.
   - A 13-minute film, "One of Many" is shown at the start of the tour through the Capitol Building.

3. Benjamin French designed the catafalque on which Lincoln's body lay in state in the Rotunda between April 19th and April 21st 1865. The catafalque for Lincoln consisted simply of pine boards nailed together and covered with black broadcloth. Over the years the base and platform have been modified and reinforced to accommodate the remains of the honored dead who lay in state in the Rotunda. The fabric has been replaced, but its draping follows the 1865 style. Presently the catafalque measures 7 feet 1 inch long, 2 feet 6 inches wide, and 2 feet high. The base is 8 feet 10 inches long, 4 feet 3-1/2 inches wide and 2 inches high. The platform is 11 feet 1 inch long, 6 feet wide and 9-1/4 inches high. The word catafalque means half casket. This is because bodies were often placed directly on the structure without being placed in a casket.

Catafalque displayed in the Capitol Visitor Center

THE CAPITOL GROUNDS

1. The Capitol grounds total 274 acres. The grounds immediately surrounding the Capitol Building, as bordered by a stonewall; cover an area of a little over 58 acres of this total.

2. Law Olmsted designed the grounds around the Capitol Building after his commission in 1874. He is also credited with designing Central Park in New York City.

3. Six massive red granite lamp piers, topped with light fixtures in wrought-iron cages, and sixteen smaller bronze light fixtures line the Capitol Plaza at the East Capitol Street entrance. The roofed bench at the East Capitol Street entrance was originally a shelter for streetcar passengers.

UNIQUE FACTS ABOUT THE CAPITOL BUILDING

1. The term *Capitoline Hill* (kăp'ĭtəlĭn') or *Capitol*, is a Latin term meaning highest of the seven hills of ancient Rome, the historic, religious, and government center of the city. The great temple of Jupiter Capitolinus was dedicated in 509 B.C.

2. The Library of Congress was located in the west wing of the Capitol Building at the time it was gutted by fire in 1851.

14

3. Running water was installed in the Capitol Building in 1832, gas lighting in the 1840s, electricity in 1885, and steam heat in 1902. The first elevator was operational in 1874 and electric air conditioning was installed in 1929. Prior to electric air conditioning being installed, a system of using ice and fans under the floors was the primary source for cooling the building.

4. The Old Supreme Court Chamber, the Old Senate Chamber, and the National Statuary Hall were restored to their mid-19th century appearance for the nation's 1976 Bicentennial celebration.

5. Over thirty layers of white paint have been removed from the exterior of the Capitol Building.

6. The first Capitol office building was constructed in 1908. Prior to 1908, the members of Congress rented their own office space in downtown Washington, D.C.

7. In 1897, electric lighting replaced gas lighting on the Capitol grounds.

8. In response to complaints from members of Congress about the poor air quality in their windowless chambers, two air-intake towers were installed to allow fresh air into the chambers of the Senate and the House of Representatives. The tower for the House of Representatives was completed in 1879 and the tower for the Senate was completed in 1889. The towers can still be seen.

9. The flags that fly over the east and west sides of the Capitol Building are 8 feet by 12 feet.

10. The tradition of flying the United States flags over the east and west fronts of the Capitol Building 24-hours a day began during World War I. It is not known when the tradition of flying the flags over the Capitol Building for any part of the day was begun.

11. Over 3,000 soldiers were barracked in the Capitol Building during the early stages of the Civil War. Later it was converted to a hospital with over 1,500 cots for patients. The soldiers referred to the building as the *Big Tent*.

12. In 1844, it was in the Capitol Building that Samuel F.B. Morse first demonstrated the telegraph. Morse tapped out the message "What hath God wrought?" from Washington, D.C. to Baltimore, Maryland.

13. There is really no front or back to the Capitol Building. What visitors refer to as the front side (facing the National Mall) is the garden side and the other side is the carriage side.

14. The Capitol Building was constructed using sandstone, limestone, marble, and concrete. The exterior walls of the Capitol Building's center structure have been treated with special consolidants and painted to match the marble wings.

15. President James Monroe (1817-1825) did not want to offend the members of the House of Representatives or Senate by taking the presidential oath of office in a particular chamber. As a result, he started a tradition in 1817 by taking the oath of office outside the temporary Capitol Building on the site where the U.S. Supreme Court Building is now located. This tradition continues as modern-day presidents take the oath of office on the exterior steps of the current Capitol Building.

16. President Andrew Jackson (1829-1837) was the first president to take the oath of office on the east portico of the current Capitol Building. This portico faces the Supreme Court.

17. President Ronald Reagan (1981-1989) was the first president to take the oath of office on the west portico of the Capitol Building. This portico faces the National Mall.

18. In addition to taking the oath of office on the porticos, some presidents have taken the oath of office in the House of Representatives Chamber, Senate Chamber, and the White House. President Lyndon Johnson took the oath of office on Air Force One after the assassination of President Kennedy in 1963.

FACTS ABOUT THE ROTUNDA AND CRYPT WITHIN THE UNITED STATES CAPITOL BUILDING

As visitors enter the interior of the Capitol Building they are presented a colorful lesson in history through paintings, statues, brassware, and woodworks. Abraham Lincoln, Thomas Jefferson, George Washington, Martin Luther King, Pocahontas, and other great contributors to history greet visitors as they enter the Rotunda. Every direction offers an opportunity to learn about the sacrifices and contributions immortalized through the hands of artists who used their considerable talents to craft several beautiful gifts to a grateful nation.

THE ROTUNDA

1. A rotunda is a high ceiling room having a circular space that is covered by a dome.

2. In 1818, work on the initial Capitol Rotunda was started and was completed in 1824. The dimensions of the first rotunda were 96 feet high from floor to ceiling by 96 feet in diameter.

3. In 1866, the current Rotunda was completed. The Rotunda is 180 feet high from floor to ceiling by 96 feet in diameter and has sandstone floors. The initial height of the Rotunda's sandstone walls was 48 feet. Everything above this height was added between 1855 and 1866.

4. The exterior bronze doors used to enter the Rotunda are referred to as the *Columbus Doors*. Sculptured by Randolph Rogers and cast in Germany in the 1850s, the doors weigh 20,000 pounds and are 17 feet high by 10 feet wide. They depict the life of Christopher Columbus. In 1871, the doors were moved from the old House of Representatives Chamber to the Rotunda.

5. Constantino Brumidi (b1805-d1880) came to the United States in 1852. Because of Brumidi's work in fresco, a process of applying pigments to fresh plaster, which was previously used by Michelangelo in his work on the Sistine Chapel in Rome, Italy, Brumidi became known as the "Michelangelo of the Capitol."

6. At the top of the Rotunda is the painting *The Apotheosis of George Washington* by Brumidi. [Apotheosis means glorification.] Brumidi painted the 4,664 square feet of surface in eleven months, completing it in 1865. Most of his painting was completed while he laid on his back beneath the 62 feet, 2-inch diameter of the painting. Brumidi received a commission of $40,000 for the painting.

7. In *The Apotheosis of George Washington*, Washington is sitting between two women who represent Liberty and Victory/Fame as he rises to heaven.

8. The thirteen maidens surrounding Washington in *The Apotheosis of George Washington* represent the thirteen original states.

The Apotheosis of George Washington

9. To ensure the figures in *The Apotheosis of George Washington* could be seen from the floor of the Rotunda, 180 feet below, the figures were painted oversized, some as tall as 15 feet.

10. There are six scenes surrounding the exterior of *The Apotheosis of George Washington*. The depictions, consisting of Greek and Roman gods among distinguished Americans, represent:

- War - Freedom, also known as Columbia, is directly below Washington in the personification of War. The scene depicts a woman fighting for liberty with a raised sword, a cape, and a helmet and shield trampling figures representing Tyranny and Kingly Power. To Freedom's left is a fierce bald eagle carrying arrows and a thunderbolt.
- Science - Minerva, the Roman goddess of crafts and wisdom, is portrayed with helmet and spear pointing to an electrical generator creating power stored in batteries next to a printing press, representing great American inventions. American scientists and inventors Benjamin Franklin, Samuel F. B. Morse, and Robert Fulton watch. In the left part of the scene a teacher demonstrates the use of dividers.

- <u>Commerce</u> - Mercury, the Roman god of commerce, is giving a bag of gold to American Revolutionary War financier Robert Morris. To Mercury's right, men move a box on a dolly, and to his left, sailors lead into the next scene – Marine.
- <u>Marine</u> - Neptune, the Roman sea-god, is shown wearing a crown of seaweed as he rides in a shell chariot drawn by sea horses. Next to Neptune is a trident. Venus, the goddess of love and who was born from the sea, is helping to lay the transatlantic telegraph cable from America to Ireland. An ironclad warship is barely showing in the background.
- <u>Mechanics</u> - Vulcan, the Roman god of fire and the forge, is standing at an anvil with his foot on a cannon next to a pile of cannonballs, with a steam engine in the background. The man at the forge is believed to be Charles Thomas, the supervisor of ironwork during the construction of the Capitol Dome.
- <u>Agriculture</u> - Ceres, the Roman goddess of agriculture, is holding a wreath of wheat and a cornucopia while sitting on a McCormick mechanical reaper. This is intended to symbolize plenty. A Young America is shown in a liberty cap holding the reins of the horses, while the goddess Flora gathers flowers next to him.

11. There are four relief sculptures above the doors of the Rotunda that show the early relationships between Native Americans and the settlers. They reflect the *Preservation of John Smith by Pocahontas – 1606* (West), *Landing of the Pilgrims – 1620* (East), *William Penn's Treaty with the Indians – 1682* (North), and *Conflict of Daniel Boone and the Indians – 1773* (South).

12. There are eight framed niches holding historical paintings on the walls of the Rotunda. Each painting measures 12 feet by 18 feet and consists of the following:

- Four scenes from the period of the American Revolutionary War, which were recommended for the Rotunda by James Madison, were painted by John Trumbull between 1819 and 1824. They consist of the *Declaration of Independence in Congress, Surrender of General Burgoyne at Saratoga, Surrender of Lord Cornwallis at Yorktown*, and *General George Washington Resigning his Commission to Congress as Commander in Chief of the Army*. Trumbull served as an aide to George Washington during the Revolutionary War. He received $8,000 for each of the four paintings.

- Four scenes of early exploration were added to the Rotunda between 1840 and 1855: *Landing of Christopher Columbus* by John Vanderlyn, *Discovery of the Mississippi by De Soto* by William Powell, *Baptism of Pocahontas* by John Capman, and *Embarkation of the Pilgrims* by Robert Weir.

13. In the painting *Baptism of Pocahontas*, one of the Indians has six toes on one foot.

14. If Miles Standish's feet (kneeling figure) were true to size in the Rotunda painting of *The Embarkation of the Pilgrims*, he would be wearing size 20 shoes.

15. Initially, the men seated in the front row of the Rotunda painting *Declaration of Independence* all had their legs crossed in the same manner. A table was inserted to eliminate this prominent feature.

Paintings on the Rotunda Wall

16. Constantine Brumidi was commissioned to complete the frescoed frieze in the belt just below the 36 windows in the Rotunda. Painted in grisaille, a monochrome of whites and browns , the 8-foot, 4-inch high by 300-foot in circumference panorama, through a series of 19 panels, traces America's history as follows:

Frieze Below Window

Panel #1-America and History, #2-Landing of Columbus (1492), #3-Cortez and Montezuma at Mexican Temple (1520), #4-Pizarro Going to Peru (1533), #5-Burial of De Soto (1542), #6-Captain Smith and Pocahontas (1607), #7- Landing of the Pilgrims (1620), #8-William Penn and the Indians (1682), #9-Colonization of New England, #10-Oglethorpe and the Indians (1732), #11-Battle of Lexington (1775), #12-Declaration of Independence (1776), #13-Surrender of Cornwallis (1781), #14-Death of Tecumsch (1813), #15-American Army Entering the City of Mexico (1847), #16-Discovery of Gold in California (1848), #17-Civil War (1861-1865), #18-The Spanish-American War (1898), and #19-The Birth of Aviation (1903).

17. In 1880, at age 74, Brumidi completed the first eight scenes of the nineteen scenes in the frieze. He died while painting *William Penn's Treaty with the Indians.*

18. In 1889, Filippo Costaggini, Brumidi's understudy, completed scenes nine through sixteen in the frieze.

19. In 1953, Allyn Cox completed the last three scenes of the frescoed frieze.

20. In 1835, near the bronze figure of General Andrew Jackson in the Rotunda, an assassin attempted to take the life of President Jackson (1829-1837). Both of the assailant's guns misfired. This was the first attempt at assassinating a United States President.

21. Lavinia "Vinnie" Ream was just age 17 when President Lincoln permitted her to sketch his daily activities. In 1866, at age 18, she was awarded a $10,000 commission from Congress to complete the marble statue of Abraham Lincoln that is displayed in the Rotunda. The statue was unveiled in 1871. She was the first woman and youngest artist to receive a government commission. Vinnie died at age 67 in 1914, and is buried in Section 3 at Arlington National Cemetery near her husband Brigadier General Richard Hoxie, who died at age 85 in 1930.

Statue of Lincoln

22. The 14,000 pound statue, 26,000 pounds if the base is included, of three female figures shows the images of suffragists Susan B. Anthony, Elizabeth Cady Stanton, and Lucretia Mott. The statue was originally in the Rotunda until the 1920s, when it was removed and placed in the Crypt. It was returned to the Rotunda in 1997.

Statue of Suffragists

23. Until the end of the 19th century, visitors had access to the walkway above the Rotunda. However, because several people collapsed from exhaustion on the nearly 300-step walkway, it was closed and remains closed to the general public.

24. A small circle in the center of the Rotunda marks the spot where the honored dead lie as mourners pay their respects to the deceased for his/her accomplishments and sacrifices.

Circle in Rotunda

25. Starting with Henry Clay in 1851, thirty American heroes and notable citizens have been granted the honor of a public viewing in the Capitol Building. The most recent of these notable Americans was former President Gerald Ford in December 2006.

26. After her death in 2004 at the age of 93, civil rights activist Rosa Parks became the first woman to be honored with a viewing in the Rotunda of the Capitol Building.

27. The remains of five presidents who died while in office have lain in state in the Rotunda. The presidents have been Lincoln (1861-1865), Garfield (1881), McKinley (1897-1901), Harding (1921-1923), and Kennedy (1961-1963).

Even though President Franklin Roosevelt (1933-1945) died while he was in office, he had requested that his body not lie in state.

28. Six former presidents who died after leaving office have lain in state in the Rotunda. The former presidents have been Taft (1909-1913), Hoover (1929-1933), Eisenhower (1953-1961), Johnson (1963-1969), Reagan (1981-1989), and Ford (1974-1977).

29. A few facts about the military honor guard who pays homage to the deceased as they lie in state:

- The members of the honor guard represent each of the branches of the military - Army, Navy, Air Force, Coast Guard, and Marines.

- Eight body bearers, four body bearers on each side of the casket, carry it into and out of the Capitol Building. If the ceremony is for a former president, an honor guard carries the flag of the United States in front of the casket. Following the casket is the officer in charge, followed by an honor guard carrying the presidential flag.

- Once the casket is placed on the catafalque in the center of the Rotunda, the duties of this team of honor guards are transferred to six other members of the honor guard. A description of a catafalque is provided in the section about the Capitol Visitor Center.

- The members of the honor guard stand at the following positions around the casket:

  - One guard at the head of the casket;
  - One guard at each corner of the casket; and
  - One guard near the foot of the casket. This guard is referred to as the *Supernumerary* or *Super*, and he would take the place of any guard who falls from his position.

- The shifts of honor guards rotate on a thirty minute basis.

- The honor guards at the head and foot of the casket are unarmed.

- The guards at the corners of the casket carry rifles. The rifles are unloaded and have had the firing pins removed.

- The flag of the United States is prominently displayed. Other flags, such as the presidential flag and state flags, are also displayed.

Even though the average casket weighs approximately 400 pounds, many of the caskets containing notable citizens weigh hundreds of pounds more. For example, President Reagan's casket weighed over 700 pounds.

Guidance under Title 4 of the United States Code states that when a president or former president dies, the flag of the United States should be lowered to half-staff for 30 days, and 10 days for a current vice president, current and former U. S. Supreme Court Chief Justices and Speakers of the House. For former vice presidents, associate Supreme Court justices, cabinet secretaries, and governors, the flag is flown at half-staff from their death to their interment.

THE CRYPT

1. The Crypt, which is in the center section of the building, was completed in 1827.

2. Despite its name, the Crypt has never been used for a funeral or burial.

3. The 40 Doric columns in the Crypt support the Rotunda above the Crypt. This style of columns is the oldest and simplest of the three ancient Greek orders of architecture, usually fluted columns with plain rounded capitols (heads).

The Crypt

4. The Doric columns were crafted from brown stone surmounted by groined sandstone arches.

5. The Crypt was initially intended to hold the remains of George and Martha Washington.

6. The remains of President and Mrs. Washington were to be enclosed in a memorial that could be viewed through an opening in the Rotunda floor. However, opposition from Southern states who did not want to see the remains removed from Virginia, a Southern state, defeated the proposal. The opening has been filled in.

7. The Crypt was also considered for the final resting place of President Abraham Lincoln after his assassination in 1865. However, Mrs. Lincoln decided to have his remains entombed at Oak Ridge Cemetery in Springfield, Illinois.

8. The star in the center of the floor denotes the points from which the streets in Washington are laid out and numbered.

The Star

FACTS ABOUT THE CAPITOL DOME AND STATUE OF FREEDOM OVER THE UNITED STATES CAPITOL BUILDING

The attention of visitors viewing the exterior of the Capitol Building is quickly drawn to the Capitol Dome. Atop one of the most prominent structures in Washington, D.C. is a statue that appears to be welcoming visitors to a building that shelters the governing bodies of the United States. As they view the Dome, and its apparent caretaker, visitors might let their curiosity run wild about how the Dome was constructed, who was responsible for constructing it, and what the statue at the top of the Dome really looks like and represents.

THE CAPITOL DOME

1. The word *Dome* comes from the Latin word *Domus*, meaning a *House*.

2. In 1824, the original Capitol Dome, which was designed after a Roman temple, was completed. It was constructed from wood covered with copper.

3. In 1855, Congress authorized the construction of a new Capitol Dome, and the old wooden Capitol Dome was removed.

4. In 1856, work on the new Capitol Dome was begun.

5. The architect of the new Capitol Dome was Thomas Walter.

6. Through the fall of 1858, Montgomery C. Meigs, then a captain in the U.S. Army Corps of Engineers, was the principal superintendent of construction for the new Capitol Dome. Meigs was later a key figure in having Robert E. Lee's Arlington estate declared a cemetery during the Civil War.

Capitol Dome

7. In 1858, William B. Franklin replaced Captain Meigs as the principal superintendent of construction for the new Capitol Dome.

8. The man who had final approval authority over the construction of the Capitol Dome was then Secretary of War Jefferson Davis. He later became President of the Confederate States of America (1861-1865).

9. The iron supports that support the Capitol Dome weigh nearly 8.9 million pounds.

10. The iron supports were lifted to the top of the Capitol Dome by steam-powered derricks. Wood from the original dome was used to power the derricks.

11. The height of the Capitol Dome, not including the statue of Freedom, is 287 feet.

12. In 1863, the exterior of the current Capitol Dome was completed. The interior was completed in 1866.

13. The cost of the completed Capitol Dome totaled $1,047,291.

14. There are 120 windowpanes in the Capitol Dome.

15. The top of the Capitol Dome has an inner-shell and an outer-shell, with a flight of stairs in between.

16. The assembly of the Capitol Dome rests on 36 supporting trusses attached to the Capitol's foundation.

17. On very hot days the Capitol Dome can expand as much as four inches.

18. Electrically charged wires on the Capitol Dome generate mild shocks to discourage birds from roosting on the dome.

19. It takes 1,750 gallons of paint to paint the top of the Capitol Dome. A red undercoat of paint protects the iron from the elements. In 1958, thirty-two coats of paint were removed from the Dome.

20. The Capitol Dome is the third largest dome of its kind in the world. The largest domes crown the tops of St. Peter Cathedral at the Vatican in Italy and St. Paul Cathedral in London, England.

THE STATUE OF FREEDOM

1. The statue on top of the Capitol Dome was originally named *Freedom Triumphant in War and Peace*. It was later referred to as *Armed Freedom*, or *Statue of Freedom*, or simply *Freedom*.

2. Thomas Crawford designed and executed the plaster model of Freedom at his studio in Rome, Italy. Crawford died in 1857, just after he completed the model.

3. Freedom consists of a figure of a woman wearing a helmet, circled with stars, on which there is a head of an eagle with long feathers and talons, a reference to the costume of Native Americans. To protect the statue from lightning, ten bronze points tipped with platinum are attached to the headdress, shoulders, and shield.

4. Freedom wears a brooch (belt) that secures her fringed robe. The letters U.S. are inscribed on the brooch.

5. Freedom's right hand rests on a sheathed sword, while her left hand holds a laurel wreath of victory and a shield with thirteen stripes representing the original thirteen United States.

Statue of Freedom at the top of the Capitol Building

6. Freedom stands on a cast-iron globe that is 7 feet in diameter. Around the sphere is the national motto, "*E Pluribus Unum* – One Out of Many."

7. The bronze statue of Freedom is 19 feet, 6 inches tall.

8. The statue of Freedom faces east, away from the Mall. This is due to the Capitol Building's east front being planned, and still serves, as the principal entrance to the building, and thus faces those who arrive from this direction.

9. Initially, the headwear worn by Freedom was that of a figure wearing a wreath and laurel, and then it was changed to a softly folded cloth liberty cap. The proposed cap was similar to the cap worn by freed slaves in ancient Rome. However, Jefferson Davis, who was then Secretary of War under President Buchanan and a citizen of Mississippi, would not accept any figure that suggested freedom for slaves, and he forced Thomas Crawford to modify the design to look like a crested Roman helmet.

10. In 1859, the final sections of the plaster model of Freedom were delivered to the United States from Rome, Italy. The statue was then cast in bronze at Bladensburg, Maryland, between 1860 and 1862. Bladensburg is located just over the Washington, D.C. border near the Capital Beltway.

11. Freedom was cast in five major pieces and then bolted together after being lifted to the top of the Capitol Dome. The bronze statue was formed from 1500 pounds of tin, 200 pounds of zinc, and 15,000 pounds of copper. The actual weight of the statue is 14,985 pounds.

12. The cost of the statue, excluding installation, totaled $23,796.

13. On December 2, 1863, a 35-gun salute signaled the dedication of the statue of Freedom. Each cannon shot represented one of the 35 states in the Union at the time of the dedication. The states consisted of the 34 states in the Union at the start of the Civil War and West Virginia, which entered the Union in June 1863.

14. Philip Reid supervised the assembly of Freedom at the top of the Capitol Dome. Reid was a former slave who acquired his freedom through the Emancipation Proclamation, which went into effect on January 1, 1863.

15. Every two years the statue receives maintenance while it remains on the Dome. This maintenance consists of cleaning the corrosion from the lady, repairing holes, caulking the gaps in the structure, and applying a thick layer of wax over the entire statue.

FACTS ABOUT THE OLD SENATE CHAMBER WITHIN THE UNITED STATES CAPITOL BUILDING

The Old Senate Chamber, which was modeled after the amphitheaters of antiquity (early years of history), is a two-story semicircular chamber measuring 75 feet long by 50 feet wide. This description of the Old Senate Chamber could be used to describe many rooms within the Capitol Building or similar rooms in many other government buildings constructed during the 19th and early 20th centuries.

THE OLD SENATE CHAMBER

1. The current chamber was completed in December 1819, and was the third chamber constructed for the U.S. Senate. The first chamber deteriorated so rapidly that it had to be reconstructed just six years after its completion. The British Army destroyed the second chamber in 1814 during the burning of the Capitol Building. The Senate met in the three chambers between 1810 and 1859, and visitors see it as it appeared during 1850-1859.

2. The two-story chamber is semicircular in shape and is 75 feet long by 50 feet wide.

3. The ceiling of the chamber is a half dome.

4. The domed and white-painted ceiling of the chamber is elaborately coffered and enriched by decorative moldings.

5. Five smaller circular skylights border a central, semicircular skylight. The skylights originally provided the chamber with natural light. It is now artificially lighted.

6. The Philadelphia firm of Cornelius and Company furnished the large brass chandelier that hangs above the vice president's desk.

7. Two visitor galleries overlook the chamber.

8. Eight Ionic columns of variegated marble support the gallery on the east wall. The columns of the Erechtheion in Athens, Greece, inspired the columns in the chamber. They were crafted from marble quarried along the Potomac River.

9. A second and much larger ladies' gallery follows the curved western wall. The gallery is carried on twelve steel columns encased in cast-iron forms, topped with Corinthian capitals. The columns were designed to simulate the cast-iron originals.

10. A wrought-iron balcony railing follows the contour of the gallery. The crimson fabric backing was intended to accentuate the decorative metal work.

11. Directly above the east gallery hangs an original 1823 porthole portrait of George Washington. The artist, Rembrandt Peale, had painted Washington from life. The portrait was purchased in 1832, during the centennial celebration of Washington's birth, for display in the chamber. The words under the figure of Washington read "Father of Our Country."

12. A curved table with richly turned and carved legs and a crimson modesty screen sits on a raised platform in the center of the room. This is the original desk of the Vice President of the United States, who serves as President of the Senate. To symbolize the importance of the desk, an elaborate canopy with a mahogany valance from which crimson fabric hangs covers the desk. A carved gilt (gold surface) eagle and shield stand above the valance.

The Vice President's Desk

13. Directly in front of the vice president's desk, but one tier down, is a larger desk of similar design. The Secretary of the Senate and the chief clerk occupied this desk when it was an active Senate Chamber.

14. A glass screen separates the vice president's dais (series of tiers) from a small lobby. This is where the senators could go to relax, yet still listen to floor proceedings.

15. Two fireplace mantels are located on the east wall behind the screen. Both mantels are originals to the chamber.

16. The two additional mantels on the north and south ends of the lobby are reproductions. The original mantels were replaced with stoves when the Supreme Court started using the chamber.

17. The 64 sets of desks and chairs in the chamber are reproductions.

18. The desks and chairs were reproduced from 1819 designs by New York cabinetmaker Thomas Constantine. The original desks and chairs were custom made from mahogany.

19. The original desks each cost $34.00 and each chair cost $48.00.

20. Today all of Constantine's desks remain in use in the current Senate Chamber. His chairs have been replaced. Senators may purchase their chairs at the time they leave office.

21. The shape of the desk reflects its position in the room. Aisle desks are narrow and angled, while center desks are wider and squarer.

22. As new states entered the Union, desks of similar design were ordered from other cabinetmakers. The four newest desks in the current chamber, those crafted for Alaska (1959) and Hawaii (1959), were built in the Senate cabinet shop.

23. Immediately behind the last row of desks is a low paneled wall. The wall separates the senators' space from a third visitor area. Furnished with red-upholstered sofas, this area was reserved for privileged visitors who gained admittance through special invitations from the senators. The niches, one on either side of the main doorway, house reproductions of the stoves that were capable of burning wood or coal.

24. The desk used by Daniel Webster, which was moved to the current Senate Chamber, is the only desk that is not a lift top desk. It is also the largest desk in the Senate Chamber.

25. The chamber floor is covered with a carpet woven from long-staple 100% virgin wool. It features a gold star pattern on a red background.

26. Every senator had a spittoon next to his desk.

27. Tradition calls for the Republican senators to be seated on the left side of the chamber and the Democrat senators on the right.

28. Tradition also calls for the senators to sit by seniority. The most senior senators sit in the front of the chamber and the junior senators sit in the rear of the chamber.

29. In 1859, the U.S. Senate moved to its current chamber.

30. In 1860, the U.S. Supreme Court was relocated to the vacated Senate Chamber, where it remained until 1935.

31. From 1935 to 1976, the chamber was used as a law library, committee room, meeting room, and storage room.

32. In 1976, the chamber was opened to visitors as part of the nation's bicentennial celebration.

33. The ladies' gallery on the western wall was restored in 1976.

34. Today the restored chamber is used primarily as a museum space open to the public on a limited basis. It is also used periodically for joint House-Senate committee conferences, important meetings, and ceremonial events. In January 1999, the chamber was used as a meeting chamber for the full body of the U.S. Senate to discuss the possible impeachment trial of President William Clinton.

Access to this chamber is limited, but a tour can be obtained through your congressional representative.

FACTS ABOUT THE NATIONAL STATUARY HALL WITHIN THE UNITED STATES CAPITOL BUILDING

The area in the Capitol Building that currently houses the National Statuary Hall previously housed the U.S. House of Representatives. After the House of Representatives moved to its current location, it was decided that the open area would be an ideal location for displaying the likenesses of notable Americans who contributed to the nation's history.

THE NATIONAL STATUARY HALL

1. From 1807 to 1857, the U.S. House of Representatives occupied the chamber now referred to as the *National Statuary Hall*.

2. After the British Army burned the Capitol Building in 1814, the Hall was constructed in its current shape of an ancient amphitheater between 1815 and 1819 under the direction of Benjamin Latrobe and his successor Charles Bulfinch. It is one of the earliest examples of Greek revival architecture in America.

3. While most of the Hall surface is painted plaster, the lower gallery walls and pilasters (columns) are sandstone.

4. Around the perimeter of the Hall stand colossal columns of variegated Breccia. The marble for the columns was quarried from along the Potomac River. The Corinthian capitals of white marble were carved in Carrara, Italy.

National Statuary Hall Showing One of the Four Fireplaces

5. A lantern in the fireproof cast-steel ceiling admits natural light into the Hall.

6. The four fireplaces on the south side of the room helped to warm the chamber during cold months.

7. The floor of the Hall is covered with black and white marble tiles. The black marble was purchased specifically for the Hall, while the white marble was scrap material from the 1857 extension to the Capitol Building.

8. Only two of the many sculptures presently in the room were commissioned for display in the House of Representatives Chamber. They are:

   - Completed between 1817 and 1819, Enrico Causici's neoclassical plaster sculpture *Liberty and the Eagle* looks out over the Hall from a niche above the colonnade behind what was once the Speaker of the House's rostrum. Giuseppe Valaperta carved the sandstone relief eagle in the frieze of the entablature. In the center is Liberty, and in her hand is the U.S. Constitution, to her right is an American eagle, and to her left is a serpent, a symbol of wisdom.

   - Completed in 1819, Carolo Franzoni's *Car of History* is located above the door leading into the Rotunda. This neoclassical marble sculpture depicts Clio, the Muse of History, riding in the Chariot of Time on a marble globe while recording events occurring in the chamber below. The wheel of the chariot contains the chamber clock, with works by Simon Willard.

9. The heavy curtains on the walls of the Hall were installed to help suppress the noise. The results were minimal.

10. A small bronze marker marks the spot in the Hall where former President John Quincy Adams (1825-1829) was fatally stricken by a heart attack in 1848. Other markers identify the spots where the desks of important members of Congress were seated. These members included such men as future Presidents Fillmore (1850-1853), Pierce (1853-1857), and Lincoln (1861-1865). Lincoln's desk was #191.

11. In 1864, Congress authorized the Statuary Hall in the Capitol Building. Each state was authorized to display no more than two figures of prominent men or women from their respective states.

12. The figures of 91 men and 9 women are displayed in the Hall and throughout the Capitol Building. Each statue must be a gift from a state, not from an individual or group of citizens.

13. In 1870, the likeness of Nathaniel Green (soldier & politician) was the first statue placed in the Hall as a gift from the state of Rhode Island.

14. In 2000, Congress enacted a law that permits the states to replace the statues of notable citizens with new statues. As a result, the dates and names for the latest of the 100 statues in the Capitol Building are subject to change. For example, in 2009, the statue of Thomas King, donated in 1931 by California, was replaced with one of former president Ronald Reagan.

15. The largest statue in the collection is of Hawaiian King Kamehameha I. The 1969 bronze statue is 9 feet, 10 inches tall, stands on a 3 feet, 6 inch granite base, and weighs approximately 15,000 pounds. It is on display in the Capitol Visitor Center.

16. In 1933, and because the collection of figures in the Hall had grown to 66, and the weight had caused the floor of the Hall to sag, Congress restricted the number of statues that may be displayed in the Hall. Currently, there are 35 statues in the Hall.

17. When the House of Representatives was in the Hall, Daniel Webster's desk was in a strategic location where the shape of the room permitted him to hear the whispered conversations of his peers as they planned their strategies in other parts of the room.

18. Presidents James Madison, James Monroe, John Quincy Adams, Andrew Jackson, and Millard Fillmore were inaugurated in the Hall when the House of Representatives was located in the Hall.

19. Of special note is what happened to the statue honoring the notable American politician John Calhoun (located in another part of the Capitol Building). On July 24, 1998, security guards confronted a man trying to force his way into the Capitol Building. The man shot to death Capitol Police Officer Jacob Chestnut and Detective John Gibson. A stray bullet put a bullet hole in the statue of John Calhoun. The hole is in the right leg of the trousers.

FACTS ABOUT THE OLD SUPREME COURT CHAMBER WITHIN THE UNITED STATES CAPITOL BUILDING

For decades following its formation, the United States Supreme Court was viewed like an orphan without a home as it was moved from one temporary location to another. One of these temporary shelters was in the bowels of the Capitol Building. As visitors enter the chamber, they view a room that may still echo with the voices of prominent judicial figures as they rendered some of the nation's most notable legal opinions.

THE OLD SUPREME COURT CHAMBER

1. This chamber was used as the Senate Chamber from 1800 through 1808. On March 4, 1801, Thomas Jefferson took the oath of office for his first term as 3rd U.S. President in this chamber. This was the first time a president took an oath of office in Washington, D.C.

2. From 1801 to 1819, the Supreme Court was convened in what became committee rooms S-146 and S-146A of the Capitol Building.

3. Benjamin Henry Latrobe constructed most of the Supreme Court Chamber. In 1815, Latrobe started to construct the chamber for the third time. After Latrobe resigned in 1817, Charles Bulfinch completed the chamber in 1819. The first chamber had to be replaced because of poor construction and the second because of the burning of the Capitol Building by the British Army in 1814.

Supreme Court Chamber

4. The old Supreme Court Chamber was the first room constructed specifically for use by the nation's highest judiciary body.

5. Latrobe's assistant, John Lenthall, was killed when the ceiling of the vaulted chamber collapsed during construction. The accident occurred when Lenthall removed the supports to the vaulted chamber before the structure had fully dried.

6. Entrance to the chamber is gained through the robing room at its southern end. Visitors view the chamber as it appeared during 1850-1860.

7. The robes in the robing room are the actual robes of former Justices. Also in the room is a bust of Roger B. Taney, the nation's fifth Chief Justice, who held the post from 1836 to 1864.

8. The coat hooks on the wall opposite the bust carry the names of the Justices on the Supreme Court from 1858 to 1860. The label *Chief* refers to Chief Justice Taney.

9. The chamber is in the shape of a semicircle, which measures 74 feet wide by 50 feet deep. The vaulted ceiling of the chamber is divided into lobes by 10 ribs.

10. Originally, the windows on the east wall of the chamber provided a view onto the Capitol Plaza. However, because the 1959-1963 expansion of the Capitol's east front blocked the windows, the windows are now artificially lighted.

11. The four busts displayed in the rear of the chamber are of the first four Chief Justices of the U. S. Supreme Court. From north to south they are John Marshall, John Ruthledge, John Jay, and Oliver Ellsworth.

Clock over Fire Place and Bust of Supreme Court Justice

12. Over the west fireplace stands a clock. It was ordered for the chamber by Chief Justice Taney in 1837.

13. The location of the chamber is near where construction of the Capitol Building was started. A wall at the entrance to the chamber is exposed to show an example of the bricks that were used to construct the building.

37

14. Above the clock is a plaster relief sculptured by Carlo Franzoni in 1817. The central figure in the relief is Justice, who is seated holding a pair of scales in her left hand, and her right hand resting upon the hilt of an unsheathed sword. Unlike many depictions of Justice, she wears no blindfold. The winged youth seated beside her is Fame, who holds up the Constitution of the United States under the rays of the rising sun. At the right side of the sculpture, an eagle protectively rests one foot upon books containing the written laws.

15. In front of the eastern arcade are mahogany desks for the nine Supreme Court Justices, which are set off from the rest of the room by a mahogany railing. Seven of these desks are 19th century originals that are believed to have been purchased for the court in the late 1830s. The chairs behind the desks represent various styles used around the year 1860. Each Justice selected his style of chair.

16. Court officials used the desks at either end of the Justices' desks. The U.S. Attorney General, the clerk, and the deputy clerk sat to the right of the Justices. The court reporters, the marshal, and the deputy marshal sat to the left of the Justices.

Bench and Chairs for Supreme Court Justices

17. The floor in the central area of the chamber is approximately one-foot lower than the level where the Supreme Court Justices sat. In this area stand four baize-covered mahogany tables that were used by lawyers presenting their cases before the Justices. Facing these tables, and lining the area's western end, are the wooden panel-back settees provided for the audience.

18. After the chamber was vacated by the Supreme Court, it was used as a reference library until the 1940s, as an office for the Joint Committee on Atomic Energy from 1955 to 1960, and as a storeroom until restoration work began in 1972. In May 1975, the chamber was opened to the public after a $478,000 renovation.

Access to this chamber is limited, but a tour can be obtained through your congressional representative.

FACTS ABOUT THE LIBRARY OF CONGRESS

Soon after winning their freedom from the British Empire, the members of Congress determined that, if they were to successfully govern the United States, reference materials covering many topics would have to be readily available. In 1783, Congress appointed a Continental Congress committee, chaired by James Madison, to assemble a reference library for members of Congress. Additionally, a bill was passed for establishing a congressional library. As time passed, this small, poorly organized set of reference material grew into the largest library in the world.

THE LIBRARY OF CONGRESS

1. On April 24, 1800, the Library of Congress was founded.

2. A sum of $5,000 was appropriated to purchase a case of maps and 740 books from dealers in London, England.

3. The first Library of Congress was located in New York City, New York.

4. In 1800, the Library of Congress was moved to Washington, D.C. when Congress moved to the new city.

5. On August 25, 1814, the British Army destroyed the first library when the Capitol Building was burned.

6. In 1815, Congress replaced the destroyed books by purchasing 6,487 replacements from Thomas Jefferson at a cost of $23,950.

7. On Christmas Eve, 1851, 35,000 of the 55,000 assembled library books were destroyed in another fire to the Capitol Building. In 1853, the restored Library was reopened.

8. Until 1897, the Library remained in the Capitol Building.

9. Three primary buildings in Washington, D.C. house the Library of Congress.

10. The three buildings - Jefferson, Adams, and Madison are connected by a series of underground pedestrian tunnels that protect the materials as they are moved from building to building.

11. Initially, access to the Library of Congress was limited to government related research. In 1897, the library was first opened to the general public.

One of the Reading Rooms in the Jefferson Building

12. In 1870, the Library of Congress was declared the National Copyright Library.

13. The Library of Congress is the world's largest library. It contains over 120 million items (books, maps, etc.). Of this number over 32 million items are books on over 650 miles of shelving.

14. The Library of Congress is the nation's oldest federal cultural institution. In addition to its primary mission of serving the research needs of the U.S. Congress, the Library of Congress serves all Americans through its popular website and twenty-two reading rooms on Capitol Hill.

THE THOMAS JEFFERSON BUILDING

1. The Thomas Jefferson Building was named in honor of President Jefferson (1801-1809) and was the first building constructed specifically as the home for the Library of Congress. Thomas Jefferson's sale of his personal library to Congress formed the nucleus of the second Library of Congress after the British Army burned the first library in 1814.

2. Between 1886 and 1897, the Thomas Jefferson Building was constructed. New Hampshire granite was used for the exterior of the building. Fifteen types of marble were used in the interior of the building.

3. In 1873, the architectural firm of Smithmeyer & Pelz (John L. Smithmeyer and Paul J. Pelz) of Washington, D.C., was awarded the $1,500 first prize for its Italian Renaissance design.

4. In 1886, John L. Smithmeyer was appointed architect of the building, and clearing of the site was begun in October of that year. Paul Pelz replaced Smithmeyer in 1888, and Paul Casey, the son of Brigadier General Thomas Casey, replaced Pelz in 1892.

5. During October 1888, General Thomas L. Casey of the U.S. Army Corps of Engineers was placed in charge of the construction. Casey is also noted for his work on the Washington Memorial. After Casey's death in 1896, Bernard Green assumed his duties.

Thomas Jefferson Building

6. Fifty American artists and twenty sculptors provided the works of art within the building. The themes of the artwork within the building are Knowledge and Learning.

7. Three sets of 14 feet by 7-1/2 feet bronze doors are at the building's main entrance. They cost $364,000 and are referred to as the *Tradition Doors*. The left door is symbolic of Tradition, the center door represents Printing and the right door Writing. The six female figures over the Tradition Doors (main entrance) to the building represent Literature, Composition, and Reflection.

8. Above the first-story windows of the building are 33 keystones. Each keystone contains a head that represents one of the ethnic groups of the world. Completed in 1891, they are referred to as the *Ethnological Heads*.

9. At the entrance to the building is the fountain *The Court of Neptune* by Sculptor Roland Hinton Perry. Constructed in 1897-1898, at a cost of $22,000, the fountain represents the events in Neptune's reign as the ruler of the seas.

Fountain – The Court of Neptune

10. In the 55-foot-wide fountain, Neptune is flanked by his sons, the tritons, mythological gods characterized by figures with the torsos of men and the fins of fishes. Two nymphs are riding wild sea horses. Other creatures, such as dolphins and turtles, are displayed.

11. Above the main windows on the second-story of the central pavilion of the building is a series of nine circular windows. These windows serve as a background for three-foot high granite portrait busts of men eminent in the history of western literature. The bust of Benjamin Franklin is the central figure. Other figures are Demosthenes, Emerson, Irving, Goethe, Maculay, Hawthorne, Scott, and Dante.

12. On the dome of the building is the *Torch of Learning*. The torch, which marks the center and apex of the Thomas Jefferson Building, is 15 feet high by 6-1/2 feet in diameter at its base. Originally, the torch was covered with a 23-carat gold leaf. It is now covered with copper.

13. The *Main Reading Room* is 160 feet high and is one of twenty-two reading rooms. The eight marble columns each support 10-foot-high allegorical female figures in plaster representing characteristic features of civilized life and thought: Religion, Commerce, History, Art, Philosophy, Poetry, Law and Science. The 16 bronze statues set upon the balustrades of the galleries pay homage to men whose lives symbolized the thought and activity represented by the plaster statues.

14. The semicircles of stained glass depict the seals of the 48 states in the Union at the time the building was constructed in 1886 and 1887. The eight statues placed around the reading room symbolize Civilized Life and Thought.

15. On November 1, 1897, the Library of Congress Building was opened to the public at a cost of $6,032,124.00. This is $200,000 less than what was appropriated by Congress. In 1980, it was renamed the Library of Congress - Thomas Jefferson Building.

16. There are hundreds of items on display in the building at any given time. However, because of their age and delicate condition, many of the exhibits are rotated for display.

THE JOHN ADAMS BUILDING

1. The John Adams Building was the second of three buildings constructed near the Capitol Building for the purpose of storing the contents of the Library of Congress.

John Adams Building

2. On January 3, 1939, at a cost of $8,000,000, the first of the annex buildings was opened to the public. Initially named to honor Thomas Jefferson, the building was renamed in 1980 in honor of President John Adams (1797-1801).

3. The exterior facade of the building was crafted from white Georgia marble.

4. In 1938, the Library of Congress Annex Bronze Doors were crafted. These seven sets of doors are 12 feet high and represent the following:

   - The center doors (west entrance) depict six figures that represent major contributors to written communication. They are Hermes, the Greek god who served as a messenger; Odin, originator of the Viking alphabet and mythical god of war; Ogma, who performed the same alphabetical task for the Iris; Itzama, chief god of the Mayans; Quetzalcoatone, god of the Aztecs; and Sequoyah, an American Indian.

   - There are two figures near the single door to the south entrance. The male is symbolic of physical labor and the female is symbolic of intellectual labor.

   - On the east side of the John Adams Building are doors with six more figures of educators who have contributed to the history of the written word. They are Thoth, Egyptian god and conveyor of speech; Ts'ang Chieh, Chinese patron saint of pictographic letters; Nabu Sumero, Akkadian god; Brahma, supreme god of the East Indian trinity; Cadmus of Greece, who planted the dragon teeth from which sprang armedme; and Tamurath, a cultural hero of Persian antiquity.

THE JAMES MADISON MEMORIAL BUILDING

1. The James Madison Memorial Building was the third of three buildings constructed for the purpose of storing the property of the Library of Congress.

2. On November 20, 1981, the building was dedicated.

    James Madison Memorial Building

3. The building contains 2,100,000 square feet of space and houses administrative offices, the Congressional Research Services, the Law Library, the Office of the Librarian, and the Copyright Office.

4. The building is considered an official memorial to James Madison (1809-1817), the 4th President of the United States.

5. A large marble statue of James Madison greets visitors to the James Madison Memorial Hall. Relatively plain in design, the primary goal of the building is to provide an efficient means of storing materials for easy retrieval.

6. Over the main entrance is a four-story relief in bronze, *Falling Books*, by Frank Eliscu. The James Madison Memorial Hall has eight quotations from Madison on its walls. The statue by Walter Hancock portrays Madison as a young man in his thirties, holding in his right hand volume 83 of the *Encyclopédie Méthodique*, which was published in Paris between1782 and 1832. At the doorways to the Manuscript Reading Room and the Manuscript Division office, are a pair of bronze medallions by Robert Alexander Weinmann. The one on the left shows the profile of Madison and the one on the right depicts Madison at work.

THE CENTRAL REPOSITORY FOR THE AUDIOVISUAL WORKS OF THE LIBRARY OF CONGRESS

In 1997, Congress approved a new repository to house the Motion Picture, Broadcasting and Recorded Sound Division of the Library of Congress. The 140,000-square-foot structure is near Culpeper, Virginia.

FACTS ABOUT THE ULYSSES S. GRANT MEMORIAL
(IN FRONT OF THE CAPITOL BUILDING)

Second only to President Abraham Lincoln, General Ulysses S. Grant is credited with saving the Union from destruction during the American Civil War. Confronting the Army of Northern Virginia almost constantly from March 1864 to April 1865 at the Wilderness, Cold Harbor, and Appomattox, Grant was quick to take advantage of the opportunities offered by Lee, and used his superior strength in manpower and overwhelming source of supplies to defeat an army that many believed unbeatable.

Grant was a man of war, not of peace. In the everyday life of peace-time-soldier, farmer, clerk, businessman and president, many historians consider Grant a failure. However, it was not the skills of a peacemaker that were needed during 1861 through 1865, but those of a warrior. It is this warrior a grateful nation pays homage to through the Grant Memorial.

THE LIFE OF ULYSSES S. GRANT

1. On April 27, 1822, Hiram Ulysses Grant, known to history as Ulysses S. Grant, was born near Point Pleasant, Ohio. He was the first of six children.

2. Grant's parents were Jessie and Hanna Grant.

3. Grant was not named until six weeks after his birth, when his first and middle names were drawn from a hat by his parents.

4. The names picked from the hat were Hiram (first name) and Ulysses (middle name), not Ulysses Simpson as he is known.

5. In 1839, at age 17, Grant entered the Military Academy at West Point, New York. He was only 5 feet, 1 inch tall and weighed approximately 120 pounds when he entered the academy. He eventually grew to 5 feet, 8 inches tall.

6. Because of confusion on the part of the congressman who appointed him and the administration officer at West Point, Grant was listed in the academy's records as Ulysses S. Grant. The S representing Simpson, the maiden name of Grant's mother.

7. Grant was listed on the rolls of new cadets as U.S. Grant. An upper classman by the name of William T. Sherman, a future Union general, jokingly stated that the letters U and S represented Uncle Sam. Thereafter, Grant's friends and relatives often referred to him as "Sam."

8. In 1843, Grant graduated from West Point with a class standing of 21st out of 39 graduates. He also received 290 demerits during his four years at the academy. Comparing Grant with Lee - Lee graduated 2nd in a class of 46, with no demerits.

9. Grant fought in the Mexican-American War of 1846-1848. It was while they served in Mexico that Lee met Grant for the first and only time prior to Lee's surrender at Appomattox, Virginia. On this occasion, Colonel Lee reprimanded Grant for a sloppy uniform. Lee did not remember the encounter when reminded by Grant at Appomattox.

10. In 1848, Grant married Julia Boggs Dent. They had four children: Frederick, Ulysses, Ellen, and Jesse.

11. In 1854, at age 32, and after four years at the West Point Military Academy and eleven years as a commissioned officer in the quarter master corps, Captain Grant resigned from the U.S. Army.

12. Even though Grant, the general, was victorious in many battles during the Civil War, his attempts at other professions usually resulted in failure. These professional failures included:

- Because he could not stand the sight of blood or to kill animals, Grant hated working at this father's tannery.
- While stationed in Oregon, Grant tried his hand at shipping ice to San Francisco. Businessmen from Alaska edged him out.
- Grant couldn't sell the cattle, hogs, and sheep he raised.
- The chickens Grant raised died on their way to market.
- Grant's attempt as a merchant resulted in his partner stealing his money and leaving town.

- A billiard room he started went bankrupt.
- Grant was fired from a job as a realtor and rent collector when he failed to collect the rent.
- As a clerk in a leather goods store, Grant often charged the wrong amounts to customers. Usually in favor of the customer.
- Grant lost his job in a customs house.
- As a farmer, Grant only raised 75 bushels of grain when his neighbors were raising as much as 500 bushels on similar acreage.
- Selling cut wood drew very few customers for Grant.
- Grant lost most of his money in an investment scheme after he left the presidency.

13. When the Civil War began Grant made several unsuccessful attempts at getting a commission in the Union Army. These attempts included commissions in the Illinois Volunteers, Illinois Regulars, Missouri Volunteers, and the Ohio Volunteers.

14. In June 1861, Grant finally received a commission in the 21st Illinois as a colonel. He was then promoted to brigadier general (one star) in August 1861 and major general (two stars) in February 1862.

15. In March 1864, Grant was promoted to the rank of lieutenant general (three stars). It was the first time the rank had been held by an officer in the United States Army since George Washington during the Revolutionary War and Mexican-American War hero Winfield Scott's promotion in 1856. Scott retired from the Army in November 1861.

16. On March 12, 1864, soon after his appointment as General-in-Chief of the Armies of the United States as a three star general, Grant started a campaign against the Confederacy that resulted in the surrender of General Lee at Appomattox, Virginia, on April 9, 1865.

17. In 1866, Grant was promoted to the rank of full general (four stars). This promotion was the first time the rank of full general had been awarded to any officer in the United States Army.

In 1976, President Gerald Ford (1974-1977) posthumously appointed George Washington General of the Armies of the United States, and specified that he would rank first among all past and present officers of the Army.

18. In March 1869, Grant was sworn in as the 18th President of the United States. His second term ended in 1877.

19. Largely due to Grant's lackadaisical attitude and a lot of corruption in his administration, his presidency is considered one of the most corrupt in U.S. history. Grant appointed twenty-four family members to government positions after his election, and many of his appointees were forced to resign from office.

20. On July 23, 1885, at age 63, Grant died from throat cancer. His wife Julia died in 1902 at age 76. Both are entombed in New York City. Grant smoked many cigars, averaging about 12 cigars each day.

THE ULYSSES S. GRANT MEMORIAL

1. In 1901, Congress authorized $250,000 for the construction of the Grant Memorial.

2. In 1903, sculptor Henry Shrady and architect Edward Casey were commissioned to design and execute the memorial. Shrady designed and executed the sculptured elements, while Casey designed the marble plaza and pedestal elements.

3. In 1906, the site for the Grant Memorial in front of the Capitol Building at the east end of the Mall was approved.

4. Shrady and Casey's design was selected over 26 other design submissions.

Grant Memorial

5. The statue of Grant, with the accompanying works, totals 252 feet in length by 71 feet in depth. The platform was constructed from Vermont marble.

6. The statue of Grant weighs 10,700 pounds.

7. The four lions located around the base of the memorial are intended to symbolize the guarding of the United States flag and the flags of the Union Army.

8. Grant is riding his favorite horse Cincinnati. The horse was presented to him in 1864 when he was a lieutenant general, and was one of seven horses he rode during the Civil War.

9. To better understand the movements of the men and horses in battle, Shrady observed staged cavalry drills at the West Point Military Academy in New York.

10. To better understand the physiological structure of horses, Shrady dissected several horses.

11. Shrady modeled the lead horse in the memorial nine times before he was satisfied.

12. In order to better reveal the rippling of their muscles, the horses used as models were sprayed with water.

13. Shrady's fingerprints, some observers say thumb prints, can be seen on the body of the lead horse.

14. The truck carrying the plaster molds to the foundry caught fire, but the molds were not damaged. The finished bronze figures also survived a fire at the foundry in New York.

15. In 1912, the 30,000-pound Artillery Group was placed on the site, the Cavalry Group in 1916, and in late 1920, the 10,700-pound equestrian statue of Grant was erected on the pedestal.

Cavalry Group – Consisting of Seven Men and Seven Horses

16. The large bronze panels on Grant's pedestal portray the U.S. Infantry. The panels, installed in 1924, were started by Shrady, but were completed by sculptor Sherry Fry after Shrady's death.

17. A plaque on the Artillery Group identifies West Point cadets Fairfax Ayres (guidon), James Chaney (lead driver), and Henry Weeks (wheel driver), class of 1908, as the models for the soldiers depicted in the group.

Artillery Group – Consisting of four men and five horses. Pulled behind the caisson is a 1857 Napoleon smooth-bore cannon with a tube weight of 1,230 pounds; tube length of 66 inches; total weight of 2,355 pounds; and fires a 12-pound ball a maximum distance of 1,660 yards.

18. The name "Grant" on the pedestal is the only inscription found on the memorial that identifies the person the memorial honors. Other inscriptions are carved in the marble or in bronze, including identifying Shrady and Casey, dedicating a section of the memorial to Shrady's friends; Alice and Dave Morris, and an inscription on the stirrup of one of the horses identifying Helen Wright. The Roman Bronze Works of New York is also identified.

19. The main figure showing Grant on his horse is 17 feet high and forty feet above the marble platform.

20. On April 27, 1922, the memorial was dedicated. The date marked the 100th anniversary of Grant's birth.

21. It took Shrady and Casey nearly twenty years to complete the memorial.

22. On April 12, 1922, at age 50, Shrady died just 15 days prior to the dedication of the memorial. Casey died in 1940 at age 75.

23. The Grant Memorial, consisting of 13 sculpted horses, is the largest equestrian statue in the United States and the second largest in the world after the monument to King Victor Emanuel in Rome, Italy.

24. During 1970-1971, the Capitol Reflecting Pool in front of the statue of General Grant was added. Looking down on the pool it would appear to be in the shape of a fan.

FACTS ABOUT THE UNITED STATES SUPREME COURT
(LOCATED BEHIND THE CAPITOL BUILDING)

The United States Supreme Court symbolizes a legal body that has been entrusted with protecting the rights of all citizens. Located behind the U.S. Capitol Building, nine of the best legal minds in the United States make decisions regarding matters ranging from race, capital punishment, and abortions, to religious freedom, taxes, and the limitations of the government. This large marble building projects an image befitting a legal body that influences the lives of every citizen of the United States.

THE HISTORY OF THE U.S. SUPREME COURT

1. Article III of the U.S. Constitution established the United States Supreme Court, which is the only court required by the Constitution. Congress creates all other federal courts.

2. The Judiciary Act of 1789 called for the Supreme Court to consist of a chief justice and five associate justices. John Jay from New York was the first Chief Justice of the U.S. Supreme Court.

3. On February 1, 1790, the Supreme Court convened its first session under the U.S. Constitution in the Merchants Exchange Building in New York City, New York.

4. In 1790, the Supreme Court moved with the federal government to Philadelphia, Pennsylvania. It was first located in Independence Hall and later in the City Hall.

5. In 1800, the Supreme Court moved with the federal government to the new Capitol Building in Washington, D.C.

6. Between 1815 and 1819, after the Capitol Building was burned by the British Army, Congress was convened on the current site of the Supreme Court Building in what was referred to as the *Old Brick Capitol.*

7. During the Civil War, the former Old Brick Capitol Building was used to confine Confederate prisoners and suspected collaborators. Captain Henry Wirz, the commandant of the Confederate prisoner of war camp at Andersonville, Georgia, was hanged on this site on November 10, 1865, for "murder in violation of the laws and customs of war." After the Civil War, the building was converted into residences until it was torn down in October 1932 for the construction of the new Supreme Court Building.

THE PRESENT DAY SUPREME COURT BUILDING

1. In 1935, the United States Supreme Court was relocated to its current location at First and East Capitol Streets, NW, Washington, D.C.

2. President William Taft (1909-1913), later the 10th Chief Justice of the U.S. Supreme Court (1921-1930), was one of the key figures in obtaining funding for the new Supreme Court Building.

3. Cass Gilbert was the primary architect of the Supreme Court Building. Neither Taft nor Gilbert lived to see the building completed. Taft died in 1930 and Gilbert died in 1934.

4. Robert Aitkin, Herman McNeil, John Donnelly, and James Fraser were the primary sculptors of the Supreme Court Building.

5. On October 13, 1932, the cornerstone of the current Supreme Court Building was dedicated by Chief Justice Evan Hughes. Among the items placed in the cornerstone were a photograph of former Chief Justice Taft and a copy of the 1932 World Almanac.

United States Supreme Court Building

6. In 1935, the Supreme Court Building was completed at a cost of $9,700,000, including furniture. This was the 146th year of the Supreme Court's existence.

7. In 1935, the Supreme Court was moved from what is now the Old Senate Chamber in the U.S. Capitol Building to the new building.

8. On October 7, 1935, the first term of the U.S. Supreme Court in its new building was convened.

9. The Supreme Court Building rises four stories above the terrace or ground floor.

10. The Supreme Court Building consists of a central building in the Corinthian architectural style, with two wings.

11. The front and back of the Supreme Court Building measures 304 feet. The sides of the Supreme Court Building measure 385 feet.

12. The oval plaza in front of the Supreme Court Building is 252 feet wide.

13. The exterior of the Supreme Court Building was constructed from Vermont, Alabama, and Georgia marble. The interior of the building was constructed from Spanish, Italian, Honduran, and African marble.

14. Sculptured from Vermont marble, the double rows of 16 Corinthian marble columns are a prominent part of the exterior of the Supreme Court Building.

15. Over 37,500 tons of marble were used to construct the Supreme Court Building at a cost of approximately $3 million.

16. The architrave above the sixteen columns is inscribed with the words "Equal Justice Under Law."

17. In 1935, the two light fixtures at the west entrance to the Supreme Court Building were installed. The turtles at the base of the lights symbolize the slow, but sure, movement of justice.

18. The bases of the two bronze flagpoles in front of the Supreme Court Building are crested with symbolic designs of the scales and sword, the book, the mask and torch, the pen and mace, and the four elements: air, earth, fire, and water. An eagle sits on the top of each pole.

19. American white oak is the primary wood used in the interior of the Supreme Court Building.

20. On each side of the main west entrance steps is a 45-ton cheek block that is the pedestal for a large figure. The male figure represents the *Authority of Law* and the female figure represents the *Contemplation of Justices*. The male figure holds a tablet backed by a sheathed sword - symbolic of law and its execution. The Latin word *Lex* on the tablet means "Law." The miniature figure the female figure holds in her hand represents *Justice*. These are the works of sculptor James Earle Fraser.

21. There are pediments over the porticos of the east and west entrances to the Supreme Court Building.

   • Sculptured by Herman A. McNeil, the pediment over the east entrance contains the phrase "Justice, the Guardian of Liberty." Moses, with the tablets of Hebraic law, is the central figure of the 18 by 60 feet symbol of law. On Moses' left is Confucius, representing the laws of China. On Moses' right is Solon, representing Greek law. The figure of a man holding a child represents the enforcement of the law, and the figure of a woman holding a baby represents tempering justice with mercy. The left soldier represents the settlement of disputes between states, and the other represents the protection of maritime and other laws. The tortoise and hare symbolize the slow, but sure, course of justice.

   • Sculptured by Robert Aitkin, the pediment over the west (main) entrance includes the phrase "Equal Justice Under Law." Liberty, who is looking into the future and has the scale of justice on her lap, is the central figure of the 18 by 60 feet symbol of law. The Roman soldiers represent Order and Authority. The remaining figures are symbolic of Council.

   • Included among the nine metaphorical figures in the pediment over the west entrance are the images of men responsible for the construction of the building. These figures include Justices William Taft and Evan Hughes, Architect Cass Gilbert, Sculptor Robert Aitkin, Justice John Marshall, and Secretary of State Elihu Root.

22. John Donnelly crafted the 17 feet high by 9-1/2 feet wide bronze doors on the west side of the Supreme Court Building. Referred to as *The Evolution of Justice*, the panels on each of the 13,000 pound doors depict historic scenes in the development of Western law. The doors slide into a wall recess when open.

23. On the other side of the bronze doors is the main corridor. It is referred to as the *Great Hall* and features a carved and painted ceiling of loral plagues. Busts of former chief justices line the corridor.

Great Hall in the U.S. Supreme Court Building

24. At the end of the Great Hall on the other side of the large oak doors is the Court Chamber where the justices hear arguments. The sides of the chamber are 82 feet by 91 feet, and rise 44 feet to the ceiling.

25. The 24 columns that stand around the chamber were crafted from Old Convent Quarry Siena marble from Italy. The walls and friezes are Ivory Vein marble from Spain, and the floor boards are Italian and African marble.

26. The chamber is decorated with drapes and a mould plaster ceiling picked out in gold leaf.

Chamber of the U.S. Supreme Court

27. Two friezes, measuring 40 feet long by 7 feet, 2 inches high and crafted from Spanish marble, are on the south and north walls of the chamber. Sculptured by Adolph Weinman, both friezes include figures of great lawgivers. The South Wall Frieze includes figures of lawgivers from the pre-Christian era such as King Solomon, and the North Wall shows lawgivers from the Christian era such as Charlemagne. Among these eighteen lawgivers are eight allegorical figures. The figures on the South Frieze are Fame, Authority, Light of Wisdom, and History; and Liberty and Peace, Right of Man, Equity, and Philosophy on the North Frieze.

28. The high windows along the north and south sides of the chamber were designed to ensure sunlight would not shine directly into the eyes of the justices on the bench or the counsel facing them.

29. The bench behind which the justices sit in the Court Chamber and the other furniture in the chamber were crafted from mahogany. In 1972, the bench was altered to its current half-hexagon shape to provide the justices with better sight and sound advantages.

30. The chairs used by the justices while sitting at the bench are crafted in the court's carpentry shop. The chairs are retained by the justices upon their retirement.

31. The justices are assembled behind the bench in the following order: The chief justice sits in the center of the bench, with the most senior justice on his/her right and the next in precedence on his/her left. The other justices alternate in a fashion so the most junior justice sits on the far right of the chief justice.

32. The two central figures above the bench depict the *Majesty of the Law* and the *Power of the Government*. Between them is a tablet of the Ten Commandments.

33. Representatives of the press are seated on the red benches along the left side of the chamber. The benches on the right are reserved for the guests of the justices.

34. The chamber has 230 seats for the public, more if you consider the chairs in the far back of the room where visitors are permitted to sit for just 3-5 minutes during a busy session, and then must surrender their seats to other temporary visitors.

35. There are two elliptical staircases in the Supreme Court Building. These self-supporting, hand-carved staircases were crafted from Alabama marble and bronze. The spiral staircases, which ascend five stories, are supported by how the steps overlap and are embedded into the wall 17 inches. Each story of a building is usually between 10 and 12 feet in height.

36. On the ground floor of the Supreme Court Building is another Great Hall. This Hall is overseen by a large statue of Chief Justice John Marshall. The statue of Justice Marshall was completed in 1883 and stood on the west lawn of the Capitol Building until 1981.

Statue of Chief Justice John Marshall

56

THE SUPREME COURT JUSTICES AND PROCEEDINGS

1. The maximum number of justices appointed to the United States Supreme Court may not exceed nine; one chief justice and eight associate justices. Initially, the Supreme Court consisted of six justices. Then the number was increased to seven, then nine, then ten, before being reduced to seven, and finally increased to nine in 1869. Congress determines the number of justices.

2. President Franklin Roosevelt (1933-1945) made an unsuccessful attempt at increasing the number of justices to 15. Even though Roosevelt failed in his attempt at increasing the number of justices, he eventually appointed eight of the nine justices who comprised the court. This is more than any other president.

3. The Judiciary Act of 1789 assigned the power to nominate justices to the President of the United States, with the approval of the U.S. Senate.

4. The Supreme Court justices are appointed to their positions for life unless they are impeached or elect to retire or step down from their positions due to ill health or other personal reasons. Supreme Court justices do not have to be attorneys, but almost all have been members of the bar.

5. Required by federal statue, the court's term begins on the first Monday in October and generally alternates between two weeks of sitting and two weeks of recesses through the end of April. The justices release their orders and opinions during the months of May and June. The court ends the term in June, but the justices continue to work on new petitions, motions, applications, and cases scheduled for the fall.

6. For two weeks each month during October through April, the justices hear an average of four oral arguments on each Monday, Tuesday, and Wednesday. The arguments are presented at or near 10 a.m., 11 a.m., with occasional sessions at 1 p.m. and 2. p.m.

7. Each argument session is limited to one hour. Thirty minutes for each side to present their argument and to answer questions from the justices.

8. The attorneys to speak first from the lectern in the center of the chamber during the morning and afternoon sessions are seated at the table on the left (10 a.m. & 1 p.m.), and the attorneys to speak second are seated at the table on the right (11 a.m. & 2 p.m.). The afternoon sessions occur only occasionally.

9. The attorneys who present their cases always start their arguments with the words "Mr. Chief Justice, may it please the court."

10. White and red lights are located before the attorney pleading his/her case. The lights are controlled by the Marshall of the Court and are used to signal the attorneys when the time for oral arguments has expired. The white light indicates that the attorney has five minutes to complete his argument. When the red light is switched on, the attorney must stop talking immediately. The attorney may save the last five minutes for rebuttal.

11. With few exceptions, the justices take at least a preliminary vote on a case the same week the oral argument is presented. The chief justice is the first to vote when the justices deliberate.

12. Between 7,000 and 8,000 petitions are presented to the Supreme Court for review each term. Of this total, the justices hear fewer than 100 petitions.

13. At least four justices must vote to hear an argument.

14. There must be at least six justices present for an argument to be presented.

UNIQUE FACTS ABOUT THE SUPREME COURT

1. A new group portrait of the justices is taken whenever a new justice is appointed and periodically updated.

2. In 1981, President Ronald Reagan appointed Sandra Day O'Connor as the first female Supreme Court justice. She retired in 2006.

3. The oldest Supreme Court tradition of placing a white quill on the table of each counsel presenting an argument continues today.

4. The library of the Supreme Court is on the third floor of the building and has a collection of more than 450,000 volumes of law and reference books, plus electronic retrieval systems.

5. The tradition of the justices wearing black robes dates back to 1800. As a result of the robes being tailored for men, who show a tie being worn, Justices Sandra Day O'Connor and Ruth Bader Ginsburg started the tradition of female justices wearing white judicial collars around the necks of their robes.

6. During his tenure as Chief Justice of the U.S. Supreme Court from 1888 through 1910, Melville Fuller started the tradition of the justices shaking hands prior to convening court sessions and private conferences to discuss decisions. It is believed that this tradition helps keep harmony among the justices.

7. As a tradition, there is a green porcelain spittoon by each of the justices' chairs. They are now used as wastepaper baskets.

8. The Supreme Court seal, shown to the right, is similar to the Great Seal of the U.S., but only has a single star beneath the eagle's claws, symbolizing the Constitution's creation of one U.S. Supreme Court.

9. The Supreme Court gym on the top floor includes a basketball court. The basketball court is jokingly referred to as the *Highest Court in the Land.*

10. The longest serving justice has been William O. Douglas. When he retired in 1975, he had served 36 years and 6 months.

11. Prior to the Supreme Court Building being opened, most of the justices worked from their homes when the court was not in session. This arrangement continued until 1937, when Justice Hugo Black started using his office in the building extensively.

12. The 1907 trials of Sheriff Joseph F. Shipp and his co-defendants have been the only criminal trials in the history of the Supreme Court where the verdicts and sentences were decided by the justices. The criminal contempt cases involved the lynching of Ed Johnson in Chattanooga, Tennessee, in 1906.

FACTS ABOUT THE WHITE HOUSE

The most popular residence in the United States is also a seat of power where decisions not only influence the policies of the United States, but the lives of men, women, and children worldwide. This large white structure on Pennsylvania Avenue has come to symbolize for generations of Americans the feeling of closeness between one of the most powerful leaders on earth and the average citizen who elected him to office. To many Americans, it matters not how many men or women serve as President of the United States, nor does it matter how many of them fulfill their quest for greatness. It does matter that this feeling of closeness remains, nurtured by a short, but impressive visit to the White House.

THE EARLY YEARS OF THE PRESIDENTIAL MANSION (WHITE HOUSE)

1. The Presidential Mansion was constructed at 1600 Pennsylvania Avenue. Known as *America's Main Street*, the avenue runs seven miles within Washington, D.C.

2. President George Washington (1789-1797) played an instrumental part in deciding where the Presidential Mansion would be located. He approved the site on June 28, 1791.

Garden Side of the White House

3. The Presidential Mansion was constructed nearly 1.5 miles from the Capitol Building.

4. The Presidential Mansion was the first large public building constructed in Washington, D.C.

5. A contest was used to encourage the submission of designs for the Presidential Mansion. The winner was to receive $500 or a medal of equal value.

6. President George Washington (1789-1797) selected James Hoban's design for the Presidential Mansion. A native of Ireland, Hoban resided in Charleston, South Carolina. Hoban also designed the state Capitol Building in Columbia, South Carolina.

7. It is believed Hoban patterned his design of the Presidential Mansion after the Leinster House in his native country of Ireland.

8. After his death on December 8, 1831, at age 69, James Hoban was buried at Mount Olivet Cemetery in Washington, D.C.

9. The initial design of the Presidential Mansion called for 36 rooms. Three of the 36 rooms were to be oval in shape. George Washington wanted the oval shape so the president and his visitors could better face each other. Upon completion, the structure was only one-fifth the size of its original design.

10. There are actually four oval rooms in the Presidential Mansion - the Blue, Green, and Yellow rooms, and the Oval Office for the president.

11. Congress appropriated $50,000 for the construction of the Presidential Mansion. The final cost of the Presidential Mansion was $232,000, or approximately $2,400,000 in 2010 inflation-adjusted dollars.

12. On October 13, 1792, construction on the Presidential Mansion was started.

13. The Presidential Mansion was constructed primarily by Irish and Scottish immigrants and slave labor. The white workers were paid wages for their labor. The owners of the slaves were paid $5.00 a month for the labor of each of their slaves.

14. The exterior of the Presidential Mansion was constructed from Arkose sandstone from the Aquia Creek quarry in Virginia.

15. Because sandstone is considered a weak stone, a combination of materials, consisting primarily of lime, rice glue, casein and lead, was used to cover the exterior of the Presidential Mansion.

16. On November 1, 1800, President John Adams (1797-1801) became the first president to occupy the Presidential Mansion. He and his family resided in the mansion for approximately four months in six usable rooms. All other presidents following Adams have occupied the Presidential Mansion/White House. Washington has been the only president not to live in the Presidential Mansion/White House. Washington left office on March 4, 1797.

17. Prior to the War of 1812, two large stone eagles guarded the north entrance to the Presidential Mansion.

18. The roof of the Presidential Mansion was originally slate. Then it was changed to iron sheets and finally to steel in 1927.

19. In 1797, the initial color of light yellow was applied to the exterior of the Presidential Mansion.

20. The British burned the mansion in 1814, destroying 1/3 of the exterior walls and the entire interior. The British Army burned Washington, D.C. in retaliation for the American Army burning the city of York, Canada, the same year.

21. There are a few places on the White House walls where the burn marks from the 1814 fire remain. One is near the kitchen and another is near the Truman Balcony. Because Truman missed sitting on his porch in Independence, Missouri, a balcony was added to the White House in 1948.

22. The Presidential Mansion was vacant from 1814 to 1817 while it was being reconstructed. President James Monroe (1817-1825) was the first president to reside in the Presidential Mansion after its destruction by the British Army.

23. In 1815, James Hoban was again hired to reconstruct the mansion he had originally designed and constructed. It cost approximately $300,000 to reconstruct the mansion.

24. In 1818, the reconstruction of the Presidential Mansion was completed. The reconstruction included painting the exterior of the mansion white versus the previous color of light yellow.

25. Between 1818 and 1979, there were at least 32 coats of whitewash and white paint applied to the exterior of the Presidential Mansion/White House. During 1979 and 1980, these coats were removed at a cost of nearly $3,000,000.

26. In 1824, Hoban constructed the south portico to the Presidential Mansion during the presidency of James Monroe (1817-1825). The north portico was completed in 1830 during the presidency of Andrew Jackson (1829-1837).

27. Until after the American Civil War, the Presidential Mansion was the largest residence in the United States.

28. The White House currently sits amid 18 acres of greenery referred to as *The President's Park*. The park consists of approximately 500 trees, 4,000 shrubs and 5-1/2 acres of turf.

29. In 1901, President Theodore Roosevelt (1901-1909) established the formal name by having the *de facto* name "White House–Washington" engraved on the White House stationery.

30. In 1902, Congress formally designated the *Presidential Mansion* as the *White House*.

THE PRESENT DAY WHITE HOUSE

1. The current White House has 132 rooms, 35 bathrooms, 147 windows, 412 doors, 28 fireplaces, 8 staircases, and 3 elevators.

2. The White House is 170 feet long by 85 feet wide by 58 feet high. The floor space of the White House totals 55,000 square feet; 67,000 square feet if the wings are included.

Carriage Side of the White House

3. The White House initially consisted of a ground floor level (formerly the basement) and two upper level floors. In 1927, during the presidency of Calvin Coolidge (1923-1929), a third upper level floor was added to the White House.

4. The 1927 addition eliminated the large attic and raised the roof. The addition also included 18 new rooms to the White House and a solarium or sky parlor over the south portico.

5. Of the four upper floors, the ground and first floors are used for public functions.

6. The third and fourth floors of the White House are the living quarters for the First Family.

7. Beneath the ground floor are two sub-floors that were constructed as bomb shelters. The floors are now used largely for storage.

8. There are four entrances to the White House, excluding service doors; i.e. kitchen, etc.

9. The East Room is the largest room in the White House. Because of its size, 80 feet long by 40 feet wide with a 22-foot ceiling, the East Room is often used for performing arts presentations attended by the president, first lady, and up to 300 guests. It was in the East Room where Mrs. Adams hung her laundry to dry, and it was also where six presidents have lain after their deaths, including Presidents Lincoln and Kennedy. Through the use of bleachers that reached nearly to the ceiling, the East Room held nearly 600 mourners during the funeral services for President Lincoln in April 1865.

10. Merriweather Lewis (famed explorer) lived in the East Room while he was the private secretary to President Thomas Jefferson (1801-1809).

11. Because of its use for large gatherings, the only piece of permanent furniture in the East Room is usually a 1938 Steinway piano.

12. The Blue Room is used for receptions. It was in the Blue Room that President Franklin Roosevelt (1933-1945) delivered his radio transmissions, referred to as *Fireside Chats*, to the American public.

13. Prior to becoming a reception room, the Blue Room was a boiler and furnace room. In 1837, President Martin Van Buren (1837-1841) began referring to the room as the Blue Room.

14. The Yellow Room is located on the third floor and is part of the private residence of the president and his family. The yellow motif was due to the influence of Jackie Kennedy, the wife of President John F. Kennedy (1961-1963).

15. The colors of the Green Room and Red Room became predominant during the presidency of James Monroe (1817-1825).

16. In 1862, it was in the Green Room that the body of President Abraham Lincoln's son William "Willie" Lincoln was viewed after his death.

17. President Thomas Jefferson (1801-1809) used the Green Room as his dining room.

Garden Side of the White House

18. In 1902, the east terrace was added to the White House. In 1942, the west terrace was added.

19. Designed by Edith Wilson to display a growing collection of White House china, the China Room was constructed in 1917 during the presidency of Woodrow Wilson (1913-1921).

20. The first time the 1,800 square-foot State Dining Room was referred to as the *State Dining Room* was during the presidency of Andrew Jackson (1829-1837). A portrait of Abraham Lincoln is a prominent part of the room that can seat 134 people.

21. The meals for White House guests are prepared in a 500 square-foot kitchen and a 250 square-foot pastry shop.

22. The White House Library was started during the presidency of Millard Fillmore (1850-1853).

23. The 27 feet by 23 feet room containing the current White House Library has a long history. A few facts about the Library are:

- Used as the White House laundry until the presidency of Theodore Roosevelt (1901-1909). In 1902, it was dedicated as a Gentleman's Ante-Room (waiting room).

- Designated as the White House Library in 1935. Used for teas and meetings by the first lady and president.

- Completely redecorated in 1961. Nearly 2,800 books are on the shelves of the library. Several writings relating to American thought and traditions have been added to the library.

24. The Lincoln Bedroom is the only room in the White House that is named after a president. Abraham Lincoln was President of the United States from March 1861 through April 1865. A few facts about the Lincoln Bedroom are:

- What is now referred to as the *Lincoln Bedroom* was used as a Cabinet Room during Lincoln's presidency.

- The Lincoln Bedroom is in a Victorian style, which is known for heavy furniture, formal fabrics, and elaborate trimmings.

- The Lincoln bed, which was crafted from dark rosewood, was purchased by First Lady Mary Lincoln in 1861. It was in this bed that Willie Lincoln died in 1862.

- The headboard of the Lincoln bed is six feet high. Over the headboard and attached to the wall is a carved canopy in the shape of a crown. Hanging from the crown is regal purple satin cloth over white lace.

- Other furniture consists of dark rococo revival furniture that was crafted by cabinetmaker John Belter.

- The carpet is a combination of emerald green, golden yellow, and deep purple.

- The walls are painted in a cream tone.

- Over the two windows are elaborate cornices (an ornamental band for covering a curtain rod). They were installed in 2004.

- The mantel over the fireplace, crafted from Opulent White marble, was installed in 2004.

- The room contains a copy of the Emancipation Proclamation, which went into effect on January 1, 1863.

- Winston Churchill, the notable Prime Minister of Great Britain, stayed in the Lincoln Bedroom during his many visits to the White House during World War II. Churchill swore he saw the image of President Lincoln in this room on more than one occasion.

25. Prior to the addition of several rooms to the White House during Theodore Roosevelt's administration (1901-1909), the administrative offices were located on the second floor of the White House. The president usually worked in the room that is now the Lincoln Bedroom, which adjoined his Cabinet Room.

26. In 1902, President Roosevelt started using an office in the West Wing. The office he used was a conventional rectangular room that was located in what is now the Roosevelt Room.

27. In 1909, President William Taft (1909-1913) directed that the size of the West Wing be expanded. Architect Nathan C. Wyeth designed the expansion of the West Wing.

28. In 1909, President Taft took over the president's secretary's office, a position that is now known as the *White House Chief of Staff*, in the center of the West Wing and changed the round-ended office to a full oval office. It was modeled after the Blue Room.

29. On Christmas Day in 1929, a fire destroyed the West Wing, including the Oval Office. It was rebuilt in 1930.

30. In 1934, in order to grant better access to a handicapped President Franklin Roosevelt (1933-1945), the Oval Office was moved to its current location on the southeast corner of the West Wing. A second floor to the West Wing was also added.

31. The Oval Office is 35 feet, 10 inches by 29 feet for a total of 1,038 square feet. The maximum height is 18 feet, 6 inches.

32. In 1942, the East Wing as it exists today was added to the White House and serves as office space for the First Lady. The East Wing also includes the president's theater, the visitor's entrance for social events, and the east colonnade.

33. In 1941, six large bulletproof glass windows were added to the Oval Office. The four doors in the Oval Office exit to the rose garden, the office of the president's secretary, the West Wing, and a small study/office for the president. The Oval Office is decorated to suit the tastes of the current president. Features that remain constant in the Oval Office are the presidential seal inlaid in the ceiling, the white mantel, and the United States and presidential flags behind the president's desk. The president also has an office in the living quarters of the White House.

34. Extensive renovations to the White House were started in 1948 during the presidency of Harry Truman (1945-1953). The cost of the 1948-1951 renovations totaled $5,700,000.

35. The renovations, completed in 1951, consisted of gutting out the insides of the White House, leaving the outside walls, installing steel beam supports, and rebuilding the insides to the specifications of the earlier White House.

36. During the 1948-1951 renovations, the number of rooms in the main structure increased from 48 to 54. Six-hundred-sixty tons of steel support the inner walls and floors. Some of the steel is set on concrete piers as deep as 27 feet below ground level.

37. In 1995, the section of Pennsylvania Avenue that runs in front of the White House was closed to motor vehicle traffic.

38. In November 2004, the renovation of the section of Pennsylvania Avenue that runs in front of the White House was completed at a cost of $23,000,000. This was the most significant improvement since it was paved with asphalt in 1876.

39. The renovated section of Pennsylvania Avenue is paved with gray granite along a 1,600 foot-long stretch of the avenue between 15th and 17th Streets. Eighty-eight elm trees were planted along the sides of the avenue.

UNIQUE FACTS ABOUT THE WHITE HOUSE

1. The White House is the oldest public building in Washington, D.C.

2. In 1826, Congress passed a law requiring that as much as possible, the furniture purchased for the White House must be of American origin and manufactured by Americans.

3. In 1801, the first toilets were installed in the White House at the insistence of President Thomas Jefferson (1801-1809). The toilets used large buckets of water suspended over the toilet to flush.

4. President Thomas Jefferson (1801-1809) opened the Presidential Mansion to public tours.

5. Only two objects known to have survived the 1814 burning of the Presidential Mansion remain in the White House. These items are:

   - Gilbert Stuart's portrait of George Washington was purchased for the Presidential Mansion in 1800 at a cost of $800. Dolley Madison saved the painting when the British captured and burned Washington, D.C. in 1814. In this portrait, there are books on the shelf behind Washington – One is titled *Constitution of the United Sates*. The word States is misspelled as Sates.

   - In the 1930s, a small medicine box was returned to the White House by a descendent of a British soldier who was present at the burning of the Presidential Mansion.

6. President Andrew Jackson (1829-1837) had running water installed in the White House - hand pumps.

7. The Magnolias planted by President Andrew Jackson (1829-1837) are the oldest trees surrounding the White House.

8. In 1913, the White House rose garden was started by Ellen Wilson, the wife of President Woodrow Wilson (1913-1921).

9. The first president to display a public Christmas tree in the White House was President Franklin Pierce (1853-1857).

10. Until the presidency of Millard Fillmore (1850-1853), all cooking in the White House was accomplished over an open fireplace. It was during his presidency that the fireplace in the kitchen was replaced with a cast-iron stove.

11. In 1878, President Rutherford Hayes (1877-1881) had a telephone installed in the White House. The one line was 500 yards long and transmitted to the office of the Treasury Secretary.

12. In 1879, the tradition of the annual Easter Egg Roll/Hunt was begun during the presidency of Rutherford Hayes (1877-1881). As many as 15,000 to 20,000 guests participate in this annual event.

13. In 1923, the tradition of the president lighting the National Christmas Tree was begun. President Calvin Coolidge (1923-1929) lit the first tree, a 48-foot Balsam Fir covered with 2,500 bulbs. Since 1954, an in-ground tree, which is periodically replaced, is located south of the White House on the Ellipse.

14. A painting of every former U.S. President hangs in the White House. The painting is completed during the president's term or after the president leaves office. Each president selects the artist who will paint the portrait. If a president dies prior to the painting being completed, the spouse or other close relative selects the artist and approves the painting.

15. As with former presidents, a painting of every former first lady hangs in the White House.

16. The small kitchen in the president's living quarters was installed during the presidency of John Kennedy (1961-1963). Mrs. Kennedy found it convenient when cooking for the Kennedy children.

17. It was during the presidency of Benjamin Harrison (1889-1893) that a flagpole flying the flag of the United States was installed on the roof of the White House.

18. In 1911, the Wright Brothers flew their plane over the White House during the presidency of William Taft (1909-1913).

19. On September 4, 1970, Presidential Proclamation 4000 was signed by President Richard Nixon (1969-1974). This proclamation proclaimed that the flag of the United States would be displayed over the White House at all times except during inclement weather.

20. It was during the presidency of William Taft that the first three automobiles were purchased for the president's use: An electric runabout, a gasoline-powered sedan, and a White steamer.

21. On March 15, 1913, President Woodrow Wilson (1913-1921) held the first presidential press conference.

22. In 1902, President Theodore Roosevelt (1901-1909) set aside a place for members of the press. President Dwight Eisenhower (1953-1961) made this area a permanent press area.

23. The current Press Room once held the swimming pool used by Presidents Franklin Roosevelt (1933-1945) through Richard Nixon (1969-1974). It was Nixon who had it covered over. In 1975, President Gerald Ford (1974-1977) had the current White House swimming pool constructed. It is 22 feet wide by 55 feet long, and is located outside on the White House grounds.

24. In 1901, as the guest of President Theodore Roosevelt (1901-1909), Booker T. Washington, a notable American educator, orator, and author, became the first African-American guest at the White House.

25. President Woodrow Wilson (1913-1921) authorized the grazing of sheep on the south lawn during World War I. The wool was sold for $52,823 to benefit the American Red Cross.

26. Bullet-proof glass and a bomb shelter were installed in the White House during World War II.

27. The president's chair in the Cabinet Room is two inches higher than the other chairs surrounding the conference table.

28. Prior to World War II, visitors could just walk into the White House for a visit. Picnics were allowed on the south lawn.

29. A tunnel was dug from the White House to the Treasury Department soon after the start of World War II. One of the Treasury's safest vaults, 30 feet below Pennsylvania Avenue, was converted into a bomb-proof shelter for the president and his staff. The shelter was never used, and in a modern war would not withstand a nuclear blast.

30. A system to detect gas was installed in the White House during the presidency of Harry Truman (1945-1953).

31. Television was installed in the White House during the presidency of Harry Truman (1945-1953).

32. Because the structure of the White House had deteriorated extensively by1947, President Harry Truman (1945-1953) moved into the Blair House until 1951. At one point, the piano in the living quarters dropped through a White House floor and the ceilings sagged 18 inches.

33. Even though it is often thought that President John Kennedy (1961-1963) was the first to use helicopters for short trips to and from the White House, it was actually President Dwight Eisenhower (1953-1961).

34. The musical salute of "Hail to the Chief," signaling the entrance of a U.S. President into a formal gathering, was begun during the presidency of James Polk (1845-1849).

35. The use of "Hail to the Chief" was discontinued at the direction of President Jimmy Carter (1977-1981), but was resumed three months later when his staff informed the president that many guests failed to notice his entrance into formal gatherings.

36. The permanent White House household staff has grown from 16 to between 85 and 100. Temporary personnel are used when necessary. President Zachary Taylor (1849-1850) was the last to use slaves as servants in the White House.

37. The person in charge of the White House household staff is referred to as the *Chief Usher*.

38. Until 1910, the presidents had to pay the salaries of the White House household staff from their personal funds. This was one of the reasons the salaries of the earlier presidents were so high for the times.

39. There are ten vehicle entrances to the White House grounds. The gates were constructed from steel.

40. The iron railing fence that surrounds the White House is eight feet high.

41. In 1842, during the presidency of John Tyler (1841-1845), guards were first assigned to the White House.

42. In 1922, the modern White House guards were established during the presidency of Warren Harding (1921-1923). The guards, originally referred to as the *White House Police*, were renamed the *Uniformed Division of the U.S. Secret Service* in 1977.

43. In 1898, the first *War Room*, which is now referred to as the *Situation Room*, was installed in the White House during the Spanish-American War. The Situation Room totals approximately 5,000 square feet.

44. It takes 570 gallons of paint to paint the exterior of the White House.

45. The largest number of children to reside in the White House at one time has been six. They were the children of President Theodore Roosevelt (1901-1909), and were referred to as the *White House Gang*.

46. The Marine Band often plays at the White House. Established in 1798, the Marine Band is nicknamed *The President's Own*. The band has performed at every presidential inauguration since 1801.

47. In 1961, President John Kennedy (1961-1963) directed the establishment of the formal reception that is now observed when the president and first lady meet foreign dignitaries at the White House.

48. As with the Capitol Building, there is really no front or back to the White House. The side of the White House facing the National Mall is the garden side or south facade and the side facing Pennsylvania Avenue is the carriage side or north facade.

49. In addition to a tennis court and swimming pool, the White House offers a president the use of a two-lane bowling alley, a 65-seat movie theater, a putting green and a basketball court. A running track was installed during President William Clinton's (1993-2001) administration.

50. The presidential china consists of 1,500 pieces.

51. At one time old furniture and pieces of presidential china were sold to pay for repairs to the White House and replace furniture and the china. This changed when Edith Roosevelt, the wife of Theodore Roosevelt (1901-1909), saw pieces of the presidential china and furniture for sale in pawnshops. As a result, china that has been broken or is no longer in use is totally smashed. All other items are transferred to the Smithsonian for disposition.

52. Seventeen White House weddings have been documented. The first occurred on March 29, 1812, during the presidency of James Madison (1809-1817) between Lucy Washington, the sister of Dolley Madison, and Thomas Todd.

53. In 1820, President James Monroe's (1817-1825) daughter, Maria, was the first daughter of a president to be married in the White House. In 1828, President John Quincy Adam's (1825-1829) son, John, was the first and currently only presidential son to be married in the White House.

54. President Richard Nixon's (1969-1974) daughter, Patricia, has been the most recent daughter of a president to be married on the grounds of the White House. She married Edward Cox in the Rose Garden on June 12, 1971.

55. Only three presidents have been sworn into office during ceremonies held in the White House. They are Presidents Rutherford Hayes in 1877, Franklin Roosevelt in 1945, and Harry Truman in 1945.

56. Of the seven presidents who have lain in repose in the White House, only two actually died in the White House - William Harrison (1841) and Zachary Taylor (1849-1850).

57. Though used before, the recurring use of the term *first lady* as it refers to the wife of the president first occurred in 1877. Reporter Mary Clemmer Ames used the term in her column in the weekly New York City newspaper *Independent* to refer to President Rutherford Hayes' (1877-1881) wife, Lucy.

58. By marrying Frances Folsom on June 2, 1886, Grover Cleveland (1885-1889) (1893-1897), at age 49, became the only president to be married in the White House. At age 22, Frances Cleveland has been the youngest first lady. The Cleveland's daughter, Esther, has been the only child of a president to be born in the White House. She was born in 1894.

59. The only bachelor president was James Buchanan (1857-1861).

60. The first child born in the White House was the grandson of Thomas Jefferson. In 1806, Jefferson's daughter, Patsy, then Mrs. Thomas Mann Randolph, Jr., gave birth to a son named James Madison Randolph. The child was named after future president James Madison.

61. Two first ladies have died in the White House - Caroline Harrison in 1892 and Ellen Wilson in 1914.

62. President James Madison (1809-1814) has been the shortest president, 5 feet tall, and the lightest, weighing 100 pounds.

63. Permanent bathtubs were installed in the White House in 1853. Since he weighed 332 pounds, President William Taft (1909-1913) had a ceramic bathtub installed in the White House that was 7 feet long by 41 inches wide, and held 65 gallons of water.

64. The presidents' salaries have been in the following increments:
   • From George Washington (1789-1797) through the first four years of Ulysses Grant's presidency (1869-1873), the annual salary was $25,000.
   • From Grant's second term (1873-1877) through the presidency of Theodore Roosevelt (1901-1909), the annual salary was $50,000.

- From William Taft (1909-1913) through the first term of Harry Truman (1945-1949), the annual salary was $75,000.
- From Truman's second term (1949-1953) through the presidency of Lyndon Johnson (1963-1969), the annual salary was $100,000.
- From Richard Nixon (1969-1974) through William Clinton (1993-2001), the annual salary was $200,000.
- Starting with George W. Bush (2001-2009) the president's current annual salary is $400,000.

(Limited by the U.S. Constitution, a president's annual salary cannot be raised during a president's current term.)

65. In 1958, Congress passed the Former Presidents Act, which gave retired presidents a pension, an office, and a staff. The pension is based on the annual salary of a cabinet secretary, such as Secretary of Defense. Starting with former president William Clinton (1993-2001), each former president receives funds for an office and staff for four and one-half years after they leave office.

66. The youngest president to **hold** the office of the presidency was Theodore Roosevelt (1901-1909). He was age 42 when he assumed the office on September 14, 1901, after the assassination of President William McKinley (1897-1901).

67. The youngest president to be **elected** to the office of the presidency was John F. Kennedy (1961-1963). He was age 43 when he took the oath of office on January 20, 1961.

68. The oldest president to be elected to the presidency was Ronald Reagan (1981-1989). He was age 73 in 1985, when he was sworn into office for his second term, and age 77 when he left office.

69. President Gerald Ford lived longer than any U.S. President. He died on December 26, 2006, at age 93 years, 165 days. This was 45 days longer than Ronald Reagan.

70. The oldest first lady has been Bess Truman, the wife of President Harry Truman (1945-1953). She died on October 18, 1982, at age 97.

71. President William Harrison (1841) served the shortest term as president, just 32 days. President Franklin Roosevelt (1933-1945) served the longest term in office, 12 years and 39 days.

72. The 22nd Amendment to the Constitution, which was ratified in 1951, states that no U.S. President may serve longer than ten years. Two 4-year terms plus a maximum of 2 years having acceded as U.S. President under a previous U.S. President's term.

73. The Constitution also stipulates that a person must be at least 35 years old and be born in the United States to serve as president.

74. The presiding U.S. President sends a commemorative wreath to the grave of a deceased former president on the anniversary of the former president's birthday.

75. Gerald Ford has been the only person to have served as vice president (1973-1974) and president (1974-1977) without having been elected to either office.

76. Each president since Herbert Hoover (1929-1933) has created a repository known as "A presidential library for preserving and making available their papers, records, and other documents and materials." Completed libraries are deeded to and maintained by the National Archives.

77. The first person of color to serve as President of the United States has been Barack Obama. As an African-American and former U.S. Senator from Illinois, the 47 year-old was sworn into office on January 20, 2009. The Bible used for President Obama's first inauguration was also used for President Lincoln's inauguration.

78. The Constitution specifies 39 words, plus the individual's name, in the presidential oath of office. The oath takes 30 seconds to recite. The vice president-elect will take the oath of office just before the president-elect. No number of words is specified for the vice president's oath of office, but usually totals around 73 words.

79. The tradition of the first lady or first gentleman holding the Bible during the swearing-in ceremony for the president was started on January 20, 1965, when Lady Bird Johnson held the Bible during the ceremony for Lyndon Johnson (1963-1969).

FACTS ABOUT THE LINCOLN COTTAGE – A PRESIDENTIAL RETREAT

Every U.S. President has had a retreat where a bit of peace from the political pressures of his office can be found. Since the presidency of Franklin Roosevelt (1933-1945), presidents have traveled to Camp David in the mountains of Maryland. However, during the second-half of the 19th century, and at 315 feet above sea level versus 33 feet above sea level for the White House, U.S. Presidents retreated to a cottage on the 3rd highest spot within Washington, D.C. This retreat has come to be referred to as the *Lincoln Cottage.*

THE ORIGIN OF THE LINCOLN COTTAGE

1. The Lincoln Cottage is located on the site of the Armed Forces Retirement Home in northwest Washington, D.C. at the intersection of Rock Creek Church Road NW and Upshur Street NW.

2. In 1842, George Washington Riggs, who founded the Riggs National Bank in Washington D. C., purchased 198 acres of farm land. The estate was initially referred to as *Corn Rigs*, derived from the estate's cornfields and the Scottish word rigs, meaning ridge or furrow.

Carriage Side of the Lincoln Cottage

3. During 1842 and 1843, Riggs had a 2-1/2-story, high-ceiling cottage built in the Early Gothic Revival style on the site. The brick exterior is covered with a pebble-dash (light-gray) stucco surface. There is also a wide, five-bay, one-story porch that has a roof that is surrounded by a wrought-iron railing and extends across the front of the cottage.

4. The cottage was referred to as *Riggs' Cottage* until 1888. The architect of the cottage was John Skirving. William H. Degges constructed the cottage.

5. The Riggs' Cottage originally had 14 rooms. At the time it was constructed it was considered a mansion second only to the White House in grandeur, and was the first house within Washington, D.C. to use natural gas versus kerosene for lighting. It even had a hand-pulled dumbwaiter, a small elevator, installed.

6. In 1851, and at a cost of $58,111, the cottage and the 256 acres of farm land surrounding it was purchased by the federal government for the site of a military asylum.

7. General Winfield Scott, a notable military leader during the war between the United States and Mexico (1846-1848), with the support of Major Robert Anderson, aide to General Scott, and Mississippi Senator Jefferson Davis, later President of the Confederate States, were instrumental in introducing a bill that would establish a military asylum for veterans on March 3, 1851.

8. On December 24, 1851, the military asylum was opened. Until 1857, when the military veterans were moved into the Scott Dormitory, now Sherman Dormitory, the military veterans lived in the cottage. It was also in 1857, in order to build political support, the commissioners of the asylum started inviting U.S. Presidents to stay at the cottage. The term *military asylum* was changed to the Old Soldiers' Home in 1859. Veterans at the asylum were referred to as *inmates*.

9. Starting with President James Buchanan (1857-1861), presidents used the cottage as a retreat. In addition to Buchanan, presidents Abraham Lincoln (1861-1865), Rutherford Hayes (1877-1881), and Chester Arthur (1881-1885) used the cottage.

10. In 1866, the year after the assassination of Lincoln, the hospital for the Soldiers' Home was relocated to the cottage. The hospital was located in the cottage until 1876, when a new hospital for the care of the residents was constructed.

11. In 1877, President Hayes began using the cottage as a retreat.

12. Beginning in 1886, and continuing for more than 30 years, the cottage served as the quarters for the band members at the Soldiers' Home.

13. In 1888, the cottage was renamed in honor of major, later brigadier general, Robert Anderson.   Anderson is known for being the commanding officer of the Union forces at Fort Sumter near Charleston, South Carolina, at the beginning of the Civil War.

14. From the early 1920s until 1954, the cottage was again used as a general barracks for the male veterans at the Soldiers' Home. In 1923, several small squad rooms were constructed for use by the male veterans.

15. From 1954 through 1969, the cottage was used as living quarters for the women veterans at the Soldiers' Home. An elevator was installed during this period. From 1969 through 2000, the cottage was used as a guesthouse and the supervisor's lounge.

PRESIDENT LINCOLN'S TIME AT THE COTTAGE

1. Lincoln first visited the cottage in March 1861. Historians believe his visit was prompted by a recommendation from out-going President Buchanan.

2. Because the elevation of the cottage is hundreds of feet higher than the evaluation of the White House, the temperature at the cottage in the summer is as much as 6 degrees cooler than the temperature at the White House.

The above is a photograph of a bronze statue of Lincoln with his horse, *Old Bob*, on the carriage side of the cottage. Lincoln rode Old Bob as he traveled the legal circuit in Illinois, and was marched immediately behind Lincoln's hearse during the funeral procession at Springfield, Illinois, on May 4, 1865.

3. The Lincoln family lived in the 14-room cottage almost continuously between June through November during the years 1862, 1863, and 1864. The Lincoln family also visited the cottage at various times throughout the year for short periods.

4. Between 1851 and 1863, the cottage was expanded with a west wing and a kitchen dependency added. In 1864, eight of the rooms in the cottage were wallpapered.

5. There were between 100 and 200 veterans living in Scott Barrack at the nearby Soldiers' Home during the years Lincoln stayed at the cottage. In addition, a force of between 150 and 180 Union soldiers were assigned to the cottage for the purpose of guarding Lincoln and his family. The assigned infantry and cavalry units consisted of the 11th New York Cavalry, the Ohio Light Guard, and the 150th Pennsylvania Volunteers.

6. It took Lincoln approximately 45 minutes to travel the distance of a little over 3 miles to or from the White House by horseback.

7. It is believed that while at the cottage during 1862, Lincoln wrote at least one draft of an executive order that became known as the Emancipation Proclamation. The *Emancipation Proclamation* is actually a pair of executive orders that abolished slavery in the states or areas of the states that were controlled by the Confederate States of America. Lincoln issued these orders under the authority set forth in Article II, Section 2 of the United States Constitution.

8. President Lincoln was at the cottage in July 1864 when Confederate General Jubal A. Early attacked Washington, D.C. On July 12, 1864, Lincoln and his wife, Mary, rode to Fort Stevens to observe the battle. The battle at Fort Stevens has been the only battle where a U.S. President was present and had come under enemy fire while in office. The fort is open to visitors.

9. In August 1864, Lincoln expressed to his friend, Ward Hill Lamon, that he believed a bullet had barely missed him while he was riding near the cottage at around 11 p.m. The bullet knocked Lincoln's hat off his head. It was after this incident that Lincoln traveled almost solely by carriage and with a military escort.

10. Lincoln's last night in the cottage was April 13, 1865. He was shot at Ford's Theatre the next night.

11. There are two gazebos near the Lincoln Cottage. The green and white one is close to the Sherman Dormitory and a white one, photographed to the right, is near the visitor center. Neither one was used by the Lincoln family as claimed by some sources.

THE CURRENT LINCOLN COTTAGE

1. The Lincoln Cottage, which was previously referred to as Riggs' Cottage and Anderson Cottage, was designated a National Historic Landmark on November 7, 1973; listed on the National Register of Historic Places on February 11, 1974; and proclaimed a National Monument by President William Clinton (1993-2001) on July 7, 2000.

2. From 1969 through the time the cottage was closed for renovations in 2000, it was used as a guesthouse and a supervisor's lounge.

3. On February 18, 2008, after a seven-year, $15 million renovation, the expanded 34-room, 10,000 square-foot cottage on 2.3 acres of land was opened to the public as a reflection on the lives of President Lincoln and his family while they lived in the cottage.

   Garden Side of the Lincoln Cottage

4. Nine of the 34 rooms are open to the public. There are four bedrooms in the cottage.

5. The simulated gaslight fixtures were re-created from a 1905 photograph of an upstairs room and a study of the old gas lines in the cottage. In addition, reproductions of the cottage's huge church-style front doors were installed, and the roof; constructed from Vermont purple slate, was refinished

6. The removal of 22 layers of paint from the interior walls of the cottage, during the seven-year renovation efforts, helped the curators determine the original colors of the walls.

7. The contents of the cottage include limited furnishings from the Civil War era, reproductions of curtains, carpet and other items from the Civil War era, and a reproduction of the Lincoln desk at which he wrote a draft of the Emancipation Proclamation. The reproduction of the desk cost $22,000. The original desk is in the White House.

FACTS ABOUT THE VICE PRESIDENT'S RESIDENCE

In response to the question about where the vice president and his family reside, the answer until 1976 was almost anywhere he pleased. The vice president, or the federal government on his behalf, would lease a residence to meet the vice president's needs. The government would pay the majority of the costs, but often the vice president would add to the allotted amount so he and his family could live in the style they had become accustomed to living. However, it was not the cost of actually leasing the residence that prompted the government to find a permanent residence for the vice president, but the cost and effort of installing security measures at each residence. As a result, the vice president now resides on the grounds of the Naval Observatory.

THE VICE PRESIDENT'S RESIDENCE

1. The vice president's residence is located at Number One Observatory Circle, Massachusetts Avenue at 34th Street, NW, Washington, D.C. The vice president's compound occupies 13 acres of the 72 acres of the Naval Observatory.

2. Margaret and Cornelius Barber, wealthy Georgetown landowners, originally owned the land on which the residence is located.

3. In 1893, the 21 room, white-brick Victorian style house with sage-green shutters was constructed.

4. The house currently consists of 33 rooms on four stories, with a pool house. Due to security concerns and the possible addition or deletion of unknown rooms, the current number of rooms is subject to change.

5. The house is owned by the United States Navy and is staffed by Navy personnel. Security is provided by both the Navy and Secret Service personnel.

6. The house was originally constructed for the superintendents of the Naval Observatory, who occupied the quarters from 1893 to 1923.

7. From 1923 to 1974, the house was used by the Chiefs of Naval Operations, United States Navy, and was designated the *Admiral's House.*

8. In 1974, Congress designated the former Admiral's House as the first official residence of the Vice President of the United States.

Vice President's Residence

9. The Navy's Chief of Naval Operations, who is a four-star admiral, now resides on the grounds of the Washington Navy Yard near South Capitol Street.

10. Gerald Ford was appointed vice president under President Richard Nixon (1969-1974) on December 6, 1973, after the resignation of Spiro Agnew on October 10, 1973. Ford was the first vice president eligible to reside in the house. However, the resignation of Nixon on August 9, 1974, occurred before renovations on the house were completed, and the then President Ford and his family moved into the White House versus the house at the Naval Observatory.

11. The next vice president eligible to reside in the vice president's residence was Nelson Rockefeller, vice president under President Gerald Ford (1974-1977). However, because he was already living in a large residence in the Washington, D.C. area, he elected not to move into the vice president's house, but did use it to entertain guests.

12. The first vice president to actually move into the vice president's residence was Walter Mondale. He was vice president under President Jimmy Carter (1977-1981).

13. The vice presidents usually furnish the residence with their own furniture. Museums, private collectors, government agencies often loan paintings and other items for use by the vice presidents.

FACTS ABOUT THE BLAIR HOUSE

Just across the street from the White House is what appears to be a small unassuming building referred to as the *Blair House*. Within its walls, military leaders, politicians, and heads of states stay during their visits to the Nation's Capital and the President of the United States. It is believed that the Blair House was purchased and renovated by the government at the request of Eleanor Roosevelt to house high-level dignitaries visiting her husband President Franklin Roosevelt (1933-1945). The house has welcomed visitors from around the world since the early days of World War II.

THE HISTORY OF THE BLAIR HOUSE

1. In 1824, the townhouse at #1651 Pennsylvania Avenue N.W. was constructed for Doctor Joseph Lovel, the first Surgeon General of the U.S. Army. It was constructed in the Federal style from buff colored limestone.

2. In 1836, Francis Preston Blair, a notable journalist and powerful advisor to Presidents Andrew Jackson (1829-1837) and Martin Van Buren (1837-1841), purchased the house for $6,500. In 1837, Blair, his wife Eliza, and three children moved into the house that was later referred to as the Blair House.

3. In 1859, Francis Blair expanded the presence of the Blair family on Pennsylvania Avenue by constructing #1653 Pennsylvania Avenue for his daughter, Elizabeth, and her husband, Samuel Lee. Lee was the third cousin of Robert E. Lee. In 1876, Montgomery Blair, the son of Francis Blair, and former Post Master General under President Lincoln (1861-1865), inherited the house.

4. The federal government purchased the Lee House (#1653) in 1941 and the Blair House (#1651) in 1942. The townhouses were joined in 1948. In 1969-1970, the townhouses located at #700 and #704 Jackson Place N.W. were purchased and joined to the Blair and Lee townhouses shortly afterwards.

5. The four interconnected townhouses form a 119-room complex totaling 70,000 square feet. The complex consists of 14 guest bedrooms, 8 staff bedrooms, 35 bathrooms, 4 dining rooms, kitchen facilities, laundry and dry cleaning facilities, an exercise room, a flower shop, and a fully equipped hair salon. The original Blair House, from which the entire Blair complex takes its name, appears on Pennsylvania Avenue as a yellow masonry structure.

6. Adjacent to the Blair House is the Trowbridge House, which was built in 1859 for mathematics professor William Petit Trowbridge. From the early 1900s, the 10,000-square-foot townhouse served as office space for the federal government. It is now used by former U.S. Presidents during their visits to Washington, D.C.

UNIQUE FACTS ABOUT THE BLAIR HOUSE

1. Before the American Civil War, such notable men as John Calhoun, Henry Clay, Daniel Webster, and Jefferson Davis used the house as a meeting place.

2. In 1850, future Civil War General William Tecumseh Sherman was married to Ellen Boyle Ewing in the house. In 1861, Colonel Robert E. Lee was offered command of the Union forces in the field in the house. Lee declined the position, resigned from the Union Army, and then accepted a commission in the Confederate Army.

3. Between 1948 and 1951, President Harry Truman and his family resided in the Blair House during the renovation of the White House.

4. On November 1, 1950, two Puerto Rican nationalists attempted to enter the Blair House in an effort to kill President Harry Truman (1945-1953). Secret Service Officer Leslie Coffelt and one assailant were killed, and two other officers were wounded.

5. In 1957, the Blair House was officially designated the *President's Guest House*. During a foreign leader's stay, the flag of that leader's nation flies over Blair House, and Blair House serves as a *de facto* diplomatic mission of that nation.

FACTS ABOUT THE NATIONAL MALL
(DEVELOPMENT, MUSEUMS, AND GALLERIES)

According to Pierre Charles L'Enfant's 1791 plan, the Mall was to be "four hundred feet in breadth, and about a mile in length, bordered by gardens, ending in a slope from the houses on each side." This simple beginning has evolved into one of the most visited sites in the United States.

THE HISTORY OF THE NATIONAL MALL

1. The National Mall was created from Pierre Charles L'Enfant's 1791 Plan.

2. Pierre Charles L'Enfant's 1791 Plan for developing the Mall was replaced by Andrew Jackson Downing's 1851 Plan.

3. Downing's Plan for developing the Mall was replaced by the 1901-1902 McMillan's Park Commission Plan.

4. The McMillan Plan, named after Michigan Senator James McMillan, called for a monumental and symbolic space. It led to what is now the Mall - a broad grassy expanse lined with non-residential buildings.

5. The McMillan Plan was designed in such a way that, if lines were drawn from one point to another, it would form a rectified axis that is shaped like a child's paper diamond shaped kite as photographed to the right. The Capitol Building rests at the bottom and the Lincoln Memorial at the top. The Jefferson Memorial is angled outward to the extreme left and the White House is angled outward to the extreme right. At an angle slanting inward from the Jefferson Memorial to the Lincoln Memorial is the FDR Memorial and at an angle slanting inward from the White House to the Lincoln Memorial is the Vietnam Memorial.

6. In 1932, the landscaping of the Mall was completed. Frederick Law Olmstead was the consultant responsible for the landscaping.

7. In 1933, the Mall was established as a National Park.

8. Originally, the Mall encompassed the area from between the United States Capitol Building to the Washington Monument. It now also includes the area from the Washington Monument to the Lincoln Memorial.

9. The distance between the steps of the Capitol Building and the Washington Monument is 1.1 miles.

10. The distance between the steps of the Capitol Building and the Lincoln Memorial is 1.9 miles.

11. The acreage of the Mall totals 309.17 acres. This is the area from the Capitol Building to the Lincoln Memorial.

12. Two forks of a small creek, which was initially referred to as *Goose Creek* and later *Tiber Creek*, joined at what is now Union Station. From this site the creek flowed to the Potomac River. Tiber Creek was named after the Tiber River, which runs through Rome, Italy. In 1871, after much of the creek had been transformed into a makeshift sewer, it was covered over and bricked up to be used as an underground sewer. The sewer is still being used today. It is because the Tiber Creek still runs underground through Washington, D.C. that large water pumps are still used in the basements of the buildings along the Mall in order to deal with occasional flooding. Specifically, the National Archives had several pumps installed when it was built in the 1930s.

13. Until 1850, there were slave pens along the Mall. During the Civil War (1861-1865) soldiers camped and trained on the Mall and cattle grazed near the Washington Monument.

14. Until 1868, notorious slum communities occupied a large area of the Mall. These communities were known by such names as *Swamppoodle* and *Murder Bay*.

15. In 1872, a 14 acre tract was given to the Baltimore and Potomac Railroad for the construction of a depot. The railroad also laid tracks north to south across part of the Mall. The depot and tracks were removed in 1909.

16. Until 1901, a central market, which was a very convenient place to sell and buy goods, was among the sites on what is now the Mall.

17. On the Mall are several buildings and museums administered by the Smithsonian Institution. This institution has a staff of approximately 6,000 workers and an annual budget of over $700 million. Approximately 70% of the funding is provided by the federal government. Information about some of the buildings and museums is provided in the following subsections.

THE SMITHSONIAN INSTITUTION BUILDING – THE CASTLE

1. The Smithsonian Institution Building was designed in 1847 and dedicated in 1855.

2. The building is the final resting place of James Louis Macie Smithson, an English chemist and mineralogist. His donation to the U.S. government led to the founding of the Smithsonian.

Smithsonian Institution Building

3. Smithson was an English citizen who was born in France in 1765. He died and was buried in Italy in 1829.

4. Until 1801, Smithson's legal name was James Louis Macie. Smithson was the illegitimate son of Hugh Smithson, the first Duke of Northumberland. When James Macie was 49 years of age he was granted permission to take his father's name.

5. In 1904, in gratitude for his generous gift to the United States, Smithson's remains were brought from Genoa, Italy, to Washington, D.C. He lies in the Crypt Room at the entrance to the Smithsonian Institution Building.

6. Smithson's will provided that if his nephew, Henry James Hungerford, died without an heir, all of Smithson's property would be bequeathed to the United States. Hungerford died childless in 1835.

7. In 1838, the Smithson estate, consisting of 104,000 gold coins valued at $508,318 was settled. The value of his estate in today's dollars would be approximately $12 million.

8. By law, the money bequeathed by Smithson is loaned to the United States government. The government pays the Smithsonian Institution interest on the loan.

Crypt of James Louis Macie Smithson

9. In 1840, the government decided that the gift would be used to start a National Institute, which would house botanical and scientific specimens donated to the national government.

10. A board of regents, whose chancellor is the Chief Justice of the United States, governs the Smithsonian Institution. The regents include the Vice President of the United States, three U.S. Senators, three members of the House of Representatives, and nine private citizens.

11. Because of its prominent towers, the Smithsonian Institution Building is often referred to as the *Castle*.

12. During the Civil War, President Abraham Lincoln (1861-1865) occasionally watched from the top of the Castle as Union troops drilled on the Mall.

13. The Smithsonian Institution Building is now used largely for the administration of the Smithsonian Institution and its holdings.

MUSEUMS OF THE SMITHSONIAN INSTITUTION LOCATED ON THE MALL

THE ARTS AND INDUSTRIES BUILDING

1. In 1881, the Arts and Industries Building was completed after 15 months of construction.

2. The Arts and Industries Building was constructed from red brick, sandstone, tile, and slate in the Modernized Romanesque style. The interior of the building consists of a four-square plan leading to a central rotunda.

Arts and Industries Building

3. The group of three female figures over the entrance to the building is titled *Columbia Protecting Science and Industry*. The figures were constructed from zinc coated with plaster.

4. The event that led to the building of the Arts and Industries Building was the 1876 Philadelphia Centennial. To spare themselves the cost of shipping their exhibits home, almost all of the exhibitors at the World Fair presented their exhibits to the United States government. Several historians believe this event is how the Smithsonian got to be referred to as the *Nation's Attic*, a term that was credited to Mark Twain for first using it. Federal laws now restrict these mass presentations.

THE NATIONAL GALLERY OF ART, WEST BUILDING

1. In 1941, the National Gallery of Art, West Building was opened to the public. There are 100 rooms of displays.

2. The exterior walls of the West Building were constructed from five different shades of pink Tennessee marble.

National Gallery of Art, West Building

3. On July 2, 1881, President John Garfield (1881) was shot at the Baltimore and Pacific Railroad Station near where the West Building is currently located. He died on September 19, 1881. A statue of Garfield is located near the Capitol Building.

THE NATIONAL GALLERY OF ART, EAST BUILDING

1. In 1978, the building containing the National Gallery of Art, East Building, was completed at a cost of $95,000,000.

2. Paul Mellon and his family foundation provided the funding.

3. The exterior walls of the East Building were constructed from three different shades of Tennessee marble.

National Gallery of Art, East Building

THE NATIONAL AIR AND SPACE MUSEUM

1. The Smithsonian's aeronautical collection began in 1876, when it was presented a group of Chinese kites after the Philadelphia Centennial Exhibition.

2. In 1946, Congress chartered the National Air Museum.

3. A national armory, constructed in 1855, was on the site of the museum until 1964.

4. In 1966, Public Law 89-509 changed the museum's name to the National Air and Space Museum.

National Air and Space Museum

5. On July 1, 1976, the current home of the museum was opened to the public. The ribbon cutting ceremony opened a 685 feet long by 225 feet wide museum that has 200,000 square-feet of floor space within exterior walls constructed from pink Tennessee marble. The ribbon cutting was accomplished by using a 10-foot arm identical to the one on the Viking Lander that was on its way to the planet Mars. The arm was activated by a signal from the Viking Lander, which took only eighteen minutes for the signal to travel from Mars to the museum.

THE NATIONAL MUSEUM OF AMERICAN HISTORY

1. In 1964, the National Museum of American History was opened to the public.

2. Until 1980, the National Museum of American History was called the National Museum of History and Technology.

3. The exterior of the 750,000 square-foot museum was constructed from Tennessee pink marble.

National Museum of American History

4. Displayed in the museum is a wide variety of artifacts that reflect the history of the United States. One of the most prominent of these artifacts is the United States flag that flew over Fort McHenry near Baltimore, Maryland, during the night of September 13-14, 1814, as the British Navy bombarded the fort. Facts about the flag include:

- Purchased for $405.90, the flag was hand-stitched in Baltimore, Maryland, during July and August 1813 by 37-year-old Mary Pickergill, a professional flag maker. She was assisted by her 13-year-old daughter, Caroline, two nieces, and an African-American servant.

- It was sewn from 266 yards of English wool with 15 cotton stars and stripes. Pickergill used the floor of Claggett's Brewery in Baltimore, Maryland, to assemble the flag.

- It currently weighs about 45 pounds without backing. With the old backing it weighed approximately 150 pounds.

- It has a red V on one of the white stripes. No one knows the origin of this letter.

- The original garrison flag was 30 feet by 42 feet in size. This is about one-fourth the size of a basketball court.

- The deep blue rectangle that forms the flag's canton, where the stars are located, measures about 16 feet by 21 feet.

Fort McHenry Flag – Shows Missing Star and Damaged Areas

- Because 8 feet of the flag has been snipped from its length, the size of the flag has been reduced to 30 feet by 34 feet.

- It has 15 stripes and 15 stars (mullet), one for each state in the Union at the time. A *mullet* is a star that has straight-sided rays. A star with wavy rays is referred to as an *estoile*.

- The stripes are about 2 feet wide and each star is about 2 feet across.

- The flag was designed to fly from a 90-foot flagpole.

- In 1813, it was presented to Major George Armistead, Commander of Fort McHenry during the War of 1812.

- It remained in Major Armistead's family until July 1907, at which time it was loaned to the Smithsonian by Armistead's grandson, Eben Appleton. In 1912, Appleton gifted the flag to the United States.

- It has had one of the original stars removed and 27 patches added.

- In 1914, a new backing of Irish linen was attached.

- In 1963, it was installed in the Museum of History and Technology. It was displayed every hour on the hour for most of the day until it was removed for repairs in 1998.

- During 1998-2006, extensive repairs were completed, which affected some of the repairs described above. These conservation efforts included the cleaning and removal of the linen backing that was put in place in 1914, the removal of 1.7 million old stitches and material, the mending of 165 areas of the flag, and attaching a new, light-weight backing.

- The *Star-Spangled Banner* was written as a poem by Francis Scott Key during the night of September 13-14, 1814, as he watched the 25-hour battle for Baltimore, Maryland. The manuscript of the poem is in the Fort McHenry museum.

- The Star-Spangled Banner became the national anthem of the United States in 1931. The words of the anthem are set to the melody of *Anacreontic Song*, which was composed around 1790 by English composer John Stafford Smith.

- By 1818, Congress limited the number of stripes on the flag of the United States to 13, one for each of the original 13 states. The stripes for Vermont (1791) and Kentucky (1792) were removed.

THE NATIONAL MUSEUM OF NATURAL HISTORY

1. In 1910, the National Museum of Natural History was opened to the public. In the 1960s, the east and west wings were added.

Museum of Natural History

2. The granite museum, which is larger than 18 football fields, was originally called the New Natural Museum.

3. One of the first of the more than 125 million specimens that welcome visitors to the museum is a large African elephant in the rotunda. The specifics about the elephant, that is often referred to as "Harry," are:

- It weighs eight tons and is 13 feet, 2 inches tall.

- J.J. Fenykovi killed it in Angola on November 13, 1955.

- It took sixteen bullets from a .416 Rigby rifle to kill it.

- It is the second largest elephant ever killed, and the largest ever mounted. The largest elephant ever killed was six inches taller and was killed in 1974 in Angola.

"Harry" the Elephant

- The hide weighed more than two tons (over 4,000 pounds) when it was removed from the carcass.

- The tusks are seven feet long. The tusks are plastic; the real ones are in storage.

95

THE NATIONAL MUSEUM OF THE AMERICAN INDIAN

1. At a cost of $199,000,000, the National Museum of the American Indian was dedicated on September 21, 2004.

2. The 450,000 square-foot museum is located on a 4.25-acre site.

3. The curving five-story museum was constructed from gold-tone Minnesota limestone.

National Museum of the American Indian

4. The exterior of the museum is intended to look like a canyon wall that has been formed by wind and water.

5. The museum faces east toward the rising sun.

6. Scattered throughout the forest, wetlands, meadowlands, and crop areas are more than forty grandfather rocks, which are viewed as the elders of the landscape, and speak to the longevity of the Native people.

7. The water feature, which runs along the north side of the museum site, recalls the tidal waterway of Tiber Creek. The Tiber Creek flows underneath the National Mall.

8. The rotunda at the entrance to the museum is 120 feet high.

9. Approximately 7,500 objects are displayed in the museum through three major exhibits and other exhibits. These major exhibits are beadwork, baskets, and pottery. Other exhibits address the lives and trials of the Indians of North, Central, and South Americas.

10. In 2009, a 12-foot-tall, 2,000 pound, bronze statue of a buffalo dancer was installed near the museum. The statue was sculptured by George Rivera, a New Mexico, Tewa-speaking, Pueblo American-Indian artist.

Buffalo Dancer

FACTS ABOUT THE NATIONAL ARCHIVES

No building within Washington, D.C. is more important to the history of the United States than the National Archives. This building, often referred to as the *Nation's Safe Deposit Box*, shelters within its walls a document that declared the United States free from England, protects documents that set forth the rights of the its citizens, and makes available for view documents that have within their borders a record of notable events in the history of the United States.

THE NATIONAL ARCHIVES

1. For many years prior to the ground breaking, the site of the National Archives was used for a large and busy Center Market.

National Archives

2. Architect John Russell Pope designed the neoclassical structure. It is an example of the beaux-arts style.

3. In 1926, Congress authorized construction of the National Archives Building. A total of $8,500,000 was appropriated for construction.

4. On September 9, 1931, the ground for the National Archives Building was broken.

5. On February 20, 1933, President Herbert Hoover (1929-1933) dedicated the cornerstone for the National Archives.

6. A total of 8,575 piles were driven twenty-one feet into the ground to support the building, before pouring a huge concrete bowl as a foundation. These reinforcements and unique foundation are needed because of the sources of water under the Mall.

7. In November 1935, 120 staff members of the Archives started working in the building.

8. In 1937, the Archives Building was completed.

9. The Archives Building is fireproof and had large pumps installed at the time of construction to deal with possible flooding.

10. The Archives Building is 330 feet long by 213 feet wide by 166 feet high.

11. The exterior superstructure of the Archives Building was constructed from limestone and the base was constructed from granite.

12. There are 72 Corinthian limestone columns surrounding the exterior of the Archives Building. Each column is 53 feet high by 5 feet, 8 inches in diameter, and weighs 95 tons. The columns were formed in sections, and as each section was finished, it was hoisted into place on top of earlier sections.

13. There are two statues each on the Constitution Avenue and Pennsylvania Avenue sides of the Archives Building. The statues were carved from 125-ton blocks of limestone.

14. The statues on the Constitution Avenue side of the Archives Building represent *Heritage* (female) and *Guardianship* (male). The female holds a child and a sheaf of wheat in her right hand as symbols of Growth and Hopefulness. In her left hand she protects an urn, symbolic of the Ashes of Past Generations. The male uses martial symbols, such as the helmet, sword, and lion skin to convey the need to protect the historical records for future generations.

15. The statues on the Pennsylvania Avenue side of the Archives Building represent *Past* (male) and *Future* (female). The inscription, "Study the Past", on the male figure is from a quotation by the Chinese scholar, Confucius: "Study the past, if you divine the future."

16. The pediment of the Archives Building facing Constitution Avenue is 18 feet high in the center by 118 feet wide. The figures were carved from individual stone blocks weighing between 13 and 50 tons each. The central figure in the pediment represents the Recorder of the Archives. The frieze above the figures is based on the flower of the papyrus plant, which is the symbol of paper. The rams represent parchment. Parchment is made from the skin of sheep. The other figures represent citizens holding documents, such as the U.S. Constitution and the Declaration of Independence. The dogs symbolize Guardianship and the winged horses symbolize Inspiration.

17. The pediment of the Archives Building facing Pennsylvania Avenue is 18 feet high in the center by 118 feet wide. The central figure represents Destiny. This figure is flanked by eagles, which represent Strength through Unity. The male and female figures on the left of the central group symbolize the Art of Peace. The warriors on the right of the central group symbolize the Art of War. The group of four people on the right represents the Romance of History. The group of four people on the opposite side represents the Song of Achievement.

18. The 12-foot limestone eagles on top of the Archives Building symbolize Guardians.

19. There are thirteen, 8-foot-high medallions on the attic frieze of the Archives Building. One represents the House of Representatives, one the Senate, and the ten cabinet-level executive departments of the federal government that surrendered their records into the keeping of the National Archives. The thirteenth medallion is the Great Seal of the United States.

20. The two, 9-foot figures in Roman armor on the sides of the central doorway of the Archives Building, Pennsylvania Avenue side, represent the Guardians of the Portal.

21. The storage space of the Archives Building is 757,000 square feet. The opening of an additional storage building in College Park, Maryland, added an additional 1.9 million square feet.

22. The entrance doors to the Archives Building from the Constitution Avenue are each nearly 10 feet wide, 11 inches thick, and 38 feet, 7 inches high. Each door weighs 6-1/2 tons (13,000 pounds), and are the largest bronze doors in the world.

23. The bronze design on the entrance floor into the Archives Building represents Legislation, Justice, History, and War and Defense.

24. The Rotunda of the Archives Building is 75 feet high from the floor to the ceiling.

25. The mural on the left side of the Rotunda is titled *The Declaration of Independence.*

26. Barry Faulkner completed the mural titled *The Declaration of Independence.* It shows 28 delegates to the 1776 Continental Congress. Thomas Jefferson is presenting the Declaration of Independence to John Hancock.

Mural – Declaration of Independence

27. The mural on the right side of the Rotunda is titled *The Constitution.*

28. The mural titled *The Constitution* was completed by Barry Faulkner, and depicts George Washington and the 28 delegates to the United States Constitutional Convention. James Madison is presenting the Constitution to George Washington.

29. Each mural weighs 340 pounds.

30. The major holdings of the National Archives date back to 1775.

31. There are billions of pages of textual material and millions of still photographs in the Archives Building.

32. The Archives Building stores only those federal records that are judged to have historical/legal value. This number totals about 1 to 3 percent of the records generated by the federal government during any given year.

33. In November 2004, the National Archives opened its document warehouse to visitors. The $7,000,000 exhibit consists of a dozen alcoves (Public Vaults) that display over 1,100 items.

THE DOCUMENTS ON PERMANENT DISPLAY IN THE NATIONAL ARCHIVES

On permanent display within the National Archives are the Declaration of Independence, the Constitution of the United States, and the Bill of Rights. Collectively, these documents are referred to as the *Charters of Freedom.*

THE DECLARATION OF INDEPENDENCE

1. Between June 11, 1776 and June 28, 1776, a Committee of Five: consisting of two New England men, John Adams of Massachusetts and Roger Sherman of Connecticut; two men from the Middle Colonies, Benjamin Franklin of Pennsylvania and Robert R. Livingston of New York; and one southerner, Thomas Jefferson of Virginia, drafted the Declaration of Independence.

2. On June 28, 1776, the committee's initial draft of the Declaration of Independence was submitted to Congress. Prior to voting for independence, Congress made 47 alterations to the draft of the Declaration of Independence.

3. On July 2, 1776, Congress voted for independence. From July 2nd through July 4th 1776, Congress made an additional 39 alterations to the draft, for a total of 86 alterations to the original draft proposed by the five committee members charged with drafting the Declaration of Independence.

4. The Declaration of Independence is made up of five distinct parts: Introduction, Preamble, Body - divided into two sections, and Conclusion.

5. On July 4, 1776, twelve of the thirteen colonies adopted the Declaration of Independence. New York did not vote. John Hancock signed/authenticated the document on the same date. However, it wasn't until August 2, 1776, that the majority of the delegates signed the document.

6. Fifty-six members of Congress signed the Declaration of Independence.

7. The Declaration of Independence is written on parchment, which is a sheep skin specially treated with lime and stretched to create a strong, long-lasting document.

8. The parchment on which the Declaration of Independence is written measures 29-3/4 inches by 24-1/4 inches. The parchment is engrossed, which is a process of preparing an official document in a large, clear hand.

9. The Declaration of Independence consists of 1,458 words, plus signatures. On the back of the Declaration of Independence is penned the words "Original Declaration of Independence, dated 4th July 1776."

10. The first formal use of the term United States of America was in the body of the Declaration of Independence.

THE U.S. CONSTITUTION

Constitution of the United States

1. On May 14, 1787, the Constitutional Convention first met in Philadelphia, Pennsylvania, to discuss the formation of the Constitution. However, a quorum was not present until May 25, 1787, and Rhode Island chose not to attend the convention.

2. On August 6, 1787, the Constitutional Convention accepted the first draft of the Constitution.

3. On September 17, 1787, the Constitutional Convention approved the United States Constitution.

4. The original seven Articles of the Constitution are: Article I-Legislative Branch; Article II-Executive Branch; Article III-Judicial Branch; Article IV- State; Article V-Amendments; Article VI-Debts, Supremacy, Oaths; and, Article VII- Ratification.

5. Article VII of the United States Constitution required the ratification of at least nine states for the Constitution to be considered established. This occurred on June 21, 1788, when the ninth state, New Hampshire, voted to ratify the Constitution.

6. Each of the states ratified the Constitution in the following order:

STATE	DATE RATIFIED	VOTE
Delaware	December 7, 1787	Unanimous
Pennsylvania	December 12, 1787	46-23
New Jersey	December 18, 1787	Unanimous
Georgia	January 2, 1788	Unanimous
Connecticut	January 9, 1788	128-40
Massachusetts	February 6, 1788	187-168
Maryland	April 28. 1788	63-11
South Carolina	May 23, 1788	149-73
New Hampshire	June 21, 1788	57-47
Virginia	June 25, 1788	89-79
New York	July 26, 1788	30-27
North Carolina	November 21, 1789	194-77
Rhode Island	May 29, 1790	34-32

7. The Constitution consists of 4,543 words, plus signatures on four pages of parchment that measure 28-3/4 inches by 23-5/8 inches.

THE BILL OF RIGHTS

1. On September 25, 1789, the first United States Congress met to discuss twelve amendments to the Constitution. On December 15, 1791, Congress ratified ten of the twelve proposed amendments, which are referred to as the *Bill of Rights*.

2. The first ten amendments are:

I.	Freedom of Speech, Press, Religion, and Petition
II.	Right to Keep and Bear Arms
III.	Conditions for Quarters of Soldiers
IV.	Right of Search and Seizure Regulated
V.	Provisions Concerning Prosecution
VI.	Right to a Speedy Trial, Witnesses, etc.
VII.	Right to a Trial by Jury
VIII.	Excessive Bail, Cruel Punishment
IX.	Rule of Construction of Constitution
X.	Rights of the States under the Constitution

3. The two Articles not included in the Bill of Rights addressed the number and apportionment of U.S. Representatives, and limiting the ability of Congress to increase the salaries of its members. Neither Article would have established a right as the term Bill of Rights is used today.

4. Congress has ratified only 27 amendments to the Constitution. The latest amendment addresses Congressional Compensation, which was ratified on May 7, 1992. This amendment was initially proposed in 1789 as one of the original twelve amendments.

LOCATIONS OF THE CHARTERS OF FREEDOM

1. Through much of the 19th century, the Declaration of Independence and Constitution were displayed in the Old Executive Office Building near the White House. The building has been renamed the Eisenhower Executive Office Building.

2. From 1924 through 1951, and with the exception of the documents being stored in vaults at Fort Knox, Kentucky, during World War II, the Declaration of Independence and Constitution were exhibited at the Library of Congress.

3. From 1952 through 2000, the Declaration of Independence and Constitution were displayed in a special helium-filled glass and bronze case in the Archives Building. Due to space limitations, only two of the four pages of the Constitution were displayed.

4. As the result of a 2001-2003 renovation to the Archives Building, all pages of the Declaration of Independence, Constitution, and Bill of Rights are displayed in an encasement that consists of an aluminum base and a titanium frame. A 3/8 inch-thick laminated tempered glass cover shields the documents. The encasements are filled with argon gas with a controlled amount of humidity to keep the parchment flexible. A special yellow filter protects the documents from light.

5. Though unsubstantiated, it is believed that each evening the Declaration of Independence, Constitution, and Bill of Rights are lowered 25 feet into a 5-ton concrete vault. However, for the sake of security, this may not be the final secured site.

FACTS ABOUT THE FORD'S THEATRE
(SITE WHERE PRESIDENT LINCOLN WAS SHOT)

On April 14, 1865, sensing the end of the Civil War, President Abraham Lincoln turned his attention to the reunification of the Union. After working a full day, the 16th President of the United States and his wife, Mary, took what was to be their last carriage ride together. During the ride and at stops along the way, they discussed what the future might bring to them. However, neither the president nor Mrs. Lincoln could envision that, in less than six hours after this quiet ride through the Maryland countryside, their plans would be destroyed by a single shot at Ford's Theatre.

FORD'S THEATRE

1. Ford's Theatre is located at 511 Tenth Street, Washington, D.C.

2. In 1833, the First Baptist Church of Washington was constructed on the future site of Ford's Theatre.

Ford's Theatre

3. In 1859, the church was vacated when the First Baptist congregation merged with the Fourth Baptist congregation.

4. In 1861, John Thomson Ford leased the building as a theater, and on November 19, 1861, presented the "Christy Minstrels," the first of multiple musical productions. The success of the shows resulted in a few days of renovations being made to the building, prior to it being reopened on December 10, 1861.

5. During February and March 1862, Ford invested $10,000 into additional renovations and the remodeling of the theater. On March 19, 1862, the theater was reopened as *Ford's Athenaeum* with a production of "The French Spy."

6. On May 28, 1862, President Lincoln attended the first of at least 12 different productions at Ford's Theatre.

7. On November 9, 1863, Lincoln saw John Wilkes Booth perform a production of "The Marble Heart."

8. On December 30, 1862, the theater was gutted by fire when a defective gas meter ignited.

9. On February 28, 1863, the cornerstone for the present structure was laid, and on August 27, 1863, the theater was reopened under the name *Ford's New Theatre* with a production of "The Naiad Queen." The above photo of the new Ford's Theatre was taken in the 1860s – Courtesy Library of Congress

10. On April 14, 1865, John Wilkes Booth assassinated President Abraham Lincoln during a performance of "Our American Cousin." The theater was closed on the same day.

11. The performance on April 14, 1865, was the last of 495 performances of various types since the theater was reopened in August 1863.

12. In 1865, the seating capacity of Ford's Theatre was 1,700 on three levels. Today the seating capacity is 658 on two levels.

13. From April 14, 1865, until after the execution of the four Lincoln conspirators Atzerodt, Herold, Powell, and Surratt on July 7, 1865, the theater remained closed and guarded. It was then released to John Ford. However, due to receiving threats that the theater would be burned down if reopened, troops were again stationed at the theater, and the theater remained closed until 1968.

14. During August 1865, the War Department began leasing the building from John Ford at a monthly cost of $1,500.

15. In August 1865, the War Department began converting the theater into a three-story office building at a cost of $28,000. In December 1865, the U.S. Surgeon General started using the building as an Army Medical Museum.

16. On April 7, 1866, Congress appropriated $100,000 for the purchase of the building. The final payment was made in July 1866.

17. From late 1865 through 1887, the building was used as an office building. The War Department Records Office occupied the first floor, the Library of Medicine was located on the second floor, and the Army Medical Museum was located on the third floor.

18. In 1887, the Library of Medicine and Army Medical Museum were moved to a new building on the Mall. All three floors of the building were subsequently used by the War Department.

19. On June 9, 1893, the collapse of the building floors resulted in 22 government clerks being killed and 68 others injured.

20. During the period of 1893-1931, the building served as a warehouse and a publications depot for the Adjutant General's Office of the War Department.

21. On July 1, 1928, the building was transferred from the War Department to the Offices of Public Buildings and Public Parks.

22. On February 12, 1932, a museum about the life of Lincoln was opened on the first floor of the building, and on August 10, 1932, the building was transferred to the National Park Service.

23. In 1946, Senator Milton Young of North Dakota introduced the first legislation for the restoration of Ford's Theatre, and President Dwight Eisenhower (1953-1961) signed a Congressional Act to restore the theater in 1954.

24. On July 7, 1964, after the completion of a restoration study, Congress authorized $2,073,000 for the restoration of the theater.

25. Between January 1965 and December 1967, Ford's Theatre was restored. On January 21, 1968, the National Park Service held dedication ceremonies for the restored Ford's Theatre.

26. On February 5, 1968, the first performance held at Ford's Theatre since 1865 was performed. The play was "John Brown's Body."

27. On February 13, 1968, the restored Ford's Theatre was opened to the general public.

THE LINCOLN ASSASSINATION

1. As early as August 1864, Booth had gathered around him a group of boyhood friends and other accomplices in an effort to capture President Lincoln. The final unsuccessful attempt at capturing Lincoln occurred in March 1865. Booth's goal was to exchange President Lincoln for Confederate prisoners of war.

2. It is believed Booth was among the crowd in front of the White House when President Lincoln made his speech after the surrender of Robert E. Lee's army on Palm Sunday, April 9, 1865. It is also believed Booth decided on this date to assassinate the president.

3. At 10:30 a.m. on April 14, 1865 (Good Friday), Booth discovered that the Lincolns were going to attend Ford's Theatre. In response, Booth assigned George Atzerodt the task of killing Vice President Andrew Johnson and Lewis Powell to kill Secretary of State William Seward. Atzerodt lost his nerve and did not attempt to kill Johnson. Powell failed to kill Seward with a knife.

4. At 8:30 p.m. on April 14, 1865, the Lincolns entered Ford's Theatre, an hour into the First Act of the play "Our American Cousin." Major Henry Rathbone and Clara Harris accompanied the Lincolns. These guests of the Lincoln's were stepbrother/stepsister, related through the marriage of Harris' father to Rathbone's mother.

5. Prior to going to Ford's Theatre, Booth stopped at the Star Saloon near the theater for a few drinks. Harry Ford lived above the saloon, and it was from his residence that he carried the Lincoln rocker on the day Lincoln was shot. The saloon was demolished in 1930.

6. Just prior to 10 p.m., Booth made the last of several trips to the theater. He walked to the back entrance to the theater and asked handyman Edman Spangler to hold his horse. Because Spangler was busy with the play in progress, he turned the horse over to a young man by the name of Joseph "Peanuts" Burroughs to hold.

7. At about 10:10 p.m., Booth took the back stairs to the 3rd level of the theater, where he was granted access to the hallway leading to the President's State Box (Boxes #7 and #8 combined). Booth then used a wooden brace to barricade the hallway door before peering through a small hole in a second door to Box #7. It is believed the door was previously drilled so the patrons enjoying the performances could be observed by theater management.

8. Waiting for Act III, Scene 2 of the play, where he knew there would be a loud response from the crowd, Booth stepped through the door to Box #7 and shot President Lincoln once behind the left ear with a .44 caliber derringer.

President's State Box

9. Responding to the shot, Major Rathbone struggled with Booth, and when the gun was knocked from Booth's hand, Booth pulled a knife and stabbed Rathbone in the left arm. It was Rathbone who removed the wooden brace that barricaded the hallway door.

10. While jumping from the state box to the stage floor, a drop of eleven and one-half feet, Booth caught his spur on the Treasury flag hanging over the front of the president's box. This misstep caused Booth to land off-balance, breaking the fibula, a small bone in his left leg. The break was three inches above the ankle.

11. Even with his injury, Booth took time as he raced to his horse in the alley to shout *Sic Semper Tyrannis*. A Latin phrase on Virginia's state flag meaning "Thus always unto tyrants."

12. Escaping through Baptist Alley behind Ford's Theatre, Booth started his twelve-day escape attempt.

13. In response to shouts for a doctor, Dr. Charles Leale, a 23-year-old surgeon, rushed to the box and had the president placed on the floor. Lincoln had stopped breathing, but his labored breaths started again after a blood clot was removed from his wound.

14. After the doctors determined Lincoln's wound was too severe for him to survive a trip to a hospital or to the White House, he was carried to the Petersen Boarding House across the street to be administered medical aid.

15. Major Rathbone, even though seriously injured by Booth's knife, escorted Mrs. Lincoln to the Petersen House, where he collapsed from a loss of blood.

THE AFTERMATH OF THE ASSASSINATION

THE MEMBERS OF THE LINCOLN FAMILY

1. After his death on April 15, 1865, President Lincoln, age 56, was buried in a tomb in Springfield, Illinois, with his two sons, Edward (Eddie) who died in 1850 at age 3 from either diphtheria or pulmonary tuberculosis, and William (Willie), who was nearly age 11 when he died in 1862 from typhoid fever. Lincoln was buried on May 4, 1865, in the same suit he wore to his 2nd inauguration a few weeks earlier.

Lincoln's Tomb in Illinois

2. In 1882, Mary Lincoln died at age 63 in Springfield, Illinois, and is entombed in a crypt near her husband's sarcophagus.

3. In 1871, Thomas "Tad" Lincoln died at age 18 from either pleurisy, an infection of the membrane surrounding the lungs, or from tuberculosis. He is entombed in a crypt near his father.

4. Robert Todd Lincoln, who was present at his father's death, became a lawyer, a successful businessman, Secretary of War, and Minister to England. He was also present at the dedication of the Lincoln Memorial in 1922. Robert died in 1926 at the age of 82, and is buried with his wife, Mary, and son, Abraham "Jack" Lincoln, at Arlington Cemetery. In response to the question as to why Robert was buried at Arlington versus next to his parents and siblings in Illinois, the answer was revealed in his wife's words, when in a letter she stated Robert "....was a personage, made his own history, independently of his great father, and should have his own place in the sun!"

110

THE CONSPIRATORS

1. On April 26, 1865, John Wilkes Booth died near Port Royal, Virginia, at age 26, from a shot to the spine. His remains were buried on April 27, 1865, at the Washington Penitentiary and later in a nearby warehouse. On June 26, 1869, Booth's remains were reburied at Greenmount Cemetery in Baltimore, Maryland.

2. On July 6, 1865, the conspirators were informed of their sentences, and on July 7, 1865, Mary Surratt (age 42), Lewis Powell (age 21), David Herold (age 23), and George Atzerodt (age 30) were hanged and buried in pine ammunition crates on the grounds of the federal penitentiary in Washington, D.C. The location is currently Fort McNair, and tennis courts now cover the site of the executions. The remains of Surratt, who was the first woman executed by the United States government, are buried in Mount Olivet Cemetery, Washington, D.C. Herold's last resting place is in the Congressional Cemetery, Washington, D.C., and Atzerodt is buried in St. Paul's Cemetery in Baltimore, Maryland. Powell's remains were claimed in 1871. However, in 1992, Powell's skull was discovered in a desk drawer in the Anthropology Department of the Smithsonian Institution. In   1994, the skull was released to his relatives, who buried it in a cemetery in Geneva, Florida, with the rest of his remains. Above is one set of the hoods and shackles worn by the prisoners.

3. Dr. Samuel Mudd, who treated Booth's broken leg, Michael O'Laughlen, and Samuel Arnold were sentenced to life in prison, and were transported to Fort Jefferson in the Dry Tortugas off the coast of Florida. In 1867 at age 26, O'Laughlen died from yellow fever at the prison. Mudd and Arnold were released from prison in 1869. Mudd died in 1883 at age 49 and Arnold in 1906 at age 72.

4. Edman "Ned" Spangler, a carpenter and stage hand at Ford's Theatre and the first person to hold Booth's horse on the night of the assassination was sentenced to six years in prison. He was released from Fort Jefferson in 1869, and died in 1875 at age 49. Spangler spent the last few years of his life with or near the Dr. Mudd family and is buried in a cemetery near the Mudd farm.

5. John Surratt, the son of Mary Surratt and an admitted co-conspirator in the kidnapping attempt of President Lincoln, escaped to Canada, then to England, then Rome, Italy. He was finally arrested in Alexandria, Egypt, in 1866, and tried in 1867 for the murder of Lincoln. The civil trial ended in a deadlock; four votes guilty and eight votes not guilty. Surratt was never again tried and died in 1916 at age 72.

HENRY RATHBONE AND CLARA HARRIS

Henry Rathbone and Clara Harris were married in 1867. However, while serving as the United States Consul to Germany, Rathbone shot and stabbed his wife to death in 1883. She was age 38. For his crime, Rathbone was placed in a mental asylum in Germany for the criminally insane, where he died in 1911 at age 74. The remains of Henry and Clara were buried in Germany, and were destroyed in 1952 after they had been declared abandoned and unattended.

THOMAS CORBETT – SHOT JOHN WILKES BOOTH

Born in London, England in 1832, Thomas "Boston" Corbett, the Union sergeant who shot John Wilkes Booth, left the U.S. Army after the Civil War with his reward of $1,653.85. Troubled by mental problems, which were probably caused by the effects of using mercury in his profession as a hatter, a maker or seller of hats, Corbett was committed to a mental asylum in Topeka, Kansas, after he drew his revolver on the members of the Kansas legislature on February 15, 1887. On May 26, 1888, Corbett escaped from the asylum, and there is no substantiated record of what happened to him after his escape. Corbett started using the nickname *Boston* after he moved to Boston, Massachusetts and decided that he liked the name.

JOHN T. FORD – OWNER OF FORD'S THEATRE

John T. Ford was in Richmond, Virginia, on the night Lincoln was shot. On April 18, 1865, he and his brothers, Harry and James, were arrested in Baltimore, Maryland, for complicity in the crime. They spent 39 days incarcerated before being released for a lack of evidence. Ford remained a successful business man, including managing several theaters, president of the Union Railroad, and acting mayor of Baltimore, Maryland. Ford died in 1894, at age 65.

PEANUTS – HELD BOOTH'S HORSE AT FORD'S THEATRE

A young man with the nickname *Peanuts* was the second person to hold Booth's horse at Ford's Theatre. Peanuts referred to himself as Joseph Burroughs and John Bohraw. After testifying under the name of Joseph Burroughs at the conspiracy trial in May 1865, no substantiated record of his later life has been found, and there is no record of his race, even though both Negro and Caucasian men claimed to be Peanuts into the early part of the 20th century.

THE DISPOSITION OF THE ARTIFACTS RELATING TO THE LINCOLN ASSASSINATION

1. The portrait of George Washington, a carved-back/cane-seat parlor chair, and a small sofa are the only three remaining items in the state box that were actually located there on the night of April 14, 1865.

2. The $8 top hat worn by Lincoln on April 14, 1865, consisting of a silk fiber finish over a paper base, has been in the Smithsonian Institution since 1867. The hat equates to a hat size of 7-1/8. Lincoln added a wide black silk mourning band to the hat in remembrance of his son Willie.

3. With the exception of Lincoln's white shirt, which was cut into pieces and given as mementos of the tragedy, the suit of clothing worn by Lincoln at the time he was assassinated is on display in Ford's Theatre. The clothing consists of a black, bloodstained double-breasted frockcoat; black broadcloth pants with bloodstains on the knee; black cotton vest, with six buttons and four pockets; black silk tie; and square-toed, goatskin, shin-high black boots. The fly on the pants, which is supposed to have three buttons, only has two, and the two remaining buttons don't match.

4. Another piece of bloodstained clothing is the overcoat that curators think was over the president's shoulders or the back of his chair at the time he was assassinated. The coat was made for Lincoln's second inauguration and embroidered in the black lining are an eagle, shields, and the words, "One Country, One Destiny."

5. On the night Lincoln was shot he was carrying gloves and had two pairs of eyeglasses, a lens polisher, a pocketknife, a linen handkerchief, a watch fob, a brown leather wallet with a $5 Confederate note, and nine newspaper clippings in his pockets.

6. The derringer used to kill Lincoln was manufactured by Henry Derringer of Philadelphia, Pennsylvania. It is 5.87 inches long with a 2-1/2 inch barrel and weighs 8 ounces. It usually fires a .44 caliber lead ball, but it is believed Booth used a .41 caliber, 6.7 gram ball. The trigger and mountings were made from German silver and there is a small box in the butt of the gun for an extra percussion cap. The derringer and the 7-1/4 inch long knife used to stab Major Rathbone are on display in Ford's Theatre. (Caliber refers to the barrel and/or bullet diameter in inches).

7. On April 22, 1865, the government confiscated the dark walnut and red-silk damask rocker on which Lincoln was sitting at the time he was shot. Secretary of War Edwin Stanton kept the rocker in his office until 1866. From 1866 to 1929, the rocker was in the possession of the War Department, Department of Interior and finally the Smithsonian. In 1921, Blanche Ford, Harry Ford's widow, petitioned the government for the return of the rocker. In 1929, it was returned to Mrs. Ford and in the same year sold at an auction to an agent of Henry Ford (Ford Motor Company) for $2,400. The rocker is on display in the Henry Ford Museum in Dearborn, Michigan.

8. Booth's red, 6 inch by 3-1/2 inch diary, actually an 1864 appointment book, with 18 pages missing, the Treasury flag on which Booth caught his spur when he jumped from the balcony, and the boot removed from Booth's leg when Dr. Mudd set it, are on display in Ford's Theatre.

9. The remains of the lead ball that killed Lincoln, a section of Lincoln's skull, a few strands of his hair, and a portion of Booth's vertebrae are at the National Museum of Health and Medicine.

10. The couch on which Booth sat while Dr. Mudd set his leg is on display at the Dr. Samuel Mudd Museum near Waldorf, Maryland.

FACTS ABOUT THE PETERSEN HOUSE
(BUILDING WHERE PRESIDENT LINCOLN DIED)

After President Abraham Lincoln was shot by John Wilkes Booth on the night of April 14, 1865, the doctor who examined the president determined the wound to his head was too serious for him to survive a trip over cobblestoned streets to either the White House or to a hospital. As a result, President Lincoln was carried to the street in front of Ford's Theatre as witnesses to this tragedy searched for a suitable place to treat the president's wound. Their search ended at the Petersen Boarding House, a small establishment almost directly across the street from Ford's Theatre.

THE PETERSEN BOARDING HOUSE

1. Built in 1849, the Petersen Boarding House is a three-story brick building with a basement. It is located across the street from Ford's Theatre.

Petersen Boarding House

2. William A. Petersen, his wife, Anna, and their six children, lived and worked in the basement of the building, while the top three floors were rented to both men and women for single and multiple-nights of lodging. William was a tailor by trade, and he and Anna had emigrated from Germany in 1841.

3. Henry Safford, a guest at the Peterson Boarding House, is credited with calling for Lincoln to be carried to the house on the night he was shot. William T. Clark occupied the room where Lincoln was carried to after the shooting. Clark, a former Union soldier, worked as a clerk at the Quartermaster General's Office and was not in the room at the time Lincoln was shot.

4. The ball fired by Booth entered behind Lincoln's left ear, traveled through his brain, and lodged behind his right eye. As many as 14 physicians attended to Lincoln after he was shot, but they could do very little to save his life. Lincoln never regained consciousness.

5.   Lincoln died in the Peterson Boarding House at 7:22 a.m., April 15, 1865, and his body was taken to the White House at a little after 9 a.m., April 15, 1865.

6.   The room in which President Lincoln died is approximately 9 feet wide by 17 feet long.

7.   The photograph to the right was taken by Julius Ulke, a boarder at the Peterson House and a professional photographer, a short time after Lincoln's death. It shows the walnut spool bed on which Lincoln died,  including the blood stained pillow. To accommodate Lincoln's 6 feet, 4 inches height, he was placed diagonally across a bed that was only six feet long.   Photo – Courtesy of National Park Service

8.   Though not substantiated, it is believed that just a few weeks prior to the assassination of President Lincoln, John Wilkes Booth, while visiting actor Charles Warwick in the rented room, had actually rested on the same bed that the president died on during the morning of April 15, 1865.

9.   In 1871, William and Anna Petersen died without a will. William died in June from a laudanum overdose, a mixture of alcohol and opium derivatives. Anna died in October from a heart attack.

10. At an auction in October 1871, the bed on which Lincoln died was sold for $80 to William H. Boyd. Boyd also purchased a bureau, gas jet, rocking chair, and engraving. In 1889, the collection, including the bed, was sold to Charles Gunther for $5,000 by Boyd's son, Andrew. In 1920, the bed and related furnishings were sold to their current owner, the Chicago Historical Society, for $250,000.

11. The blood-spotted pillow and pillowcase on which Lincoln's head rested were displayed on the bed in the Petersen Boarding House until 1994. The items are now in the possession of the Chicago Historical Society in Chicago, Illinois.

12. The furnishings in the room where Lincoln died are similar in appearance to those of April 15, 1865.

13. On one of the walls of the room where Lincoln died is a reproduction of the *Village Blacksmith* and over the bed is a copy of Rosa Bonheur's *Horse Fair*. The wallpaper is a reproduction of the original pattern, and the bed and chairs closely resemble those originally in the room at the time of Lincoln's death.

14. The front parlor, a common area used by the boarding house guests, looks today very much like it did the morning of April 15, 1865, and is where Mrs. Lincoln spent much of the previous night. The reproductions of Victorian style furnishings consist of a couch, chairs, small tables, writing desk, and fireplace. The wallpaper in the room is a pattern from the time period.

Front Parlor

15. The back parlor is where former Union Corporal James Tanner took shorthand notes from witnesses of the tragedy as interviewed by Secretary of War Edmond Stanton. Tanner had lost both of his legs during the Civil War, and is buried at Arlington Cemetery.

16. The house remained in the Petersen family until November 1878, when it was sold to Louis Schade for $4,500. Schade published the *Washington Sentinel* newspaper in the basement.

17. In 1893, former Ohio resident **O**sborn **H. I. O**ldroyd (OHIO) (1843-1930) moved into the Petersen House and displayed his over 3,000 books and artifacts about the life of Abraham Lincoln. From 1883 to 1893, Oldroyd had lived in the Lincoln House in Springfield, Illinois. First as a renter, then as a curator.

18. In 1896, the federal government purchased the house for $30,000 and retained the services of Oldroyd. In 1927, the federal government paid Oldroyd $50,000 for his collection of books and artifacts. Some artifacts were returned to the Lincoln House.

19. In 1932, Oldroyd's collection, which formed the nucleus of the Lincoln exhibits, was moved to Ford's Theatre.

20. The historical bronze marker at the entrance to the house was installed in 1924, replacing an 1883 marble tablet.

FACTS ABOUT THE UNITED STATES HOLOCAUST MEMORIAL MUSEUM

It is said "Those who cannot remember the past are condemned to repeat it." The United States Holocaust Memorial Museum (USHMM), through a series of audio/visual recordings and nearly 1000 artifacts provides a window into a part of history where an insurmountable amount of pain, suffering, and destruction of life was inflicted on the people of Europe by a madman and his executioners. And it is through these educational tools that the unknowing are enlightened and are encouraged to immediately oppose any form of persecution and genocide.

FACTS ABOUT THE HOLOCAUST BETWEEN 1933 AND 1945

1. First used by the Greeks as early as the fifth century B.C., the word *holocaust* was derived from the words *olos* meaning "whole" and *kaustos* or *kautos* meaning "burnt", and was accepted to mean a sacrifice wholly consumed by fire or a great destruction of life, especially by fire. However, since the early 1930s, the word Holocaust has been associated with the systematic persecution and annihilation of the people of Europe, especially Jews, by Nazi Germany and its collaborators between 1933 and 1945.

2. The Holocaust was inflicted on the people of Europe primarily by the National Socialist German Workers' Party (Nazi Party), a political party that gained power in Germany during 1933, and remained in power until the end of World War II in 1945. The Nazi Party embraced a combination of military dictatorship, socialism, and fascism. A fascist government always has one class of citizens that is considered superior (good) to another (bad) based upon race, creed, or origin.

3. The following provides some of the different categories of civilian and military victims of Nazi atrocities from 1933 through 1945. **(Due to a lack of universally accepted statistics, some of the figures offered by the author may conflict with other sources.)**

- Jews – Originally referred to as Hebrews, many non-Jews associate the term Jew with the religion of Judaism. It is also a term associated with a person's non-religious status as a citizen of an ancient tribe or nation, such as the Children of Israel. However, the Nazis did not distinguish between the religious and social characteristics in their persecution of the Jews.

- Gypsies - The Roma and Sinti peoples are the groups most frequently referred to as Gypsies. They are believed to have originally migrated from India, eventually arriving in Europe between the 12th and 15th centuries. Because of the color of their skin, language, race, and social structure, the nomadic Gypsies were considered by the Nazis as outcasts from the European society. Even through the unreliability of the pre-Holocaust population figures make it difficult to determine, an estimated 220,000 to 500,000 Gypsies were murdered by the Nazis.

- Non-Jewish Civilians - As many as 1.9 million Polish, 3 million Ukrainian, 1.5 million Russian and 1.4 million Byelorussian non-Jewish civilians perished during the occupation of their countries by the Nazis between 1939 and 1945.

- People with Mental or Physical Disabilities – These victims were largely Germans whose physical or mental disabilities were opposite to the Nazis' philosophy of a strong Aryan race, therefore, seen as inferior. More than 200,000 people with mental and physical disabilities were murdered at the hands of the Nazis through Operation T4. The term Aryan race was used by the Nazis to designate a master race of non-Jewish Caucasians.

- Soldiers of the Soviet Union - Of the 5.7 million Soviet soldiers who were captured by the Nazis between 1941 and 1945, more than 3 million died in captivity.

- Homosexuals – They were persecuted by the Nazi leadership because it was believed that a homosexual's degenerate behavior posed a threat to the capacity of the state and the masculine character of the German male. Of the estimated 50,000 to 60,000 German homosexuals incarcerated by the Nazis, an estimated, but unsubstantiated, 10,000 died in captivity.

- Jehovah Witnesses – These German citizens were persecuted by the Nazi because they practiced a religion that did not accept the Nazi ideology, refused to recognize any God other than Jehovah, and refused to serve in the military. Approximately 11,000 Jehovah Witnesses were imprisoned and over 1,000 died during incarceration.

4. The Nazis hated the Jews because the Nazis were racists of the worst kind. The Nazis considered themselves and the German people a master race of Aryans, superior to all other races.

5. In response to the question as to why the Jews did not resist the Nazis. It was simply a matter that the Jews, like so many other victims, failed to believe until it was too late that a civilized nation, even one controlled by the Nazis, could intend to murder them all. When the Jews finally realized that the Nazis did intend and had the means, they lacked the strength of arms to effectively respond. However, there were several acts of resistance; including uprisings in the camps and ghettos and through partisan efforts.

6. The persecution of the Jews in Germany began in 1933, when the Nazi regime started to systematically deprive German Jews of their civil rights, property, freedom, and lives. In 1933, Germany's Jewish population totaled approximately 565,000, or 1% of the German population of 62 million. The post-World War II population of the German Jews had been reduced to approximately 35,000, for a 94% reduction of the Jewish population in Germany. Approximately 169,000 Jews left Germany between 1933 and 1938.

7. The persecution of Jews, by the Nazi regime in the 21 countries occupied by the Nazis, started at the beginning of World War II in Europe in 1939. The Jewish population in Europe totaled approximately 9.5 million in 1933. The post-World War II population of European Jews had been reduced to approximately 3.5 million, for a 63% reduction of the Jewish population.

8. Of the estimated 6 million Jews murdered by the Nazis and their collaborators from the start of the war in Europe on September 1, 1939, to the end of the war in May 1945, it is estimated that over 4 million of the victims were in Poland and the Soviet Union.

9. It is estimated that as many as 1.5 million children under the age of 18 were murdered during the Holocaust. This figure includes more than 1.2 million Jewish children, thousands of Gypsy children, and thousands of mentally and physically handicapped children.

10. Between 1933 and 1945, the Nazis constructed over 20,000 prime and satellite concentration camps throughout Europe. Dachau was the first concentration camp. It was built at a site northwest of Munich, Germany, for political prisoners.

11. The largest concentration/death camp complex built by the Nazis was Auschwitz I, II, and II near Krakow, Poland. Built between 1939 and 1942 for men, women and children, an estimated 1 million to 1.1 million Jews and non-Jews perished at the complex from 1939 through 1945.

12. The Nazis established over 1,000 ghettos to confine Jews, Gypsies, and other undesirables into tightly packed areas of Eastern European cities. Turning the ghettos into *de-facto* concentration camps. The first ghetto was established in 1939 in Poland.

THE CONSTRUCTION OF THE HOLOCAUST MUSEUM

1. Timeline for the construction of the United States Holocaust Memorial Museum:

   - October 7, 1980 - Public Law 96-388 established the United States Holocaust Memorial Council.
   - April 13, 1983 – 1.9 acres of land owned by the federal government for construction of the museum building is transferred to the Council. The land was previously occupied by a building that housed part of the U.S. Department of Agriculture.
   - October 16, 1985 – Ground breaking ceremonies take place.
   - October 5, 1988 – Cornerstone for the museum is laid.
   - August 2, 1989 – Construction on the museum begins.
   - October 8, 1986 – 15th Street, adjacent to the future museum entrance, is officially renamed Raoul Wallenberg* Place.
   - April 17, 1990 – Two milk cans containing soil and ashes from different concentration camps and extermination camps are buried under the basement level of the Hall of Remembrance.
   - April 22, 1993 – The neoclassical structure, which was designed by American Architect James Ingo Freed**, is dedicated after nearly four years of construction.
   - April 26, 1993 – Museum opens to the public. His Holiness, the 14th reincarnation of the Dalai Lama*** is the first visitor.
   - The museum dedicates the plaza on Raoul Wallenberg Place to General Dwight David Eisenhower**** and to the soldiers who fought under his command.
   - October 12, 2000 – President William Clinton signs Public Law 106-292 granting permanent status for the Museum.

* Raoul Wallenberg (1912-19??) was a Swedish diplomat who is credited with saving as many as 100,000 Hungarian Jews from slaughter by the Nazis during World War II. He was captured by the Soviet Union at the end of the war and was never heard from again.
** James Ingo Freed (1930-2005) was born in Germany. As a Jew, he migrated to the United States in 1939. In addition to the Holocaust Museum, Mr. Freed works include the Ronald Reagan Building in Washington, D.C., and the U.S. Air Force Memorial in Arlington, Virginia.
*** Dalai Lama is a lineage of religious leaders of the Gelug School of Tibetan Buddhism.
****General Dwight D. Eisenhower (1890-1969) was a United States general and the Supreme Commander of Allied Forces in Europe during World War II. He was also the 34th U.S. President.

2. The Holocaust Museum has a hybrid brick and limestone exterior, is 312 feet long by 91 feet tall, and is 265,000 square feet in size. Of this total square footage, some of the major components of the museum include: The Permanent Exhibits which occupy 36,000 square feet (S/F), Temporary Exhibits - 8,000 S/F, Archives/Research Center - 100,000 S/F, Hall of Witness - 6,000 S/F, and Hall of Remembrance - 3,600 S/F. Private contributions paid for the majority of the $90 million for the building's construction and $78 million for the  exhibits, for a total of $168 million.   U.S. Holocaust Memorial Museum

3. Visitors enter the museum, which has five floors and a lower level, through the *Hall of Witness* on the first floor. As described by the representatives of Pei Cobb Freed & Partners, Architects, LLP, the museum is "organized internally around the skylit of the Hall of Witness, a three-story arrival, distribution and circulation center that infuses stairs, walls, layered space and shadows with suggestive disquiet. Devoid of literal reference to the Holocaust, it speaks instead through dualities of dark /light, transparency /opacity, openness / constriction."

Hall of Witness – Credit Alan Gilbert, Courtesy USHMM

FACTS ABOUT THE EXHIBITS IN THE HOLOCAUST MUSEUM

The permanent exhibits are displayed on floors two through four. They start with the *Nazi Assault – 1933 to 1939* on the fourth floor, the third floor with the exhibit *The Final Solution – 1940 to 1945*, and finally to the *Last Chapter* on the second floor. The fifth floor contains the library and archives.

Fourth Floor – The Nazi Assault – 1933 to 1939

1. The fourth floor chronicles the events in Nazi Germany from 1933 until the outbreak of World War II on September 2, 1939, when Germany invaded Poland. The films "The Nazi Rise to Power" and "Anti-Semitism" can be viewed on this floor.

2. The four major themes covered on the fourth floor are: (1) The creation of a police state after the Nazis gained control of Germany; (2) Implementation of Nazi Policies; (3) Groups Deemed Enemies of the State; and (4) Refugee Crisis.

3. Specific major exhibits on this floor are: (1) Americans Encounter the Camps; (2) The Terror Begins, (3) Nazi Propaganda; (4) The Science of Race; (5) *Kristallnacht*, German for "Crystal Night" or the "Night of Broken Glass;" (6) The Search for Refuge; and (7) Nazi Euthanasia.

4. Engraved on the glass walls of the corridor that passes over the lower floors are some of the names of the 5,000 European towns, villages, and *shtetls* – "Jewish communities," destroyed during the Holocaust. Designer James Freed wanted to "…..convent the feeling of constantly being watched, of things closing in."

Third Floor – The Final Solution – 1940 to 1945

1. The focus of the third floor is on the victims and survivors of the Holocaust through audio recordings, photographs and artifacts. These include: (1) Experiences at the concentration camps, extermination camps, and ghettos; (2) Armed resistance in the camps and ghettos; and (3) Efforts to preserve the evidence of the Jewish life under the Nazis.

123

2. Specific major exhibits on this floor consist of: (1) Warsaw Ghetto Milk Can; (2) Railway Car; and (3) Arrival at the Killing Centers, Prisoners of the Camps, and Auschwitz Barrack.

3. The German term *Die Endlosung* or "Final Solution" to the Jewish question, was first officially used by the Nazis at the Wannsee Conference held in Berlin, Germany, on January 20, 1942. The Final Solution refers to the efforts of the Nazis to annihilate the Jewish people through a system of death squads, concentration camps, death camps, and ghettos in Europe between 1942 and 1945. Wannsee is a suburb of Berlin, Germany.

4. The displayed milk can is one of the three original cans used by Jewish historians confined to the Warsaw Ghetto in Warsaw, Poland, to store records that documented the lives of the estimated 400,000 Jews confined in the ghetto. Even through the Jews totaled 30% of the population of Warsaw, they were confined in just 2.4% of the total city. Next to the milk can is a reproduction of the 11-foot-high wall that confined the Warsaw Jews.

5. Starting in October 1941, the use of railroads to transport Jews and other so called undesirables to ghettos, concentration camps, and killing centers contributed immeasurably to the success of the Nazis' killing machine. The maximum length of a train was 50 cars, traveled at a maximum speed of 30 miles per hour, and transported from 50 to as many as 100 men, women, and children in each car, for a total of 1,000 to 5,000 victims per train. The 44 parallel tracks that led to the railroad station at Auschwitz is an example of how efficiently the railroads worked.

6. The railway car on display is believed to be an authentic 15-ton car that represents the type of car that transported Jews to camps and ghettos. The dimensions of the car are 31 feet, 6 inches in length; 14 feet high from the bottom of the wheel to the highest point of the car; 13 feet, 2 inches wide, including roofing; and approximately 11 feet wide inside the car. The railway car, built around 1920, and on loan from Poland, was hoisted into the museum during the construction of the building.  Railway Car - Credit Arnold Kramer, Courtesy of USHMM

7. Exhibited is a cast of a sign that hung over the entrance to the Auschwitz death camp. The words *Arbeit Macht Frei* in German means "Work Sets You Free." Similar signs were placed at the gates to various concentration and death camps, such as Dachau. The words were accepted by prisoners as a ray of hope that if they worked hard they would be set free from the camp. To their captors, the sign was another psychological tool for controlling the prisoners, and the only way the prisoners would be set free would be their extermination through work.

Sign Over Gate - Courtesy USHMM

8. Among the exhibits is a reproduction of a barrack at Auschwitz-Birkenau death camp in Poland. The three-level bunk was intended to sleep from 15 to 18 prisoners.

9. The mound of 4000 shoes is just a small part of the estimated 800,000 shoes that were worn by the prisoners at the Majdanek extermination camp near Lublin, Poland. The shoes were to be given to German families who occupied the *Lebensraum,* which means "living space," as the land was captured by the German armies.

Mound of Shoes – Credit Thomas Arledge, Courtesy of USHMM

10. The *Tower of Faces*, with the top part of the exhibit being displayed on the fourth floor, is a three-story tower of about 1,000 photographs that record the everyday lives of the 3,000 to 4,000 residents of the Lithuania *shtetl* – "Jewish community" of Eisiskes between 1890 and 1941. Among the 29 Jews who survived the destruction of their *shtetl* by the Nazis and their Lithuanian collaborators on September 25-26, 1941, was four-year old Yaffa Sonenson. Yaffa migrated to the United States in 1954, and in 1979 with her husband, David Eliach, began her quest "to rescue this one village from oblivion" by collecting nearly 6,000 photographs from

archaeological excavations, former residents of Eisiskes, and the relatives of the victims.

Tower of Faces – Courtesy of USHMM

11. Next to the reproduction of the crematorium furnaces, which were used at the Mauthausen extermination camp, is a reproduction of an airtight metal door used on the gas chambers at the Majdanek camp. The peephole in the upper center of the door permitted the guards to observe the results of their deeds.

12. The glass walls through which the first floor can be seen, is a continuation of the names of the 5,000 European towns, villages, and *shtetls* – "Jewish communities" destroyed during the Holocaust that was started on the fourth floor. Designer James Freed stated "I was thinking of the Warsaw ghetto. The bridges that the Jews had to cross over to get from one part of the ghetto to another, so they wouldn't contaminate others." The term "Others" refers to non-Jews.

Second Floor – Last Chapter

Specific major exhibits on this floor consist of: (1) Danish Rescue, with the exhibit of a small boat; (2) Rescuers Wall; (3) Resistance; (4) Liberation; and (5) The Testimony Theater- crafted from stones from Jerusalem.

Hall of Remembrance and Other Exhibits

1. After exiting the exhibits, visitors have an opportunity to enter the *Hall of Remembrance* to reflect on what they saw, pray, and light a candle for the victims. It has 6 sides and the 6 sides symbolize the 6-point Star of David. The skylight has 6 sides. On the sides of the Hall are the names of major concentration camps, death camps, and reference to death marches. It was in these and other camps that many of the 6 million Jews perished.

Hall of Remembrance

2. The eternal flame in the Hall of Remembrance is perched on a rectangular block of black marble. Beneath the marble are 38 urns that contain dirt from 38 of the concentration camps in Europe. The urns were placed beneath the marble by Jewish Holocaust survivors. A 39th urn contains dirt from Arlington National Cemetery in Virginia, where American soldiers are buried, and is intended to commemorate the American liberators of the camps.

3. The black marble panel on the wall behind the eternal flame has the inscription: **"Only guard yourself and guard your soul carefully, lest you forget the things your eyes saw, and lest these things depart your heart all the days of your life. And you shall make them known to your children and to your children's children."**

Eternal Flame, Black Marble Block, and Marble Panel

4. It is from one of the two stands in the Hall that the President of the United States delivers his speech during his annual visit to the USHMM on *Holocaust Remembrance Day*. The president's visit falls beyond a date after Passover, March/April, but within the time span of the Warsaw Ghetto Uprising, January18, 1943 through May 16, 1943. This would be during April or May of each year.

5. Other exhibits include the following:

   • Located on the lower floor, the *Children's Wall*, opened in 1993, incorporates more than 3,000 colorful tiles painted by U.S. children and is dedicated to the 1.5 million children murdered by the Nazis. Many of the tiles call for peace, hope, remembrance, and freedom. A quotation from Yitzhak Katzenelson appears above the tiles: "The first to perish were the children...From these a new dawn might have risen."

   Children's Wall – Credit Max Read, Courtesy USHMM

   • Located on the first floor, the exhibit *Remember the Children: Daniel's Story*, is an exhibition for children that was opened in 1993. It presents the history of the Holocaust in ways that children can understand. The exhibit is entered through the Hall of Witness. The fictional story is about the lives of a German Jewish boy and his family from around the time the Nazis took power in 1933 until the end of World War II in 1945, including their lives in a ghetto and at a concentration camp.

FACTS ABOUT THE U.S. BUREAU OF ENGRAVING AND PRINTING

Visitors to the U.S. Bureau of Engraving and Printing (BEP) just might hear someone shout out "show me the money" at some point during their tour of the agency's facilities. And they won't be disappointed. Billions of dollars of U.S. currency are printed each year within the walls of the BEP in Washington, D.C. and Fort Worth, Texas. The tours and displays at these facilities certainly provide every visitor, no matter if they are young in years or in spirit, their money's worth.

HISTORY OF THE U.S. BUREAU OF ENGRAVING AND PRINTING

1. The United States Bureau of Engraving and Printing (BEP) is responsible for printing Federal Reserve notes (paper money) for the Federal Reserve and producing a variety of government security documents. The BEP also produces Treasury securities, identification cards and naturalization certificates among other documents. It does not produce coins, which are minted by the U.S. Mint.

2. The engraving and printing of federal notes was first authorized by an 1857 act of Congress. Two additional acts in 1862 required that there be engraved signatures and an imprinted Treasury seal on all notes, and authorized such engraving to be done at the Treasury Department using government personnel and equipment.

3. In 1862, an experimental engraving and printing operation was established in the Treasury Department, from which personnel and equipment were drawn to organize the First Division of the National Currency Bureau under the 1863 National Banking Act. The First Division, responsible for engraving and printing federally backed bank notes, and known informally as the Bureau of Engraving and Printing as early as 1866, was formally separated from the National Currency Bureau by an 1869 administrative order.

4. The BEP was established under the Department of the Treasury by an 1869 administrative order, with the first bureau chief being appointed on March 17, 1869. The BEP was first recognized in law by an 1869 act that prohibited the engraving and printing bureau from doing private contract work. An 1874 act authorized appropriations for providing the services.

5. By 1877, the Bureau of Engraving became the sole producer of all United States currency, revenue stamps, government obligations and other security documents. The addition of postage stamp production in 1894 made the BEP the nation's security printer. Stamps and passports are no longer being printed by the BEP.

LOCATIONS OF THE U.S. BUREAU OF ENGRAVING AND PRINTING

1. Between 1862 and 1880, the Bureau of Engraving and Printing (BEP) and its predecessor the First Division of the National Currency Bureau (NCB), was located in the basement of the U.S. Treasury building at 1500 Pennsylvania Avenue in Washington, D.C. The NCB initially employed two men and four women to separate and seal $1 & $2 notes that were printed by private bank note companies.

2. In 1878, land was purchased for the site of the original BEP building. In 1880, the fireproof building, at a cost of $300,000, was occupied. Between 1911 and 1914, and at a cost of $2.88 million, the original BEP building was expanded into a new building between 14th and 15th Streets in Washington, D.C.

U.S. Bureau of Engraving and Printing

3. The main building of the BEP is a fireproof building built in a neoclassical style, has a steel superstructure, and is constructed from concrete and Indiana limestone with a granite trim exterior. Stone columns cover the 505-foot length of the building's front. The building is also 296 feet deep and 105 feet high, with four wings that extend toward 14th Street.

4. In May 1938, at a cost of $2 million, an annex to the BEP was completed on 14th Street, just opposite the main BEP building.

5. The <u>annex</u> building is 570 feet long by 285 feet wide and constructed entirely of reinforced concrete with a limestone façade. The structure consists of a central support running from 14th Street to 13th Street, with five wings extending north and south.

Annex Building – BEP

6. In 1991, a second BEP facility was opened at 9000 Blue Mound Road in Fort Worth, Texas. The new facility was built for three primary reasons: Help keep up with the demand for notes; Ensure there was a backup facility for the one in Washington, D.C.; and reduce the cost of shipping currencies to the western part of the United States.

7. Approximately 2,800 employees work at the BEP facilities. Since 1908, all jobs have been government positions. The employees work shifts that keep the facilities operating 24-hours a day.

Interesting Side-Fact – Due to the affects of polo, President Franklin Roosevelt (1933-1945) had difficulty walking. When he traveled by train, the president's railroad car was moved to the loading platform in the basement of the BEP annex building, where the president would more easily board or leave the train.

FACTS ABOUT THE CURRENCY OF THE UNITED STATES

1. In mid-1775, the Continental Congress authorized paper currency, which was redeemable in Spanish Milled Dollars - large silver coins of 8 Real denominations (pieces of eight) struck at the Spanish colonial mints in Mexico and South America. However, it quickly depreciated to a face value of less than what the paper was printed on. Thus, the saying "not worth the paper it's printed on."

2. The coinage system of the United States was established after the Constitution was ratified. The first coins were struck in 1793 at the Philadelphia Mint. From 1793 until 1861, the U.S. government saw no need for a national paper currency.

3. From 1830 through 1861, and because of the need for money to be in circulation, individual states authorized about 1,600 banks to issue paper currency. This currency, which resulted in as many as 30,000 variations in design, was backed by the amount of money the bank had on deposit.

4. On July 17, 1861, Congress authorized the federal government to begin issuing paper money to fund the Civil War and to deal with the shortage of cooper, silver, and gold coins. The shortage was due to people hoarding the coins. The 1861 paper currency was referred to as *Demand Notes*, which meant they could be redeemed for coins upon demand. The Demand Notes were replaced by *Legal Tender Notes* in 1862. By the end of the war in 1865, the national debt had topped $2.7 billion, or $37 billion in 2008 inflation-adjusted dollars.

5. The difference between the Demand Notes and Legal Tender Notes is substantial. The bearer of the Demand Notes could demand that the paper currency be replaced with coins. The Legal Tender Notes were backed only by the good faith and credit of the United States government. However, the government started backing some of the paper currency with gold in 1865. This practice was discontinued in 1933. A similar practice for silver certificates was started in the 1870s, but was discontinued in 1968.

6. The Demand Notes and Legal Tender Notes were printed on both sides. The backs of the Legal Tender Notes were inked entirely in green. This use of the color green soon led to the notes being referred to as *Greenbacks*, a term that remains synonymous with U.S. currency to this day.

7. Prior to 1929, currency notes measured 7.42 inches by 3.13 inches. Since 1929, all denominations of paper currency notes are the same size, measuring approximately 2.61 inches (6.63 centimeters) by 6.14 inches (15.60 centimeters). Each note weighs about one gram. There are 454 grams in a pound.

8. Until 1945, currency notes in denominations of $500, $1,000, $5,000, and $10,000 were printed. In 1969, these high value notes were removed from circulation.

9. Since 1969, only the $1, $5, $10, $20, $50 and $100 currency notes are printed, and the $2 note on a limited basis. The portraits on the notes are $1 – Washington, $2 – Jefferson, $5 – Lincoln, $10 – Hamilton, $20 – Jackson, $50 – Grant and $100 – Franklin.

10. It is estimated that the life span of a $1 bill is 21 months, $5 – 16 months, $10 – 18 months, $20 – 24 months, $50 – 55 months, and $100 – 89 months.

11. Beginning with the 1996 series, serial numbers on notes consist of 2 prefix letters prior to the numbers, 8 numerals, and 1 letter suffix. The exceptions are on the $1 and $2 notes, which have 1 prefix letter. No two notes of the same kind, denomination, and series have the same serial number.

12. The motto "In God We Trust" was first stamped on the U.S. 2-cent coin in 1864, and larger coins the next year. It was not until 1957 that the motto first appeared on paper currency. Though unsubstantiated, it is believed the motto was placed on the notes as a form of moral comparison between the United States and the Communist Soviet Union during the Cold War.

13. Of the notes printed, 95% are used to replace earlier notes, and the $1 note accounts for 45% of the currency production. A portrait of George Washington was first put on the $1 note in 1869. The current version of the $1 note has existed since 1963. Martha Washington is on the 1886 and 1891 silver certificates and is the only image of a woman on a note.

14. During Fiscal Year 2008, October 1, 2007 through September 30, 2008, BEP printed 7.7 billion notes at an average cost of 6.4 cents per note.

FACTS ABOUT PRINTING NOTES AT THE BEP

1. There are 65 steps in printing sheets of currency. The first process is dry intaglio printing, which has been used since 1968. This is when fine-line engravings are transferred to steel plates from which an impression is made on sheets of distinctive paper. Ink is applied to the plates – each plate containing 32 note impressions – and then wiped clean, leaving ink in the engraved lines.

2. Using 20 tons of pressure, the plate is pressed against the back of the paper, then the front, so as to actually press the paper into the lines of the plate to pick up the ink. After the faces are printed, the sheets are then typographically overprinted with <u>Treasury Seals</u> and <u>serial numbers</u>. Each side must dry for 72 hours. The press speed is 7,300 sheets per hour.

3. Approximately 18 tons of ink are used each day to print the 35 to 40 million notes. A faster drying ink was introduced in 1943, which eliminated the need to place tissues between sheets, thus increasing the speed of printing notes.

4. Currency paper is composed of 25% linen and 75% cotton, with plastic security threads and red and blue synthetic fibers distributed throughout the paper. Since 1879, the paper has been supplied to the BEP by Crane & Co., Inc. in Dalton, Massachusetts. The paper is delivered with water marks and facial images.

5. The printing plate used in this process is created from hand-cut engravings called *master-dies*. Highly skilled artists called *engravers* draw images into soft steel to make the dies. There are separate dies for the different images on the bill, such as the portrait of the president, the lettering, and other designs.

6. Plate capacity on power presses increased from 4 to 8 notes per sheet in 1918, to 12 notes in 1929, to 18 notes in 1952, and to 32 notes in 1968.

7. After the sheet of 32 notes is dried and inspected by a computer using 800 electronic eyes, with 3% to 4% being rejected, it is cut into two sheets of 16 notes before the notes are stamped with the serial numbers and the Federal Reserve and Treasury seals.

8. Once the notes are printed they are cut into two notes, then into single notes, and are finally wrapped into bricks of 4,100 notes before they are shipped to one of 12 Federal Reserve Districts, then to local banks where they are released to the public.

FACTS ABOUT THE WASHINGTON MONUMENT

Through successful careers as a farmer, member of Congress, Commander of the Continental Armies during the Revolutionary War, President of the Federal (Constitutional) Convention and President of the United States - George Washington is revered as the "Father of Our Country."

Among Washington's many duties as president, he strongly influenced the selection of the permanent site for the nation's capital city and within the city the location of many of the primary government buildings. Because of his influence on Washington, D.C., it is only appropriate that a tribute to this honored citizen be constructed on a prominent site within a city that bears his name. This tribute is in the form of the Washington Monument.

THE LIFE OF GEORGE WASHINGTON

1. In 1656, the first members of the Washington family emigrated from England.

2. On February 11, 1732, George was born at Pope's Creek Plantation (later called Wakefield) in Virginia. He was the oldest of the six children from the marriage between Augustine and Mary Ball Washington. In 1752, his birth date was changed to February 22, when England adopted the Gregorian calendar.

3. In 1743, Washington's father died when George was only age 11. His mother died on August 26, 1789, at age 81.

4. Between 1754 and 1759, Washington served as commander of the Virginia militia. He was age 22 when he assumed this position and played an active role in the French and Indian War (1754-1763) - the name given to a war between France and Britain for control of North America.

5. On January 6, 1759, Washington married Martha Dandridge Custis, a wealthy widow with two children - John Parke Custis and Martha Parke Custis. He was age 26 and she was age 27.

6. In 1774 and 1775, Washington served as a member of the First and Second Continental Congresses.

7. From 1775 through 1783, Washington served as Commander-in-Chief of the Continental armies. He was age 43 when he accepted command of the armies.

8. In 1787, Washington presided over the Federal (Constitutional) Convention that drafted the United States Constitution.

9. On April 30, 1789, at age 57, Washington was inaugurated in New York City as the first President of the United States under the U.S. Constitution. Washington's second term started on March 4, 1793, and ended on March 4, 1797.

   As established through the 12th amendment to the U.S. Constitution in 1804, March 4th remained the inauguration date for elected U.S. Presidents until the 20th amendment was ratified in 1933. The 20th amendment changed the beginning of the president's term to noon on January 20th following the date of election, even if the 20th falls on a Sunday.

10. On December 14, 1799, Washington died at age 67 from complications of a throat infection. Historians believe Washington would have probably lived longer, but the medical practice of bleeding was still being used to treat sickness. Bleeding is when a patient is intentionally cut to allow the sickness to flow from the body. A form of treatment that was used well into the 1800s.

PLANNING THE WASHINGTON MONUMENT

1. In 1783, a national monument honoring George Washington was first considered by Congress.

2. Because George Washington was still alive at the time the first efforts to build a tribute to him were started, the structure is considered a monument rather than a memorial.

3. In 1833, the Washington National Monument Society was formed. In the same year Congress authorized the construction of the Washington Monument and transferred land to the Society.

4. In 1836, Robert Mills' design for the monument was selected.

5. The initial monument design, a blend of Greek, Babylonian and Egyptian architecture, provided for a decorated obelisk 600 feet high by 70 feet square at the base. It was to rise from a circular colonnaded building 100 feet high by 250 feet in diameter, surrounded by Doric columns (one for each state in the Union), each 12 feet in diameter by 45 feet high. (There were 30 states in the Union in 1848.) The cost of this version of the monument was estimated at $1,250,000.

Sketch of the initial design of the Washington Monument by Robert Mills – Courtesy of the National Archives. Mills referred to his design as a "National Pantheon."

6. An 1876 Congressional Act authorized the completion of the monument, transferred the responsibility for completing the monument from the Washington National Monument Society to the U.S. Army Corps of Engineers, and appropriated $2 million.

7. After the monument was formally deeded to Congress from the Washington National Monument Society in 1877, it was decided that the design for the monument would be limited to a 55-foot square Egyptian obelisk - an upright four-sided pillar, gradually tapered as it rises, with the top terminating in a pyramid. It was also decided that the height of the monument would be 10 times the square of the monument – 555 feet. And in addition, the new design eliminated the colonnaded building and columns.

THE CONSTRUCTION OF THE WASHINGTON MONUMENT

1. On July 4, 1848, Benjamin B. French, Freemasons Grand Master of the District of Columbia, dedicated the first of two cornerstones installed in the monument.

   French wore the same apron and sash and used the same gavel that were worn/used by George Washington in 1793 to dedicate the first cornerstone of the U.S. Capitol Building.

2. The first cornerstone, quarried near Baltimore, Maryland, weighs 24,500 pounds.

3. Sealed in the first cornerstone of the Washington Monument is a zinc box. The box contains money – bills and coins, a Bible, newspapers, reports of government agencies, and a program of the Smithsonian Institution.

4. Guests at the dedication of the cornerstone included Congressman Abraham Lincoln, Dolley Madison, Mrs. John Quincy Adams, President James Polk, and George Washington Parke Custis.

5. Because of a need for firmer ground, the location of the monument is about 350 feet east from the original planned location.

6. In 1849, the state of Alabama offered a large stone to be used in the construction of the monument. Presently there are 193 inscribed memorial stones and 2 descriptive stones installed around the interior steps of the monument, for a total of 195 stones. Most of the stones date from 1849 to 1855. Sixteen stones were installed during the 20th century.

7. The construction of the monument progressed at the following pace during the given years:

- 1848-1854 - 0 to152 feet
- 1855-1858 - 153 to 176 feet
- 1880 – 150 to 176 feet (removed)*
- 1880 - 150 to 172 feet
- 1881 - 173 to 250 feet
- 1882 - 251 to 340 feet
- 1883 - 341 to 410 feet
- 1884 – 411 to 555.5 feet and 1/8 inch

Washington Monument

*In 1880, an inspection of the 26 feet of secondary stones that had been set in 1858 atop the original 150 feet level revealed that the shaft had disintegrated and the facing stones had been displaced and were chipped and crumbled. As a result, between July 15, 1880, and August 7, 1880, three courses of stone were removed from the monument. This alteration, which is particularly noticeable in damp weather, was to leave a permanent dividing line on the monument at the 150-foot level (27% up from the base of the monument).

8. The monument consists of the following materials at various levels:

    - There are two walls from the ground level to a height of 150 feet. The inner-wall was constructed from Gneiss, and the outer-wall from Ashlar marble. The area between the inner-wall and exterior-wall is filled-in with rubble.

    - There are also two walls from 150 to 450 feet. However, the inner-wall was constructed from granite and the outer-wall was constructed from Ashlar marble. The area between the inner-wall and exterior-wall is not filled in, and the walls butt-up against each other.

    - There is a single wall above the 450-foot level, and the wall is constructed from Ashlar marble.

9. Due to the lack of money and the event of the Civil War, construction on the monument slowed dramatically between 1858 and 1880.

10. Lieutenant Colonel Thomas Casey, Army Corps of Engineers, was instrumental in reinforcing the base of the monument and completing the structure above the 150-foot level.

11. After the U.S. Army assumed responsibility for the monument, engineers inspected the foundation and determined it too weak to support the proposed structure. The problem was corrected in 1880 by using a new building material known as concrete to reinforce the foundation. The concrete pad is over 13 feet thick and extends out 23 feet from the previous edge of the foundation.

12. On December 6, 1884, construction on the outside of the monument was completed when a marble capstone was placed on the top of the monument.

13. On February 21, 1885, the Washington Monument was dedicated. This was a day before the actual anniversary of Washington's 153rd birthday. The Saturday ceremony occurred because Sunday was considered a day of rest and religion.

14. The final cost of the monument totaled $1,187,000.

15. On October 9, 1888, the monument was officially opened to the public – 40 years, 3 months and 5 days after the first cornerstone was dedicated. It remained the tallest man-made structure in the world until the 1,063-foot iron Eiffel Tower in Paris, France, was opened on March 31, 1889.

THE CHARACTERISTICS OF THE WASHINGTON MONUMENT

1. The shape of the monument is of an Egyptian obelisk. Because obelisks are of Egyptian origin, construction of the Washington Monument in this style showed the Masons' mystic connection with the Egyptian stone builders. Washington became a mason at age 21, and was a master mason at the time of his death.

2. The Egyptian obelisk is also referred to as *Cleopatra's Needle*, in reference to the notable Queen Cleopatra.

3. The monument was constructed on a 37-acre site that was initially proposed for a monument site to honor Washington by Pierre Charles L'Enfant in his 1791 plan for the city. L'Enfant proposed an equestrian statue of George Washington.

4. The foundation of the monument has a depth of 36 feet, 10 inches, covers an area of 16,001 square feet, and weighs 36,912 tons.

5. The width at the base of the monument is 55 feet 1-1/2 inches. The height of an obelisk is approximately ten times its width. Thus the height of the monument is 555.5 feet and 1/8 inch or the approximate height of a 55-story building.

6. The monument weighs 90,854 tons.

7. The first 152 feet of the monument's exterior marble came from a quarry near Texas, Maryland (Baltimore County).

8. The top four courses/rows of the more white marble in the middle of the monument were extracted from a quarry near Sheffield, Massachusetts. The darker marble above the Sheffield marble was extracted near Cockeysville, Maryland (Baltimore County).

9. The granite for the inner-walls is from a quarry in Maine.

10. The width of the monument at the observation level is 34 feet, 5-1/2 inches.

11. The walls are 15 feet thick at the at the base of the monument, 18 inches thick at the observation level, and 6 inches thick at the top of the monument.

12. Each side of the capstone is 3 feet wide. The capstone weighs 3,300 pounds.

13. The surface of the monument totals 93,600 square-feet. There are 36,491 stone blocks in the monument. Of this number, 11,098 blocks are on the face of the monument.

14. The pyramidion, the area at the top of the monument that slants inward to a peak, consists of 262 pieces of white marble stones 7 inches thick. The 300-ton pyramidion is supported by 12 ribs that rise from the walls of the shaft.

15. On December 6, 1884, a 100-ounce pyramid tip (apex), crafted from solid aluminum and cast in Philadelphia, Pennsylvania, was placed at the top of the monument as part of a lightning rod system. Aluminum was also used because it would not deteriorate and stain the monument. The height of the tip is 8.9 inches and the width 5.6 inches. At a cost of $225.00, the apex was the largest piece of aluminum cast up to that date in the United States.

16. The market price of aluminum in 1884 was approximately $1.00 per ounce, which was about the same price as silver at the time.

17. Prior to being placed on the top of the monument, the aluminum tip was exhibited at Tiffany's in New York City, where people could jump over it and claim they "jumped over the top of the Washington Monument."

18. Engraved on the four sides of the aluminum tip is the official record of the monument's construction. The <u>west face</u> reads "Cornerstone laid on bed of foundation, July 4, 1848. First stone at height of 152 feet laid August 7, 1880. Capstone set December 6. 1884." The <u>east face</u> reads the Latin words *Laus Deo* meaning "Praise be to God." On the <u>north face</u> are the names of the monument's commission members, and on the <u>south face</u> are the names of Thomas Casey, Chief Engineer and Architect, and his assistants: George Davis, Bernard Green, and P.H. McLaughin.

UNIQUE FACTS ABOUT THE WASHINGTON MONUMENT

1. There are 897 steps leading to the top of the monument. The monument is the highest freestanding masonry structure in the world.

2. The top of the Washington Monument is higher above sea level than the top of the Capitol Building, but lower than the top of the Washington National Cathedral.

3. During the Civil War the grounds surrounding the unfinished monument were used as a site to slaughter army beef and drill Union troops.

4. In 1933, the U.S. Park Services took over the administration of the Washington Monument from the U.S. Army Corps of Engineers.

5. In 1854, and <u>though unsubstantiated</u>, it is believed that members of the *Know-Nothings* stole the monument stone donated by Pope Pius IV, broke it into pieces, and threw it into the Potomac River. In 1982, a replacement stone was installed in the monument.

   The American Party was a political party during the 1840s and 1850s whose members were against immigration, especially German and Irish Catholic immigration. The Know Nothings were a semi-secret sub-group of this party, who when asked about their activities, which were occasionally criminal activities, replied "I know nothing."

6. Construction on the monument had been delayed so long that it was referred to as the *Deep Hole Monument*.

7. On August 7, 1880, a second cornerstone was dedicated at the 150-foot level of the Washington Monument. During the ceremony, President Rutherford Hayes (1877-1881) scratched his initials and the date on a coin and placed the coin in the mortar.

8. In 1931, aircraft signal lights were installed on the monument cap.

9. Major repairs were made to the monument during the years 1934-1935, 1964, and 1998 through 2000. Lightning has hit the monument several times, and it cost $15 million to repair the damage from a 2011 earthquake.

10. The observation area is located at the 500-foot level, with an exhibit room ten feet below. Visitors can enjoy the view from this level through eight observation windows – two on each side of the monument. After Congress was deeded the monument in 1877, it decided to add windows to the design of the monument. The windows could be closed by inserting marble slab shutters pivoted on bronze hinges.

View from top of the Washington Monument showing the World War II Memorial, Reflecting Pool, and Lincoln Memorial

11. In 1897, a workman fell from the Washington Monument. In 1915, a woman jumped down the elevator shaft from the 450 landing. In 1924, a woman fell while trying to save her three-year-old child who had slipped on the stairs. The child survived, she didn't. In 1926, bars were installed over the windows of the monument after two men jumped from the pyramidion, and the most recent suicide occurred in 1949 when a man jumped down the elevator shaft.

12. In 1937, a circle of 48 U.S. flags, one for each of the states in the Union at the time, was added to the site. In 1959, flags for Alaska and Hawaii were added to the circle. (A 1971 Proclamation authorized the flying of "our national colors" day and night.)

13. In 1901, the first electric elevator was installed in the monument. Previously, steam engines powered the elevators. Replacement evaluators were installed in 1926 and 1959. The current elevator system, excluding the current elevator cab, was installed in 1998.

14. The current 25-passenger elevator cab, installed in 2002, has glass panels in the doors. These panels allow the passengers to view a few of the 193 commemorative stones on the 290 and 160-foot levels as the elevator descends. The trip up the monument takes 70 seconds, and the trip down takes 2 minutes and 18 seconds.

15. In 1958, safety glass was installed over the openings on all sides of the observation level. In 1975, bullet-proof glass was installed over the openings at the observation level.

16. In 1971, visitors were no longer allowed to walk up the stairway. In 1976, the same restriction was placed on walking down the stairway.

17. In August 1998, and due to the possibility of terrorist acts against the United States, a series of concrete jersey barriers were erected around the monument. In 2005, the concrete barriers were replaced with granite walls that fold into the landscape.

18. The Marble Lodge next to the Washington Monument was constructed in 1889 to provide offices, serve as an archive, and provide comfort stations for visitors. The initial cost of the lodge was $11,650, with an additional $930 paid for expenses relating to changing the site of the lodge.

Marble Lodge

19. At the peak of construction in 1884, there were 118 workmen working on the monument. The daily wages for an average 10-hour workday were: Master Stone Cutter - $5, Marble Cutters - $3.50, Blacksmith - $3.50, and Stone Setter - $4.25.

20. A 30-mile-per-hour wind will cause the monument to sway 0.125 inch. The monument is closed when high winds occur.

FACTS ABOUT THE WORLD WAR II MEMORIAL

No other historical event has been more catastrophic than World War II. Lead by the dictators of Germany and Italy, and the militaristic government of Japan, it was Germany's invasion of Poland on September 1, 1939, that ignited a period of destruction that engulfed the world, and left an estimated 60 million men, women, and children dead, and an incalculable number of others displaced and homeless.

Just prior to World War II, ten other countries had larger military forces than the United States, including Greece and Belgium. From this small beginning of ill-equipped soldiers, sailors, and airmen grew one of the largest and best-equipped military the world has ever known. Drawn from the ranks of farmers, factory workers, coal miners, secretaries, and businessmen, these men and women set aside their way of life to become what author Stephen Ambrose described as "Citizen Soldiers."

The World War II Memorial honors all of these citizen soldiers, sailors, marines, and airmen; and the career members of the military and merchant marines. It also honors the citizens on the home front, the nation at large, and the highly moral purpose and idealism that motivated the nation's call to arms.

THE PARTICIPATION OF THE UNITED STATES IN WORLD WAR II

1. Hostilities for the United States during World War II officially started on December 7, 1941, when the Empire of Japan attacked the U.S. Pacific Fleet at Pearl Harbor, Hawaii. This attack left the United States with 2,433 dead and 1,178 wounded. It also resulted in the sinking of 18 warships and 188 planes destroyed.

2. On December 8, 1941, the United States declared war on Japan.

3. On December 11, 1941, Germany and Italy declared war on the United States.

4. Some of the major battles the United States fought during World War II include: The naval battles of the Coral Sea and Midway (1942); the invasions of North Africa (1943), Sicily (1943), and Normandy (1944); and the battles for the Philippines (1944) and Iwo Jima (1945).

5. On September 3, 1943, Italy agreed to surrender to the Allies. The formal surrender occurred on September 8, 1943.

6. On May 7, 1945, German forces surrendered to the Allies. Victory in Europe (VE-Day) occurred on May 8, 1945.

7. On August 15, 1945, Japan agreed to surrender to the Allies. The formal surrender occurred on September 2, 1945.

8. On December 31, 1946, President Harry Truman's Presidential Proclamation officially terminated hostilities by the United States.

9. World War II lasted 2,193 days and claimed an average of 27,600 lives each day.

10. The U.S. Presidents during World War II were President Franklin D. Roosevelt (1933-1945) from December 7, 1941 through April 12, 1945, and President Harry S. Truman (1945-1953) from April 12, 1945, through the end of the war.

11. The population of the United States at the end of World War II (1945) totaled 140,000,000.

12. The strength of the United States military in 1940, the year prior to the United States entering World War II, totaled approximately 457,000 officers and enlisted personnel.

13. A total of 16,353,659 Americans, 11.7% of the population of the United States, served in the military during World War II (1941-1945).

14. Approximately 1,100,000 African-Americans served in the military during World War II.

15. Approximately 250,000 Hispanic-Americans served in the United States military during World War II.

16. Approximately 44,000 Native-Americans served in the United States military during World War II.

17. Approximately 25,000 Asian-Americans, which included Chinese, Japanese, and Hawaiians, served in the United States military during World War II.

18. Over 200,000 American women served in uniform during World War II. The women who served included:

    - Over 150,000 - Women's Army Corps (WAC) (Of this total 60,000 served in the Army Air Force.)
    - 18,000 - Navy's Women Accepted for Voluntary Emergency Service (WAVES)
    - 1,074 - Women Air Service Pilots (WASPS) flyers, plus support personnel
    - 50 – Women Auxiliary Ferrying Squadron (WAFS) flyers, plus support personnel
    - 10,000 - Coast Guard (SPARS)
    - 22,000 - Marine Corps Reserves

19. The average enlisted soldier during World War II was 26 years of age. After completing basic training, he averaged 5 feet, 8 inches in height, weighed 151 pounds, had a 35-inch chest, and a 31-inch waist. The German and Italian soldiers had similar physical characteristics, but the average height of a Japanese soldier was only 5 feet, 3 inches tall and weighed about 130 pounds.

20. Nearly half of the soldiers were high school graduates and one in ten had at least some college education.

21. Military personnel during World War II spent an average of 33 months on active duty.

22. Approximately 73% of the military personnel served overseas.

23. Military personnel deployed overseas spent an average of 16 months overseas.

24. The following table provides statistics about the men and women who served in the United States military and merchant marines during World War II.

Military Branch/ Mariners	Number Who Served	Battle Deaths	Other Deaths *	Wounded – Not Mortal	Total Casualties
Army (Including the Army Air Force)	11,260,000 (Including 3.4 million in the Army Air Force	234,874	83,400	565,861	884,135
Navy	4,183,466	36,950	25,664	37,778	100,392
Marines	669,100	19,733	4,778	68,207	92,718
Coast Guard	241,093	574	1,343	-	1,917
Sub-Total	16,353,659	292,131	115,185	671,846	1,079,162
U.S. Mariners	215,000	9,300	Unknown	11,000	20,300
Total	16,568,659	301,431	115,185	682,846	1,099,462

*Accidents, sickness, etc.

25. The following table provides statistics about the percentages of combat deaths and wounded versus the number of men and women who served in the United States military and merchant marines.

Military Branch/ Mariners	Number Who Served	Battle Deaths	% of Combat Deaths vs. Served	Wounded Not Mortal	% of Wounded vs. Served
Army (Including Army Air Force)	11,260,000	234,874	2.09%	565,861	5.03%
Navy	4,183,466	36,950	0.88%	37,778	0.90%
Marines	669,100	19,733	2.95%	68,207	10.19%
Coast Guard	241,093	574	0.24%	-	0%
Sub-Total	16,353,659	292,131	1.79%	671,846	4.11%
U.S. Mariners	215,000	9,300	4.32%	11,000	5.11%
Total	16,568,659	301,431	1.81%	682,846	4.12%

26. Of the men and women who served in the United States military and merchant marines during World War II, 416,616 sacrificed their lives. Of this total, 72% were battle deaths.

27. Of the 416,616 men and women who sacrificed their lives, 78,976 were declared missing in action.

28. A total of 130,201 U.S. military personnel became prisoners of war (POW) during World War II. Of this total 14,072 died while they were POWs, nearly 11% of the total number of POWs.

29. Nearly 40% of the U.S. military personnel held as POWs by Japan died while in captivity. A little over 1% of the POWs held by Germany died in captivity.

30. There were 19,000 U.S. civilian men, women, and children, internees during World War II. Approximately 11% of the civilian internees held by Japan died while in captivity. Nearly 3.5% of the civilian internees held by Germany died in captivity.

31. Of the servicemen and servicewomen who died overseas during World War II, 233,181 were returned to the United States for reburial.

32. Specially designed metal transportation caskets were used to transport the remains to the United States. Many of these same caskets were first used to transport the remains of the soldiers killed during World War I. The military refers to the ritual of returning a fallen comrade to the United Sates from a foreign country as a "dignified transfer."

33. Over 400 servicewomen, including 38 WASPS, died while serving their country during World War II.

34. The Medal of Honor was awarded to 464 men for acts of valor during World War II. Of this total; 286 served in the Army, 82 served in the Marine Corps, 57 served in the Navy, 38 served in the Army Air Corps, and 1 served in the Coast Guard.

35. Of the 464 Medals of Honor awarded; 22 were to Asian-Americans, 12 to Hispanic-Americans, 7 to African-Americans, and 3 to Native-Americans.

36. The financial cost to the United States for World War II totaled approximately $304 billion. Allowing for inflation-adjusted dollars, this equates to approximately $3.6 trillion in 2010 dollars.

37. The first eight Presidents of the United States after President Truman (1945-1953) all served in the military during World War II. These men were Eisenhower, Kennedy, Johnson, Nixon, Ford, Carter, Reagan, and George H. W. Bush. Carter was in the Naval Academy during the war.

THE WORLD WAR II MEMORIAL

1. The World War II Memorial is located on the National Mall at the site of the Rainbow Pool and east end of the Reflecting Pool.

2. In 1987, the idea of a World War II Memorial was conceived.

WWII Memorial from top of Washington Monument

3. In October 1996, architect Friedrich St. Florian, the former Dean of Rhode Island School of Design, was chosen to design the memorial. His design was selected over nearly 400 other designs.

4. On Veterans Day, November 11, 1995, President William Clinton (1993–2001) dedicated the memorial site.

5. On August 27, 2001, preparation work for the memorial was started. In September 2001, construction of the memorial was started.

6. On May 29, 2004, the memorial was dedicated.

7. President George W. Bush (2001-2009) accepted the memorial on behalf of the citizens of the United States.

8. The dimensions of the memorial are:

   - Length from the back of the Pacific Arch to the back of the Atlantic Arch: 384 feet.

   - Width from the back of the basin behind the Freedom Wall to the bottom of the Ceremonial Entrance: 279 feet.

9. The memorial is on a 7.4-acre site.

10. Two-thirds of the acreage consists of grass, planting, and pools.

11. The *Ceremonial Entrance* on 17th Street is the main entrance to the memorial.

12. The Ceremonial Entrance is 48 feet, 3 inches wide by 147 feet, 8 inches long, curb to plaza.

Entrance to World War II Memorial

13. Stone carver Nicholas Benson was the primary carver of the words carved throughout the memorial. The following words greet visitors to the World War II Memorial at the Ceremonial Entrance:

"HERE IN THE PRESENCE OF WASHINGTON AND LINCOLN, ONE THE EIGHTEENTH CENTURY FATHER AND THE OTHER THE NINETEENTH CENTURY PRESERVER OF OUR NATION, WE HONOR THOSE TWENTIETH CENTURY AMERICANS WHO TOOK UP THE STRUGGLE DURING THE SECOND WORLD WAR AND MADE THE SACRIFICES TO PERPETUATE THE GIFT OUR FOREFATHERS ENTRUSTED TO US: A NATION CONCEIVED IN LIBERTY AND JUSTICE."

14. At the Ceremonial Entrance are three wide steps that descend into the heart of the memorial. Three large lawn panels break up the three steps. This space can be used to seat as many as 3,000 attendees during ceremonial events.

15. Two United States flags fly over the Ceremonial Entrance. Located at the base of each flagpole are the crests for each branch of the military and the merchant marines.

16. Raymond Kaskey, whose deceased father was a veteran of World War II, sculptured every bronze piece displayed at the memorial, including the 4,048 gold stars on the Freedom Wall.

17. Kaskey sculptured the bas-relief panels along the steps entering the memorial. There are 24 bas-relief panels: 12 for the Atlantic theater of the war and 12 for the Pacific theater. The panels depict human elements of World War II and are based on archival photographs taken during the war as they relate to America's vast agricultural, industrial, military, and human resources.

18. Each bas-relief contains a minimum of eight figures. Each relief took approximately 250 hours to sculpt.

19. There are 276 faces in the bas-relief panels. Kaskey used living persons as models for the faces of the people in the panels; including six World War II re-enactors, his assistant, himself, and even the UPS deliveryman.

Bas-Relief Panel of D-Day Invasion at Normandy

20. The bronze figures were cast in a foundry in Chester, Pennsylvania.

21. The memorial includes 17,000 pieces of granite.

22. The largest stone weighs 17 tons.

23. The memorial consists of two primary granite stones. The Kershaw stone from South Carolina is used for the vertical elements and the Green County stone from Georgia is used for the main plaza paving stone.

World War II Memorial

24. Two green stones, Rio Verde and Moss Green, are used to accent paving on the plaza. Both were quarried in Brazil.

25. The two 49-foot memorial arches (pavilions), one each on the north and south sides of the memorial, represent the Atlantic and Pacific theaters of the war.

26. Each arch is 43 feet above grade and 23 feet square.

Arch – Representing the Pacific Theater

27. Each arch has four bronze pillars, four bronze eagles, and one bronze laurel.

28. The four pillars within the arch represent each major military branch - Army, Army Air Force, Navy, and Marines. An eagle rests on each of the pillars.

29. Each eagle weighs about 2,600 pounds and has a wingspan of about ten feet. The eagles hold a ribbon that supports a laurel wreath; commemorating victory.

Eagles holding the Victory Wreath

30. An X-ray machine was used to ensure the welds, holding the eagles and wreaths to their supports, were welded correctly.

31. The inlaid on the floor beneath the wreath and eagles is the World War II victory medal with the inscription *Victory on Land, Victory at Sea, and Victory in the Air*.

Victory Medal

32. In front of each arch is a semicircular fountain that lists the names of the major battles for that theater of the war.

33. The 56 granite pillars in the memorial are 17 feet above grade, 4 feet, 4 inches wide, and 3 feet deep.

Stone Pillars

34. The pillars represent the 48 states of the United States, and Alaska, Hawaii, Puerto Rico, Guam, the Philippines, American Samoa, the U.S. Virgin Islands, and the District of Columbia at the time of the war. Alaska and Hawaii became states in 1959.

35. The names on the pillars start with the original 13 states from the right side of the Freedom Wall (facing 17th Street), and alternate from right to left in the order the states ratified the U.S. Constitution – Delaware, Pennsylvania, etc.

36. The opening in each pillar behind the wreaths symbolizes the loss of military members from each state, territory, and the District of Columbia.

37. Each pillar is adorned with two sculptured bronze wreaths, one on each side, for a total of 112 wreaths. The oak leaves in the wreaths represent the industrial strength of the United States, and the wheat represents the agricultural strength.

38. There are 56 bronze ropes between the pillars. This arrangement signifies the unprecedented unity of the nation during the war.

Bronze Ropes

39. The curved *Freedom Wall*, centered at the back of the memorial, pays tribute to the Americans who lost their lives during the war.

40. The Freedom Wall is 84 feet, 8 inches wide by 9 feet high from the plaza floor, with a radius of 41 feet, 9 inches.

41. There are 4,048 sculptured gold stars on the Freedom Wall. Each star represents the death of about 100 Americans in the war. The stars are set against a textured bronze background.

Freedom Wall – With the inscription "Here We Mark the Price of Freedom"

42. A star symbolizes service to the nation. If a family member was serving in the military, a blue star was displayed in the window of the family's house for each family member serving. A gold star was displayed for each family member who had died serving his/her country. This tradition of displaying stars continues to be used by families of servicemen and servicewomen.

43. The *Circle of Remembrance* is located in the northwest corner of the memorial.

44. The Circle of Remembrance is a circular garden of about 38 feet in diameter enclosed within a two-foot-high stone wall. Wooden benches are located around the perimeter.

45. The *World War II Plaza* was designed to fit around the original Rainbow Pool.

46. The Plaza is 337 feet, 10 inches long by 240 feet, 2 inches wide and 6 feet below grade.

47. The *Rainbow Pool* is 246 feet, 9 inches long by 147 feet, 8 inches wide. The two fountains in the pool shoot water 30 feet into the air. The pool was initially completed in the early 1920s and was reduced in size by 15% for the memorial.

Rainbow Pool and Fountains

48. The Rainbow Pool and fountains symbolize the significance of the oceans and seas during World War II.

49. To help ensure visitors aren't showered by the flow of water from the fountains on windy days, an automatic system controls the height of the spray. On the top of the Atlantic Arch is a wind gauge. It signals an underground system to lower or raise the height of the water as the wind increases or decreases.

50. The 900 bronze-green drain grates surrounding the plaza allow for drainage. They are in the shape of a star within a star, surrounded by a circle. The symbol of a white star within a white circle was the identification marking placed on American vehicles (tanks, jeeps, etc.) during the war. A star within a dark background with bars on both sides of the star was the identification marking placed on American aircraft during the war.

Drain Grate

51. The bronze-green color of the bronze wreaths, figures, grates, etc. is the result of rubbing chemicals on the bronze.

52. On the walls are portions of speeches made by notable participants of the war, e.g. Presidents Roosevelt and Truman, and Generals Eisenhower and MacArthur.

Eisenhower's D-Day Speech

53. There is an engraving of Kilroy on the outside wall of the memorial near the pillar for the state of Delaware. The engraving consists of a bald little man peeking over a wall with the words "Kilroy Was Here" over his head. This form of graffiti was drawn by servicemen wherever they were stationed or camped, including battle areas, during World War II.

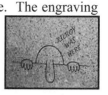
Kilroy

UNIQUE FACTS ABOUT THE MEMORIAL DEDICATION

1. The World War II Memorial was dedicated 58 years, 270 days after the formal surrender of Japan on September 2, 1945. Japan was the final Axis power of Germany, Italy, and Japan to surrender to the Allies at the end of World War II.

2. It was noted during the ceremony that May 29th would have been the 101st birthday anniversary of the great American comedian Bob Hope, who often entertained the troops during World War II, the Korean War, and the Vietnam War. It also marked the 87th birthday anniversary of former President John F. Kennedy (1961-1963), who served in the Navy during the war.

3. Former presidents George H. W. Bush (1989-1993) and William Clinton (1993-2001) attended the ceremony.

4. At the time of his commission on June 9, 1943, George H.W. Bush was credited with being the youngest U.S. naval aviator during World War II. Lt Bush was also awarded a Distinguished Flying Cross for combat against the Japanese on September 2, 1944.

5. Approximately four million veterans of World War II were living at the time of the memorial dedication. The average age of the remaining veterans was 82 years. Fifty of the 464 Medal of Honor recipients from World War II were still living at the time the memorial was dedicated in 2004.

6. Because World War II veterans were dying at a rate of over 1,000 each day in 2004, it was decided to open the memorial to the public on April 29, 2004, even though the official dedication was not until May 29, 2004. Regrettably, some veterans died during their trips to or from the memorial.

FACTS ABOUT THE THOMAS JEFFERSON MEMORIAL

During his long life, Thomas Jefferson accomplished more than almost any other ten people combined. As a statesman, he was a major contributor to the drafting of the Declaration of Independence, served in Congress, performed duties as secretary of state and vice president, and was twice elected to the presidency. As an inventor, he is credited with inventing many effort saving devices, and as a horticulturist, he experimented with as many as 170 types of fruits and 330 varieties of vegetables and herbs. Jefferson was also paradoxical. He wrote that "all men are created equal," but owned slaves. Prior to becoming president, he believed periodic revolts by citizens were good for a country, but had citizens imprisoned for protesting his presidential policies. He believed personal property should be protected by the government, but forced the American Indians from their lands in the East. He was appalled by the decadency he found in Paris, but participated in and enjoyed many of the large parties.

Even with his faults, many Americans, including some of the nation's greatest presidents, considered Jefferson second only to Washington as the nation's best president. The Jefferson Memorial is a tribute to this exceptional man and his accomplishments.

THE LIFE OF THOMAS JEFFERSON

1. On April 13, 1743, Thomas Jefferson was born at Shadwell, Albemarle County, Virginia.

2. Jefferson's father was Peter Jefferson, a land surveyor and landowner. His mother was Jane Randolph, the daughter of a prominent Virginia family.

3. Jefferson was a good reader and writer at the young age of six. His studies included Greek and Latin.

4. Jefferson taught himself how to play the violin and eventually became very good at playing the works of Mozart.

5. On August 17, 1757, Jefferson's father, Peter, died at age 49. Thomas was only 14 years of age at the time of his father's death. On March 31, 1776, his mother, Jane, died at age 56.

6. In 1760, at age 16, Jefferson entered William and Mary College in Williamsburg, Virginia. He graduated in 1762 with honors.

7. In 1767, at age 24, Jefferson was admitted to the Virginia bar as a lawyer.

8. In 1769, at age 26, Jefferson was elected to the Virginia House of Burgesses. Established in 1619, the House was the first representative government group in the American colonies.

9. In 1772, Jefferson married Martha Wayles Skelton. He was age 28, and she age 25.

10. On September 6, 1782, at age 34, Martha died from weakness incurred from giving birth to a child. Jefferson never remarried.

11. Jefferson and Martha were the parents of six children - five girls and one boy. Only their first born, Martha (Patsy) (1772-1836) and another daughter, Mary (Polly) (1778-1804), lived to adulthood.

12. In 1775, Jefferson was selected to represent Virginia in the Congress of the United States. He helped draft 160 bills while a member of this governing body.

13. In 1776, at age 33, Jefferson was credited with being the primary author of the Declaration of Independence. With alterations the Declaration of Independence was approved by Congress in 1776.

14. From 1779 through 1781, Jefferson served as governor of Virginia. While governor of Virginia, Jefferson pushed for and was very successful in ensuring religious freedom. (Being an atheist was a capital offense in Virginia, and no Jew, Catholic or Quaker could hold government positions in Massachusetts.)

15. In 1783, Jefferson was elected to the Congress of the Confederation of States.

16. In 1784, Jefferson was appointed the U.S. Minister to France.

17. In 1789, President George Washington (1789-1797) appointed Jefferson the first Secretary of State for the United States.

18. In 1797, Jefferson became Vice President of the United States under John Adams (1797-1801) after losing to Adams by only three electoral votes in the presidential election. Election rules at that time directed that the presidential candidate who received the most votes from the U.S. Electoral College was elected president, and the presidential candidate who received the next highest number of votes was elected vice president. This election system was changed in 1804, when the 12th Amendment to the Constitution required separate ballots for the president and vice president.

19. The presidential election of 1800 was very unique. Democratic-Republicans Thomas Jefferson and Aaron Burr both received more votes than Federalist John Adams for the presidency. This situation, which was due to the Democratic-Republican electors' attempt to name both a president and a vice president from their own party, cast a tie vote between Jefferson and Burr. The House of Representatives settled the tie by selecting Jefferson as the 3rd President of the United States and Burr as vice president.

20. Among his accomplishments, President Jefferson started the military academy at West Point (1802), purchased the Louisiana Territory from France for $15,000,000 (1803), and directed the Lewis and Clark expedition to explore the land purchased from France (1804-1806).

21. At the end of his presidency in 1809, Jefferson left Washington, D.C., never to return to the city during the remaining 17 years of his life.

22. In 1819, Jefferson founded the University of Virginia.

23. On July 4, 1826, Jefferson died at age 83. He and John Adams (2nd U.S. President), age 90, both died on the 50th anniversary of the adoption of the Declaration of Independence by the Continental Congress. Jefferson died a few hours prior to Adams.

THE JEFFERSON MEMORIAL

1. In 1913, when Franklin Roosevelt made his first trip to Washington, D.C. as Assistant Secretary of the Navy, one of his first actions was to view the tribute to Thomas Jefferson. He discovered no such tribute.

2. In 1933, when Franklin Roosevelt returned to Washington, D.C. as the 32nd President of the United States, he and other admirers of Jefferson took steps toward initiating the construction of a memorial to Jefferson.

3. Architect John Russell Pope designed and oversaw the construction of the Jefferson Memorial. After his death in 1937, architects Otto Eggers and Daniel Higgins assumed the project.

4. In November 1938, work was started on the memorial, and on December 15, 1938, President Franklin Roosevelt (1933-1945) presided over the official groundbreaking for the memorial. The same spade (shovel) that was previously used for the ground breaking for the Lincoln Memorial and Arlington Memorial Bridge was used for the Jefferson Memorial.

5. On November 15, 1939, President Roosevelt was present at the laying of the memorial cornerstone. The cornerstone contains copies of the Declaration of Independence; the Constitution of the United States; *The Life and Morals of Jesus of Nazareth*, written by Jefferson; *The Writings of Thomas Jefferson* (10 volumes), edited by Paul Ford; the 1939 Annual Report of the Thomas Jefferson Memorial Commission; the signatures of Franklin D. Roosevelt and members of the Memorial Commission; and copies of the four leading Washington newspapers at the time - *Washington Post, Washington Evening Star, Washington Times-Herald*, and *Washington Daily News*.

6. On April 13, 1943, fifty-eight years after the dedication of the Washington Monument, and at a cost of $3,192,312, the Jefferson Memorial was dedicated in Potomac Park. President Roosevelt was present at the ceremony.

7. The memorial is an adaptation of the Pantheon in Rome, Italy.

8. The original Declaration of Independence was displayed at the Jefferson Memorial during the dedication ceremony. It was the 200th anniversary of Jefferson's birth.

9. The memorial stands on a 2.5-acre site.

10. The exterior of the memorial has a full diameter of 183 feet, 10 inches. The memorial weighs 32,000 tons.

11. The height of the memorial from the roadway to the top of the dome is 129 feet, 4 inches.

Jefferson Memorial

12. The exterior of the memorial's dome is 103 feet from the ground.

13. The diameter of the memorial's interior is 86 feet, 3 inches.

14. The height of the memorial from the floor to the ceiling of the dome is 91 feet, 8 inches.

15. The height of the memorial exterior, from the floor to the top of the dome, is 95 feet, 8 inches.

16. The dome is 4 feet thick.

17. The piers that support the memorial were driven 138 feet, 3 inches into the ground and bedrock. Until the end of the 19th century the site on which the memorial is located was under water.

18. The memorial stands on a granite circular base.

19. The exterior dome and columns of the memorial were crafted from Danby Imperial Vermont marble.

20. The interior wall panels of the memorial were crafted from Georgian white marble.

21. The ceiling of the memorial dome was crafted from Indiana limestone.

22. The floor of the memorial's interior was crafted from Tennessee pink marble and the pedestal to the memorial was crafted from Missouri gray marble.

23. Fifty-four columns support the memorial. The exterior columns are 41 feet high and the inner columns are 39 feet, 2 inches high. The columns are approximately 5 feet in diameter.

24. The entrance to the memorial is from the plaza on the north/tidal basin side of the memorial.

25. In 1941, Rudulph Evans was awarded a $35,000 contract to provide preliminary models of Jefferson and the final plaster cast from which the statue of Jefferson would be cast from bronze.

26. The statue of Jefferson was initially formed from plaster and painted to look like bronze. Use of these materials was due to the shortage of bronze during World War II (1941-1945).

27. On April 22, 1947, a full bronze statue replaced the plaster statue of Jefferson.

28. The bronze statue of Jefferson is 19 feet tall and stands on a 6-foot-high black Minnesota granite pedestal. A ring of Missouri marble surrounds its base. The dates of Jefferson's birth and death (1743-1826) are inscribed in bronze numbers on the front of the pedestal.

Statue of Thomas Jefferson

29. The statue of Jefferson is 6 feet, 5-1/2 inches wide.

30. The statue of Jefferson is hollow, weighs 10,000 pounds, and is 3/16 inch thick.

31. Over nine months, the statue of Jefferson was cast in 12 pieces through 21 separate castings.

32. The statue of Jefferson may be viewed through the four colonnaded openings of the memorial—two on the east-west axis and two on the north-south axis.

33. The four panels surrounding the statue contain a series of Jefferson's best quotations. A fifth quotation is located above the panels. The quotations are from the following works:

- The first panel is quoted from the Declaration of Independence of 1776.

- The second panel is quoted from the Act for Religious Freedom passed by the Virginia Assembly in 1779.

- The third panel is a composite of thoughts from Jefferson's Summary of a View of Rights; Notes on Virginia; a January 4, 1787 letter to George Washington about the business of state; an August 13, 1780 letter to George Wythe about laws for educating the common people; and Jefferson's autobiography.

Panel - Jefferson Quotation

- The fourth panel provides insight into how Jefferson regarded the evolvement of the Constitution and other aspects of government. It was quoted from a July 12, 1810, letter to Samuel Kercheval.

- The quote "I have sworn upon the altar of God eternal hostility against any form of tyranny over the mind of man" that circles the dome above the four panels is from a September 23, 1800, letter written by Jefferson to Dr. Benjamin Rush.

34. Above the north entrance portico of the memorial, facing the tidal basin, is a 10-foot high by 65-foot wide pediment. The pediment (relief) is titled *The Drafting of the Declaration of Independence.*

35. Sculptor Adolph A. Weinman completed the pediment.

36. The figures in the pediment represent the men who worked with Jefferson in drafting the Declaration of Independence. Seated on the right of Jefferson are Benjamin Franklin and John Adams. On the left of Jefferson are Roger Sherman and Robert Livingston.

CHERRY BLOSSOM TREES AND JAPANESE STONE LANTERN NEAR THE JEFFERSON MEMORIAL

1. In January 1910, 2,000 cherry trees arrived in Washington, D.C. as gifts in the name of the city of Tokyo, Japan. However, the trees were infested with insects and had fungus disease; and had to be destroyed. Dr. Jokichi Takamine, a Japanese chemist, paid the cost of both the initial and replacement trees. On March 27, 1912, the first of the replacement trees were planted during a ceremony attended by Helen Taft, wife of President William Taft (1909-1913) and Viscountess Iwa Chinda, wife of Japanese Ambassador Sutemi Chinda.

Cherry Blossoms

2. The 3,020 cherry trees of twelve varieties were given to the United States as a symbol of peace between the two nations. Only about 150 of the original trees remain. The first two trees planted, which were Yoshino cherry trees, were planted at a site that is south of what is now Independence Avenue. The trees are still living.

3. In 1915, the United States gifted flowering dogwood trees to the people of Japan. The dogwood is Virginia's state tree.

4. There are currently more than 3,700 cherry trees growing in three main park locations. These locations are: Around the tidal basin in West Potomac Park, in East Potomac Park (Haines Point), and on the Washington Monument grounds. A few other locations hold additional trees.

5. The older trees are referred to as *Witnesses,* which makes reference to the fact that they have witnessed many years of historical events.

Cherry Trees in Bloom and Jefferson Memorial

6. *Hanami* is the Japanese word for the act of "viewing cherry blossoms."

7. The cherry trees bloom in late March or early April each year for an average of 10 days. The trees do not bear fruit.

163

8. The Cherry Blossom Festival was started in 1935, the Cherry Blossom Pageant was introduced in 1940, and the crowning of the Cherry Blossom Princess was begun in 1948.

9. On November 18, 1938, as part of a series of protests against the removal of the cherry trees around the tidal basin during the construction of the Jefferson Memorial, several women chained themselves to the trees. Their efforts, and those by other members of an activist group referred to as "Dowagers," with coverage by local newspapers, and support offered by local businesses, influenced the government's decision to reduce the size of the memorial, transplant existing trees, and plant additional trees.

10. On December 11, 1941, four of the cherry trees were vandalized after the bombing of Pearl Harbor by Japan. In an effort to avoid further vandalism, the cherry trees were then referred to as *Oriental Flowering Trees* until after World War II.

11. Hidden among the cherry trees near the Tidal Basin rests a 20-ton granite stone lantern. Crafted in 1651, it was presented to the city of Washington, D.C. in 1954 as a symbol of Japanese-American friendship.

- The lantern is located on the opposite side of the Tidal Basin from the Jefferson Memorial (off to the left) near Independence Avenue.

- The lighting of the 8-foot high lantern, which once stood on the grounds of the To-ei-zan Temple in Tokyo, Japan, has for years signaled the start of the Cherry Blossom Festival.

Japanese Stone Lantern – Crafted in 1651

- The lantern consists of the following six parts from top to bottom: (1) Houju – a sacred gem is believed to possess the power to banish evil, cleanse corruption, and satisfy wishes; (2) Kasa – acts as an umbrella over the fire box; (3) Hiburkuro – where the fire is lit; (4) Middle base of lantern; (5) Sao – the shaft that supports the lantern; and (6) Kidan – platform or podium.

164

FACTS ABOUT THE FRANKLIN DELANO ROOSEVELT MEMORIAL

Franklin Delano Roosevelt, often referred to as *FDR*, is believed by many historians and citizens to be one of the most capable presidents elected to the nation's highest public office. Born into a wealthy New York family, Roosevelt enjoyed a privileged and sheltered life. But even with his background as a member of the socially elite, he is recorded in history as the key to the survival of many poverty stricken Americans during the Great Depression of the 1930s; a decade of severe economic decline, and the world's defense and victory against the dictatorships of Germany, Japan, and Italy during World War II. The memorial to FDR is a tribute to a man who forbade physical limitations from keeping him from fulfilling his destiny, and to his wife, Eleanor, who did much to influence the greatness of the 32nd President of the United States.

THE LIFE OF FRANKLIN DELANO ROOSEVELT

1. The name Roosevelt means *Field of Roses* in Dutch.

2. The Roosevelt family crest is *Three Roses*.

3. On January 30, 1882, Franklin Delano Roosevelt was born at his family's Springwood Estate near Hyde Park, New York. He was an only child.

4. Roosevelt's middle name, Delano, was his mother's maiden name.

5. Roosevelt's father, James, was age 54, and his mother, Sara, was age 28, when Franklin was born.

6. In 1904, Roosevelt graduated from Harvard University. He also attended Columbia Law School, but did not graduate.

7. On St. Patrick's Day, March 17, 1905, Franklin Roosevelt, age 23, married Eleanor Roosevelt, age 20 and a 6th cousin once removed. President Theodore "Teddy" Roosevelt (1901-1909), the brother of Eleanor's father, Elliott, who died in 1894, gave the bride away.

8. Franklin and Eleanor were the parents of six children: Anna Eleanor (1906-1975), James (1907-1991), Franklin Delano Jr. (1909), Elliott (1910-1990), Franklin Delano Jr. (1914-1988), and John (1916-1981). Because their first son to be named Franklin died in infancy, they named another son Franklin.

9. From 1910 through part of 1913, Roosevelt served as a state senator for the state of New York. He also served as Assistant Secretary of the Navy from 1913 through 1920 and was the Democrat nominee for Vice President of the United States in 1920.

10. On August 10, 1921, at age 39, and while vacationing at his summer home near New Brunswick, Canada, Roosevelt was disabled from the waist down by poliomyelitis (polio).

11. From 1928, until he took office as President of the United States in 1933, Roosevelt served as Governor of New York.

12. On November 8, 1932, Roosevelt was elected the 32nd U.S. President and took the oath of office on March 4, 1933.

13. Roosevelt was elected to an unprecedented four terms as President of the United States (1933-1945). He was the first and only president to serve more than two full elected terms.

14. Roosevelt served as president for 12 years, 39 days, from March 4, 1933 to April 12, 1945.

15. Roosevelt was the only president to be sworn into office during the months of January and March: March 4, 1933, January 20, 1937, January 20, 1941, and January 20, 1945. Presidents elected since Roosevelt have all been sworn into office on the 20th of January following the November they are elected.

16. Roosevelt suffered a cerebral hemorrhage, which is the rupturing of a blood vessel in the brain, at 1 p.m. on April 12, 1945, while he was at Warm Springs, Georgia. He died at 3:35 p.m. the same day. His remains were returned to the White House on April 14th, where they lay in repose in the East Room. On April 15, 1945, Roosevelt's body was taken to his Springwood Estate home at Hyde Park, New York, where he was buried the same day.

THE LIFE OF ANNA ELEANOR ROOSEVELT

1. On October 11, 1884, Anna Eleanor Roosevelt was born as the oldest of four children. Her siblings were Elliott (1889-1893), Gracie (1891-1941), and Margaret (1892-1941).

2. In 1892, when Eleanor was only 8 years old, her mother, Anna, died from diphtheria, an illness of the upper respiratory tract.

3. In 1893, Eleanor's brother, Elliott, died from scarlet fever, a bacterial disease. In 1894, her father, Elliott, died from depression and alcohol related illnesses when Eleanor was just age 9.

4. As a child, Eleanor endured pain from a curvature of the spine, which required her to wear a steel brace for years. In addition, and because many of Eleanor's relatives considered her homely, slow moving, and uncoordinated, they called her *Granny* for many of her early years.

5. After the death of her mother, Eleanor lived with her grandmother, Valentine G. Hall. Eleanor was educated by private tutors until she was 15, at which time she was sent to England to attend preparatory school, but did not attend college. During her younger years Eleanor had contact with needy and impoverished people through charity programs supported by her family.

6. Due to Franklin's disability, Eleanor became his legs. She traveled an average of 200 days each year during the presidency of her husband. During these trips she talked to people from all walks of life, and reported her findings to the president. Eleanor was assigned the call sign *Rover* by the U.S. Secret Service.

7. Eleanor's strong influence on the American civil rights movement benefited minorities, especially African-Americans and women. Prior to World War II there were only five African-American officers in the military. At war's end this number had grown to over 7,000. The number of women (19 million) working in the factories at the peak of war production had grown from less than 1% to 60% of the workforce. Over 100,000 African-American workers were also employed. Because Eleanor was such a thorn in the military's backside, the Army's Chief of Staff, assigned a general officer to handle the demands of the first lady.

8. After World War II, Eleanor was appointed a member of the United States' delegation to the United Nations and played an important part in drafting and gaining approval of the United Nations' Declaration of Human Rights.

9. Eleanor died on November 7, 1962, at age 78, from tuberculosis and heart failure at her Manhattan apartment in New York City. She was buried beside her husband at the family's Springwood Estate in Hyde Park, New York, on November 10, 1962.

THE FRANKLIN DELANO ROOSEVELT MEMORIAL

1. In 1946, the idea for a Franklin Delano Roosevelt Memorial was conceived.

2. In 1955, a commission to plan the memorial was established.

3. In 1959, the site for the memorial was selected.

4. Two previous more grandiose designs for the memorial were accepted, but later withdrawn. The 1960 design looked like great slabs of paper on edge containing engraved FDR memorandums. The 1966 design consisted of a series of high walls at various angles containing engraved FDR memorandums.

5. Work on the third version of the memorial was begun in the mid-1970s. In 1978, the design was approved by the Memorial Commission and the Commission of Fine Arts.

6. Florida Senator Claude Pepper was the driving force behind the approval of the FDR Memorial. Senator Pepper, an avid supporter of Roosevelt and his New Deal policy, died shortly after the project was approved.

7. In September 1991, the ground was broken for the memorial.

8. In October 1994, on-site construction of the memorial was begun.

9. On May 2, 1997, President William Clinton (1993-2001) dedicated the memorial.

10. The memorial is located on a 7.5-acre site in West Potomac Park.

11. The final cost of the memorial totaled $48,500,000. Of this amount $42,900,000 was funded through federal appropriations, with the remaining $5,600,000 donated by private contributors.

12. Lawrence Halprin designed the memorial. Halprin died in 2009, at age 93.

13. The memorial includes sculptural groups and inscriptions by Leonard Baskin, Neil Estern, Robert Graham, Thomas Hardy, George Segal and John Benson.

14. John Benson engraved the large and small quotations into the stones.

15. John Benson's prior works included the inscriptions on the John F. Kennedy Memorial at Arlington Cemetery and the East and West Buildings of the National Gallery of Art. He also participated in designing the inscriptions for the Vietnam Veterans Memorial.

16. President Roosevelt's words are engraved into Red Dakota granite.

17. Visitors wander through a zigzag path among the rough granite walls to pass by the sculptures, the engraved quotations, and the waterfalls.

18. Because water was a constant in Franklin Roosevelt's life, it was chosen as the theme for the memorial. Roosevelt was an avid boater, a former Assistant Secretary of the Navy, held wartime summits aboard Navy ships, and died in Warm Springs, Georgia, a health spa he helped create and frequently visited.

19. Approximately 100,000 gallons (378,500 liters) of water are recycled every minute through the entire monument.

20. The memorial consists of nine artworks.

21. The memorial contains six waterfalls.

22. There are 21 FDR quotations engraved into the memorial.

23. Construction of the memorial required 31,439 pieces of cut stone, which included 75,000 square feet of granite pavers and ten miles of steel.

24. Four thousand pieces of granite blocks were used to form the walls.

25. The memorial walls are 12 feet high.

26. Four rows of granite blocks are in each wall.

27. The walls and paving stones are Pink Carnelian granite.

28. The benches and other gray stones are Minnesota granite.

29. Over 8,200 cubic yards of concrete were used to construct the memorial.

30. The memorial contains enough stones to erect an 80-story building.

31. The memorial stones weigh 6,000 tons.

32. Nine hundred steel pilings were used to support the memorial stones. The pilings were sunk 80 feet deep before they hit bedrock.

33. If a flood washed the ground away from under the memorial, the memorial would still remain standing.

34. The memorial is divided into four rooms, punctuated by two meditative spaces. The dates for each period of Roosevelt's presidency are engraved in the granite walkway at the entrance to each room.

35. Each room not only represents one of Roosevelt's four terms, but the social climate of the country at the time - depression, social reforms, war, and peace.

36. The journey through the memorial begins in a paved forecourt, where a long granite wall announces the memorial's subject – "Franklin Delano Roosevelt, 1882-1945."

37. Also in the forecourt is a bronze statue of President Roosevelt that welcomes visitors to the memorial. The statue, which cost $1.65 million to construct, was dedicated by President Clinton (1993-2001) on January 10, 2001, and shows Roosevelt in a wheelchair similar to the one Roosevelt designed. See information about the controversy surrounding the statue at the end of this section.

Statue of President Roosevelt in Wheelchair

Room 1 - The Early Years (1932-1936)

1. The Presidential Seal on the wall is an interpretation of the Presidential Seal at the time of FDR's first inauguration in March 1933. The seal is intended to remind visitors that FDR is being remembered above all else for his role as President of the United States.

2. The Presidential Seal weighs 1,000 pounds and represents a bird in flight. The bird is an American Bald Eagle.

3. The Presidential Seal consists of sheet bronze that has been arc welded together.

4. Sculptor Thomas Hardy was age 77 when he completed the Presidential Seal.

Presidential Seal as of 1933

5. A 30-foot-wall titled *The First Inaugural* represents optimism and new beginnings in the midst of the Great Depression. FDR waves from an open car during his first inaugural parade in 1933.

Room 2 –Social Policy (1936-1940)

1. This room represents the social programs of the New Deal, many of which were intended to combat the Great Depression.

171

2. *The Breadline* is a sculpture of five men in a bread line outside a closed door. It represents unemployment and the hard times of many citizens during the depression. Unemployment at the peak of the depression was 24.9% of the workforce or 13,000,000 workers.

3. *The Fireside Chat* is a sculpture of a man listening to one of Roosevelt's 30 speeches broadcasted from the White House or from his home in Hyde Park, New York. These so called chats were attempts by the president at keeping the average citizen informed and providing encouragement. The first fireside chat occurred on March 12, 1933, and dealt with the bank crisis. The last chat on June 12, 1944, dealt with a war loan (bond) drive.

4. *The Rural Couple* is a sculpture of a weary couple set against an old barn door. Times were hard for people in both rural and urban areas. Many farmers lost farms that had been in their families for many generations. In 1933 alone, banks foreclosed on 200,000 farms.

Room depicts Breadline, Rural Couple, and the Fireside Chat

5. Real people modeled for all of the figures depicted in the Breadline, the Rural Couple, and the Fireside Chat.

6. In this room is a 30-foot-long bronze mural that depicts 54 social programs implemented during Roosevelt's presidency. The five bas-relief panels titled *Social Programs* pay tribute to FDR's New Deal legislation. The five nearby columns carry the images of the mural in reverse, as if one had been cast from the other. Some of these New Deal programs still exist today - Social Security, Unemployment Insurance, and Workman's Compensation.

7. Robert Graham, who sculptured FDR's first inaugural and the five bas-relief panels and columns, is also credited with casting the Olympic Gateway at the entrance to the Los Angeles Memorial Coliseum for the 1984 Olympic Games.

8. Visitors can view the Potomac River from an opening in the landscape of the memorial.

9. The four-tiered waterfall pays homage to the Tennessee Valley Authority (TVA). Established in 1933, during Roosevelt's presidency, the dams constructed by the TVA were instrumental in providing jobs, preventing floods, and providing electrical power. Nine out of ten rural Americans did not have electricity in their homes at this time.

Room 3 - The War Years (1940-1944)

1. The piles of broken granite blocks surrounding the words "I Hate War" represent the bombed-out ruins of World War II.

2. On September 1, 1939, war began in Europe. The United States entered the war as a result of Japan bombing Pearl Harbor, Hawaii, on December 7, 1941.

3. The bronze statue of Roosevelt is 8 feet, 7 inches high.

4. The chair on which Roosevelt is seated has casters on the legs. This is the only suggestion that Roosevelt was handicapped. The leg braces worn by Roosevelt weighed nearly 10 pounds.

Statues of Roosevelt and his dog Fala

5. Roosevelt stood 6 feet, 2 inches tall and weighed 185 pounds.

6. The dog next to Roosevelt is his Scottish terrier Fala, a 1940 Christmas gift from Augustus Kellogg through Roosevelt's cousin Margaret Suckley. Fala's full name was *Murray the Outlaw of Fala Hill*. Fala was known to stand on his hind legs when the national anthem was played.

7. The statue of Fala stands 34-inches high from the front paws to the tips of its ears. Its length totals four feet from the tip of Fala's tail to the tip of his nose.

8. Fala died in 1952 and is buried at the foot of FDR's gravesite on the Roosevelt's Springwood Estate in Hyde Park, New York.

9. Room 3 contains the largest stone in the memorial. This stone is 21 feet, 6 inches long by 6 feet high.

Room 4 – Seeds of Peace (1944-1945)

1. The Funeral Cortege is a 30-foot long by 6-foot high bas-relief depicting the grief of mourners following on foot behind FDR's horse-drawn casket. Roosevelt died on April 12, 1945, at age 63, from a cerebral hemorrhage.

2. The sculptor, Leonard Baskin, drew inspiration for this bronze relief from studying ancient Greek, Egyptian, and Chinese sculptures.

3. The statue of Eleanor Roosevelt stands in front of the seal of the United Nations. Eleanor was a member of the U.S. delegation to the United Nations (U.N.) and she played an important part in drafting the U.N. Declaration of Human Rights.

4. The bronze statue of Eleanor is the only statue of a first lady displayed at any of the presidential memorials or monuments within Washington, D.C.

5. The statue of Eleanor is 7 feet, 3 inches high. Eleanor has been the tallest first lady. She was 6 feet tall.

Statue of Eleanor Roosevelt

6. After studying several photographs of Eleanor, sculptor Neil Estern noticed that the lapels on Eleanor's overcoats were often folded over and unpressed. This observation caused Mr. Estern to insert this notable trend into the likeness of the first lady.

7. The water flowing over the final waterfall, "The Grand Finale," symbolizes the excitement at the end of World War II. It cascades over orderly granite blocks in a loud grand finale. War ended in Europe in May 1945 and in the Pacific in September 1945.

8. A series of granite steps near the last waterfall were crafted into the shape of an amphitheater. On the steps are inscribed the major events of FDR's life.

9. Weighing 76,000 pounds, a foundation block located in Room 4 is the heaviest stone in the memorial.

10. Upon leaving through the rear of the Roosevelt Memorial, visitors can see the Jefferson Memorial across the tidal basin.

UNIQUE FACTS ABOUT THE FDR MEMORIAL

1. As a rebuttal to those who believed Franklin Roosevelt should be portrayed in a wheelchair or on crutches, Lawrence Halprin stated "He didn't want people to focus on it (Roosevelt's handicap). This memorial is not meant to solve the problems of the handicapped. It is meant to be historically correct."

2. Just weeks prior to the dedication of the memorial, President William Clinton (1993-2001) bowed to pressure. He directed that a figure of President Roosevelt (1933-1945) showing him in a wheelchair be included in the memorial. Only a few photographs and a 15 second film clip are known to exist that show President Roosevelt on crutches or unable to walk on his own.

3. Prior to his death, Franklin Roosevelt requested that no memorial be dedicated to him after his death. However, in 1965, friends and admirers of Roosevelt placed a small memorial near the  National Archives. The memorial consists of a piece of granite the size of Roosevelt's desk with the inscription "In Memory of Franklin Delano Roosevelt, 1882 – 1945" engraved onto its surface.

FACTS ABOUT THE MARTIN LUTHER KING, JR.
NATIONAL MEMORIAL

Doctor of Philosophy (Dr.) Martin Luther King Jr. is often associated with non-violent activism for the improvement of civil rights. His "I Have a Dream" speech at the Lincoln Memorial in Washington, D.C. on August 28, 1963, was just one of many speeches, marches, and rallies organized under the leadership of a man whose efforts contributed immeasurably to the passage and enforcement of such civil rights bills as the 1964 Civil Rights Act and the 1965 National Voting Rights Act. This national memorial to an inspirational and spiritual civil rights leader offers visitors an opportunity to reflect on the life and accomplishments of an African-American who did much to enrich the lives of his and future generations of Americans.

THE LIFE OF MARTIN LUTHER KING, JR.

1. Dr. King's parents were the Reverend (Baptist) Michael "Martin Luther" King and Alberta Williams King (school teacher). Martin died from a heart attack in 1984 at age 84. Alberta, at age 69, was shot and killed in 1974 by a deranged anti-Christian.

2. Michael King, Jr. was born on January 15, 1929, in Atlanta, Georgia. He had an older sister, Christine, and a younger brother, Alfred Daniel. Alfred died in 1969 from an accidental drowning.

3. At the times of their births, King Sr. was named Michael King and King Jr. was named Michael King, Jr. In 1934, when the son was five, "Daddy" King changed his own name to Martin Luther King and his son's name to Martin Luther King, Jr. when both were baptized to honor the German Protestant religious leader Martin Luther (b1483-d1546). In 1957, Martin Luther King, Jr. amended his birth certificate to reflect this change.

4. In 1952, Dr. King met his future wife, Coretta Scott, while he was attending Boston University and she was studying concert singing at the New England Conservatory of Music in Boston. They were married on June 18, 1953, and were the parents of four children.

5. Dr. King's formal education consisted of:

- In 1944, he entered Morehouse College in Atlanta, Georgia, at age 15, skipping his ninth and twelfth high school grades without formally graduating from high school.

- In 1948, he graduated from Morehouse College, previously known as Atlanta Baptist College, at the age of 19 with a Bachelor of Arts degree in sociology. His father had graduated from Morehouse College in 1930.

- In 1951, he graduated from Crozer Theological Seminary in Chester, Pennsylvania, with a Bachelor of Divinity degree.

- In 1955, he received a Doctorate of Philosophy in systematic theology from Boston University in Boston, Massachusetts.

6. Notable accomplishments by Dr. King include:

- In 1953, at age 24, he became pastor at the Dexter Avenue Baptist Church in Montgomery, Alabama.

- In 1955 and 1956, he led the historical bus boycott in Montgomery, Alabama. The 385-day boycott of the bus system ended racial segregation on public buses in Montgomery.

- Beginning in 1956, he was arrested and incarcerated multiple times. These include:

    - January 26, 1956 – Arrested for driving 30 mph in a 25 mph zone in Montgomery, Alabama. Fined $14.00.
    - February 21, 1956 – Arrested for organizing the Montgomery boycott. Fined $500.
    - September 3, 1958 – Arrested and charged with loitering, later changed to disobeying a police officer, in Montgomery, Alabama.
    - February 17, 1960 – Arrested for Tax Evasion – Alabama State Income Tax Returns. Acquitted on May 28, 1960.
    - May 4, 1960 – Arrested for driving without a Georgia driver's license in DeKalb County, Georgia.
    - October 19, 1960 – Arrested for civil disobedience during a sit-in at a lunch counter in Atlanta, Georgia. Charges were dropped on October 25, 1960, and he was released from Fulton County Jail.

- October 25, 1960 – Immediately after being released from the Fulton County Jail, he was arrested, tried in DeKalb County, and sent to Reidsville State Prison for violation of his probation for driving without a license on May 4, 1960. He was released from prison on October 27, 1960.
- December 16, 1961 – Arrested for disturbing the peace by obstructing the sidewalk and parading without a permit in Albany, Georgia.
- July 10-12, 1962 – Served part of 45-day sentence for December 16, 1961 arrest.
- July 27-August 10, 1962 – Arrested for prayer vigil at City Hall in Albany, Georgia.
- April 12-19, 1963 – Arrested for protesting against the segregation of a department store and unfair hiring practices in Birmingham, Alabama.
- June 11, 1964 – Arrested for demanding service at a whites-only restaurant in St Augustine, Florida.
- February 1, 1965 – Arrested for participating in the Voting Rights March in Selma, Alabama.
- October 30-November 2, 1967 – Served four-day contempt of court sentence for actions relating to the 1963 protests in Birmingham, Alabama.

- In 1957, he was one of the co-founders and first president of the Southern Christian Leadership Conference. This organization was created to organize and conduct non-violent protests in the service of civil rights reform.

- In 1959, he moved to Atlanta, Georgia, to become co-pastor of his father's church - Ebenezer Baptist Church.

- In 1963, he led the civil rights March on Washington, D.C., where he delivered his "I Have a Dream" speech. It took Dr. King just over 16 minutes to present his 1665-word speech.

- For 1963, he was selected as the "Man of the Year" by Time Magazine as someone who had "done the most to influence the events of the year."

- In 1964, at age 35, he was awarded the Nobel Peace Prize for his work to end racial segregation and racial discrimination. He donated the $54,123 prize to the furtherance of the civil rights movement. At the time of the award he was the youngest recipient of the peace prize.

- In 1965, he was awarded the American Liberties Medallion by the American Jewish Committee for his "exceptional advancement of the principles of human liberty."

- After his death, he was awarded a 1971 Grammy Award for Best Spoken Word Recording for his "Why I Oppose the War in Vietnam" recording. He was also awarded the Presidential Medal of Freedom in 1977 and the Congressional Gold Medal in 2004.

7. At 6:01 p.m., on April 4, 1968, at the age of 39, Dr. King was struck by an assassin's bullet at the Lorraine Motel in Memphis, Tennessee. After surgery at St. Joseph Hospital, he died at 7:05 p.m. on the same day.

   Previous attacks on the life of Dr. King include: (1) Having a bomb explode on the porch of his home in Montgomery, Alabama, on January 30, 1956; (2) Another bomb (unexploded) was discovered on his porch on January 27, 1957; (3) On September 20, 1958, during a book signing in New York City (Harlem) for his first book *Stride Toward Freedom – The Montgomery Story*, he was stabbed in the chest with a letter opener by a paranoid schizophrenic African-American woman. The letter opener touched, but did not cut the aorta – the largest artery in the body. The doctors told King that if he had coughed or sneezed before the opener was removed he would have probably bled to death; and (4) A motel in Birmingham, Alabama, where he was registered as a guest, was bombed on May 11, 1963.

8. On April 9, 1968, Dr. King's body was buried at South View Cemetery in Atlanta, Georgia. On January 12, 1970, Dr. King's body was exhumed and reburied at the Martin Luther King Memorial Center, just down the street from his birth home at 501 Auburn Ave., Atlanta, Georgia. The center is next to the Ebenezer Baptist Church, where Dr. King was baptized, was a pastor between 1959 and 1968, and where his final funeral services were conducted in 1968.

9. In 2006, Coretta King was buried beside her husband after her death from cancer at age 78.

Tomb of Martin Luther and Coretta King

10. On November 2, 1983, President Ronald Reagan signed a bill creating a federal holiday to honor Dr. King. The holiday was first observed on January 20, 1986, and is celebrated on the third Monday in January of each year. Since 2000, all 50 U.S. states officially observe the Dr. Martin Luther King holiday.

THE MARTIN LUTHER KING, JR. NATIONAL MEMORIAL

1. The memorial is on a four-acre crescent-shaped site in the West Potomac Park on the northwestern side of the tidal basin, near the Roosevelt Memorial and across the basin from the Jefferson Memorial. There is also a visual line to the Lincoln Memorial.

The Martin Luther King Jr. Memorial

2. The $120 million memorial was conceived in January 1984 by the Silver Spring, Maryland Chapter of Dr. King's fraternity – Alpha Phi Alpha. The memorial was later authorized on November 12, 1996, with the site being approved on December 2, 1999, and the ground breaking occurring on November 13, 2006. The memorial was opened to the public on August 22, 2011.

3. The dedication was originally scheduled for August 28, 2011; the 48th anniversary of the day Dr. King delivered his 1963 "I Have a Dream" speech at the Lincoln Memorial. However, due to Hurricane Irene the dedication of the memorial was delayed.

4. President Barack Obama dedicated the memorial on October 16, 2011.

5. October 16, 2011 also celebrated the 16th anniversary of the *Million Man March,* a gathering of several thousand mostly Black men on the Mall in 1995 to advocate "unity, atonement, and brotherhood."

6. The dedication of the memorial was the first time a U.S. citizen had been honored through a memorial or monument on the Mall who was not honored for his government service (president, members of the military, etc.).

7. In 2000, the design submitted by San Francisco-based ROMA Design Group was selected as the winning design for the memorial from approximately 900 entries representing 52 countries.

8. In 2007, Chinese master sculptor Lei Yixin, who was born in 1953 in Changsha, Human, China, was selected to complete the likeness of Dr. King. His signature is on the Stone of Hope.

9. A total of 337 concrete structural piles were driven into the ground as deep as 50 feet to support the memorial site.

10. The memorial consists of 1,600 metric tons of granite.

11. The three main elements of the approved design include the curved *Inscription Wall*, the *Mountain of Despair,* and the *Stone of Hope.*

12. The Mountain of Despair and Stone of Hope elements were formed from 159 blocks of granite in China and assembled and finished on site in Washington, D.C. by Yixin and his 10-man team from China. To reduce the weight of the structure, the cores of these elements were filled with concrete.

13. Two large stone slabs form an entrance at the middle of the Inscription Wall. These slabs represent the *Mountain of Despair*, which is referenced in Dr. King's 1963 "I Have a Dream" speech, and the quotes on the slabs are from this speech.

Mountain of Despair

The distance between the two stone slabs forming the Mountain of Despair was intentionally keep narrow to symbolize the difficulty of getting through the Mountain of Despair in order to reach the Stone of Hope.

14. Through the entrance between the two sides of the Mountain of Despair is a third stone pushed back as if it was part of the stones in the forefront. This *Stone of Hope*, which is 30 feet, 8 inches high, was crafted from 35 granite blocks.

15. The blocks that form the Stone of Hope range from just over one-foot high to just over four feet high, with the largest block weighing 55 tons. (The 55-ton block is located just below Dr. King's shoulder, and includes his arms and hands.)

16. Standing on the Stone of Hope is the image of Dr. King in a business suit with his arms crossed. The image of King was formed from a slightly pink hued stone to better display King's features. The pale granite, quarried in China, has flecks of black and gray, and because of its pink hue has the nickname "shrimp pink." The sculpture rests on a 2 ½-foot concrete slab.

Statue of Martin Luther King

As an adult, Dr. King stood between 5 feet 6 ½ inches and 5 feet, 7 inches tall. His draft registration card at age 18 listed him as 5 feet, 7 inches tall.

17. The sculpture of Dr. King is based on a 1966 photograph taken of King at his office in Atlanta, Georgia. The photograph, taken by photographer Robert Fitch, shows King standing at his desk, with a photograph of Indian leader Mohandas Gandhi on the wall in the background.

Mohandas Gandhi (1869-1948) was a political and ideological leader of India. Dr. King drew inspiration from Gandhi's use of satyagraha, which is the use of mass civil resistance against any barrier of civil rights, and from Gandhi's nonviolence philosophy.

18. The photograph of Dr. King was reproduced from a reversed negative of the 1966 photograph. This caused the right-handed King to be shown holding his pen in his left hand. Unfortunately, the sculpturing of King's likeness had progressed to the point where the error could not be corrected. As a result, the pen was replaced with a scroll.

19. Inscribed on the Stone of Hope are additional words from Dr. King's speech at the Lincoln Memorial on August 28, 1963.

20. The Inscription Wall is approximately 450 feet long, weighs 194 tons, and covers an area of 2,350 cubic feet.

21. On the surface of the wall are 14 quotes from Dr. King's speeches, books, and letters. The inscriptions, from 1955 through 1968, are inscribed on 355 granite panels that arc around the memorial. The Inscription Wall

22. The quotes on the Inscription Wall are intended to build on the words and life of Dr. King through the themes of *Justice*, *Democracy*, *Love*, and *Hope*.

23. Stone carver Nicholas "Nick" Benson, from Newport, Rhode Island, and his three-man team, chiseled the lettering on the memorial. Using only mallets and chisels for most of the work, the men formed the letters from a font originated by Benson by using a combination of classical Greek/Roman lettering in a contemporary scan serif script. (Because of the difficulty in forming the letters, only six or seven letters were formed each day.)

Nick Benson is a third-generation stone carver who also carved the inscriptions on the World War II Memorial (Dedicated in 2004). His father, John E. Benson, carved the inscriptions on the Franklin D. Roosevelt Memorial (Dedicated in 1997). And his grandfather, John H. Benson, carved the inscriptions on the Iwo Jima Memorial (Dedicated in 1954).

24. An additional 185 Yoshino Cherry trees and 32 American Elm trees were added to the site during the construction of the memorial. In addition, plants consisting of jasmine, English yew, and liriope were added to the landscape.

FACTS ABOUT THE KOREAN WAR VETERANS MEMORIAL

In a short period of five years after the end of World War II, the United States was again engaged in a conflict far from its shores. This time it was Korea, an Asian country divided at the 38th parallel between a communist north and a democratic south. After the initial attacks and victories by North Korea, the combined forces of South Korea, the United States, and their allies forced the armies of North Korea beyond the 38th parallel to a point close to the border of Communist China. These victories by the forces of the United Nations prompted military intervention by China, and led to a long and destructive conflict that threatened to explode beyond the borders of Korea. The Korean War Veterans Memorial is a tribute to the men and women who served and sacrificed in what has become known as the *Forgotten War*.

THE KOREAN WAR

1. In 1945, near the end of World War II, the Allies agreed that in order to expedite the surrender of the Japanese military forces on the Asian peninsula, the Soviet Union would accept the surrender of the Japanese above the 38th parallel, and the United States would accept the surrender of the Japanese below the 38th parallel.

2. Instead of the areas above and below the 38th parallel reuniting after the surrender of the Japanese military, they remained divided and became North Korea and South Korea.

3. On June 25, 1950, the military forces of North Korea invaded South Korea.

4. The United States and 21 other members of the United Nations immediately went to the aid of South Korea. Fifteen countries actually provided combat troops, with the United States providing most of the armed forces and supplies.

5. For political reasons, President Harry Truman (1945-1953) referred to the war as a conflict. Only Congress can declare war.

6. On October 14, 1950, Chinese forces crossed into North Korea.

7. On July 27, 1953, an uneasy armistice agreement was signed. Many historians believe threats by President Dwight Eisenhower (1953-1961) to use atomic weapons forced China and North Korea to negotiate.

8. Of the 1,500,000 U.S. servicemen and servicewomen who served in the Korean War; 33,651 died from battle wounds and 3,262 died from accidents, disease and other non-battle related incidents. An additional 103,000 U.S. servicemen and servicewomen were wounded during the conflict.

9. To compare the casualties of the Korean War with those of World War II and the Vietnam War: Deaths resulting from World War II totaled 292,131 killed in battle and 115,185 non-battle related deaths. Vietnam had over 47,000 service personnel killed in battle and over 10,000 non-battle related deaths.

10. The following is a breakdown of the number of casualties, captured personnel, and missing in action for U.S. troops, and the total for all United Nations (U.N.) troops:

CASUALTIES OF THE KOREAN WAR		
STATUS	U.S. MILITARY FORCES	UNITED NATIONS FORCES
Killed	36,913	610,987
Wounded	103,284	1,064,453
Missing	8,177	470,267
Captured	7,140	92,970

*Official Department of Defense records support the number of service members who died of combat and non-combat incidents in the immediate Korean area as 33,651 combat deaths and 3,262 non-combat deaths, for a total of 36,913. Previously, the total was listed as 54,246 deaths attributed to the Korean War. However, on

June 25, 2000, the Department of Defense corrected the 54,246 total fatalities by removing, from the list of Korean related deaths, the deaths of military personnel whose deaths occurred as a result of events outside the borders of Korea (i.e., United States, Europe, etc.).

**Resulting from a correction of non-combat casualties suffered by the United States in Korea, the number of U.N. deaths associated with the Korean conflict was dropped from 628,833 to 610,987.

11. An estimated 2,000,000 Chinese and North Korean military personnel lost their lives during the conflict. It is also estimated that over 3,000 advisors from the former Soviet Union provided in-country support to North Korea during the Korean War.

12. A total of 135 U.S. servicemen have been awarded Medals of Honor for military service in Korea. Of this number, 96 sacrificed their lives performing their heroic acts of valor. In 2011, the most recent Medals of Honor for service in Korea were awarded to Army Privates Anthony T. Kaho'ohanohano of Pukalani, Hawaii, and Henry Svehla of Belleville, N.J. They had previously been awarded the Distinguished Service Cross, the second highest military decoration, for their actions.

13. There were two commanders of U.S. military forces over the course of the war. The first commander was General Douglas MacArthur, who was relieved of duty by President Harry Truman (1945-1953) on April 11, 1951. The second commander was General Matthew Ridgeway, who replaced MacArthur. MacArthur was age 71 when Truman relieved him of his duties.

THE KOREAN WAR VETERANS MEMORIAL

1. In October 1986, Congress authorized the creation of a Korean War Veterans Memorial.

2. President Ronald Reagan (1981-1989) appointed a 12-member board of Korean War veterans to direct the construction of the memorial.

3. In 1989, a team from State College, Pennsylvania, submitted the plan initially approved for the memorial. However, the board later withdrew its acceptance of the plan.

4. The 1992 memorial plan submitted by Cooper-Lecky Architects was accepted and implemented.

5. On June 14, 1992, President George H. W. Bush (1989-1993) formally broke ground for the memorial.

6. On July 27, 1995, the memorial was dedicated. This date marked the 42nd anniversary of the armistice that ended hostilities in the Korean War. President William Clinton (1993-2001) and South Korean President Kim Young Sam attended the dedication.

7. The total cost of the memorial was $16,500,000.

8. The memorial stands on a 2.2-acre site.

9. A total of 223 piles were driven into bedrock 30-60 feet deep to support the statues and the wall.

10. The memorial's most prominent feature is the triangular *Field of Service.*

11. There are 19 U.S. servicemen depicted in the Field of Service.

Servicemen in Field of Service

12. The lines of trees behind the servicemen are being used as a background. They also symbolize the act of the United Nations troops coming to the aid of South Korea from west to east.

13. World War II veteran Frank Gaylord sculptured the servicemen.

14. The formation of the servicemen depicts a squad on patrol and evokes the experience of American ground troops in Korea.

15. The actual 19 statues and their reflections on the wall total 38 servicemen. The number 38 is symbolic of the 38th parallel, which is the border between North Korea and South Korea. The number 38 can also represent the number of calendar months in which combat actions were conducted between June 1950 and July 1953, before a ceasefire was agreed to by the combatants.

16. The 19 stainless steel figures stand between 7 feet, 3 inches and 7 feet, 6 inches high.

17. Each figure weighs approximately 1,000 pounds.

Lead Figure of Squad, plus Reflections on Wall

18. Of the 19 figures, one figure represents the Air Force, one represents the Navy (medic), and the others represent the Army and Marines. The one member of the squad wearing a winter cap versus a helmet is an Air Force observer.

19. Of the 19 figures, 12 represent Caucasian servicemen, 3 represent African-American servicemen, 2 represent Hispanic-American servicemen 1 represents Asian-American servicemen, and 1 represents Native-American servicemen.

20. The figures of the servicemen are walking through a simulated rice paddy on a windy and cold day. Strips of granite and scrubby juniper bushes suggest the rugged Korean terrain. The strips also help limit erosion.

21. The servicemen are wearing cold weather clothing and ponchos. Gaylord chose this particular design for two reasons: (1) To provide motion to the figures as the ponchos flow in the wind, and (2) To represent the type of weather the soldiers often fought in during the war. During the winter-months, troops fighting in the mountains had to deal with temperatures as low as 30 degrees below zero.

Servicemen

22. Fully equipped, a combat soldier carried an average of between 75 and 80 pounds of food, clothing, and equipment.

23. The clothing and equipment used by the military during the Korean War was largely left over from World War II. The following list provides the average equipment issued to a soldier:

- M1 Steel Helmet with liner. (This 1940 helmet replaced the M1917A helmet used by U.S. troops during World War I.)
- M1928 Haversack (Backpack)
- M1923 Dismounted Cartridge Belt
- M1938 Dismounted Leggings
- M1940 Boots (Replaced by black boots during the 1950s.)
- M1910 Canteen, Cup & Cover
- M1910 Entrenching Tool & Cover (Shovel)

24. The M before a type of weapon, clothing, etc. represents the word Model and does not represent Military. The numbers following the letter M usually represent the year the item was first manufactured or accepted by the government.

25. Many of the servicemen in the squad carry an M1 rifle, the standard weapon for U.S. ground troops in Korea. Designed by John Garand, this semi-automatic rifle weighs 11.2 pounds, fires .30 caliber bullets from an 8-round clip, and has an effective range of 500 yards. Over 5.5 million M1 rifles were produced between 1936 and 1957.

26. One of the servicemen walking near the front of the squad is carrying an M1918 Browning Automatic Rifle (BAR). Used in WWI, WWII, Korea and the early stages of the Vietnam War, it fires a .30 caliber bullet from 20-round clips, weighs 20 pounds, has a firing rate of between 300-600 rounds per minute, effective firing range of 500 yards, and a maximum firing range of 3,500 yards.

27. The weapon carried by the Air Force member of the squad is an automatic/semi-automatic M1 carbine. The carbine weighs 6 pound, 9 ounces, fires .30 caliber bullets from 30-round clips, and has a maximum range of 300 yards. Veterans described the M1 carbine as very ineffective after 150 yards. Beyond this range, the bullet seldom passed through winter clothing. It was used between 1942 and the 1960s.

28. The officer/squad leader is probably carrying under his poncho a gas pressured .45 caliber automatic pistol. The weapon weighs 2 pounds, 5 ounces, has a 7-shot magazine, and an effective firing range of 50 yards. The Model 1911 Colt 45 was first fielded in battle in the Philippines during 1911 and 1912.

29. Two squad members are carrying a .30 caliber air-cooled Browning machine gun, tripod, and ammunition. This machine gun was used previously during World War II, fires .30 caliber bullets, weighs 31 pounds, with a length of 3 feet, 6 inches, and a maximum range of 3,500 yards, and an effective range of 500 yards.

30. One of the squad is carrying a large radio, evident by the large hump on his back and an antenna sticking out from beneath his poncho. This radio, referred to as an AN/PRC (Angry) 29, could transmit long and short distances.

31. Two members of the squad are carrying a small portable radio capable of receiving and transmitting over short distances. This SCR-536 two-way radio, referred to as a BC-611 Handie-Talkie, could be used to contact other squads in the area or low flying aircraft. The servicemen are probably lieutenants or a rank no higher than captain and no lower than corporal.

32. The high mural on the south side of the statues pays tribute to the military personnel who served in many roles during the Korean War.

33. The mural was designed by Louis Nelson.

34. The mural was crafted from Academy Black granite from California.

Reflections of Servicemen on the Mural

35. The mural consists of 41 panels, is 164 feet long by 13 feet high at its highest point, is 8 inches thick, and weighs 100 tons.

36. Displayed on the surface of the mural are more than 2,500 photographic archival images. These images show various support and combat personnel in their military roles. The images were selected from over 15,000 images obtained from the National Archives.

37. The images on the mural were formed by first scanning period photographs into a computer, then using a computer-generated stencil to sandblast the images onto the surface of the mural. The images of the servicemen and servicewomen represent many of the combat, medical, and support functions associated with military service in the Korean War.

38. In addition to the sandblasted images of servicemen and servicewomen on the mural, there are images of several types of military equipment used during the conflict.

39. The United Nations Wall is the granite curb on the north side of the statues. It lists the 22 United Nations countries that provided combat troops or medical support in defense of South Korea.

40. Encircled by a grove of linden trees, at the top of the Field of Service, is the *Pool of Remembrance*. It is dedicated to the servicemen and servicewomen who sacrificed their lives during the Korean War.

Pool of Remembrance

41. Engraved on a nearby wall are the total casualties of the United States and the forces of the United Nations along with the words "FREEDOM IS NOT FREE."

42. The Pool of Remembrance is 30 feet in diameter and was crafted from black granite from Canada.

43. To the south of the memorial are three beds of Rose of Sharon hibiscus plants. This plant is the national flower of South Korea.

FACTS ABOUT THE LINCOLN MEMORIAL

As the 16th President of the United States, Abraham Lincoln (1861-1865) led the United States through one of the most trying times in its short history, the American Civil War (1861-1865). A notable accomplishment considering Lincoln was born and raised in the wilderness, lost his mother at an early age, taught himself how to read and write, was self-educated in the practice of law, and served as a state legislator and U.S. Congressman without the aid of formal schooling. Many historians rate Lincoln as a man of considerable personal strength, political savvy, and compassion, whose presidency is equal to those of Washington and Jefferson.

Immediately after Lincoln's death, efforts were begun to erect a memorial in Washington, D.C. to honor the man who many believed saved the Union. However, it was not until the 20th century that any successful steps were taken by Congress to erect a memorial to Lincoln in the nation's capital. Their efforts resulted in a magnificent tribute to Lincoln in the form of the Lincoln Memorial.

THE LIFE OF ABRAHAM LINCOLN

1. In 1637, Abraham Lincoln's great-great-great-great grandfather, Samuel Lincoln, migrated from England to Massachusetts. In 1649, Samuel married Irish immigrant Martha Lyford.

2. Lincoln's parents were both born in Virginia. Thomas Lincoln in 1778 and Nancy Hawks in 1784. They married in 1806.

3. On February 12, 1809, Abraham Lincoln was born at Nolin Creek near Hodgenville, Kentucky. Lincoln was born in Kentucky, raised in Indiana, and spent his adult life in Illinois.

4. In 1812, Lincoln's brother, Thomas, died in infancy.

5. In 1818, Lincoln's mother, Nancy, died at age 34. She died from milk sickness, a disease obtained from drinking the milk of cows that had grazed on poisonous white snakeroot.

6. In 1819, Lincoln's father married Sarah Bush Johnson. Lincoln was very close to his stepmother. Lincoln's stepmother outlived her stepson. She died in 1868 at age 80.

7. In 1828, Lincoln's sister, Sarah Lincoln Grigsby, died at age 20 while giving birth to a baby boy. He also died the same day.

8. In 1832, Lincoln lost his bid for the Illinois General Assembly.

9. In 1834, Lincoln was elected to the Illinois General Assembly. It was in this same year that he began his studies of law. A license to practice law in Illinois was issued in 1836.

10. In 1835, Ann Rutledge, Lincoln's friend and unsubstantiated first love, died at age 22 from typhoid.

11. In 1838, Lincoln was re-elected to the Illinois General Assembly.

12. In 1839, Lincoln met Mary Todd and married her on November 4, 1842. He was age 33, and she was age 24. He often referred to her as *Molly* or *Mother*. She referred to him as *Abe* or *Father*.

13. In 1846, Lincoln was elected to the U.S. House of Representatives as a member of the Whig party, and served a single two-year term.

14. In 1851, Lincoln's father, Thomas, died at age 73. Lincoln was not close to his father and did not attend his father's funeral.

UNIQUE FACTS ABOUT ABRAHAM LINCOLN

1. Between the period when Lincoln left the U.S. House of Representatives in 1848 and his election as U.S. President in 1860, events in his life included fathering two additional sons to increase his family size to four sons; buried his son, Edward, in 1850; was elected to the Illinois legislature in 1854, but did not serve; and was defeated for a seat in the U.S. Senate in 1854 and 1858.

2. Lincoln served a full term as President of the United States from March 4, 1861 to March 4, 1865 (Republican Party), and started a second term on March 4, 1865 (National Union Party).

3. Lincoln was the first president to be born outside the thirteen original states of the United States.

4. At 6 feet, 4 inches tall, Lincoln has been the tallest president. On this tall frame rested an average weight of between 180 and 185 pounds carried over size 14 shoes.

5. Lincoln was the first president to wear a beard while in office. His decision to grow a beard was influenced by an October 15, 1860, letter he received from Grace Bedell, an 11-year-old girl from Westfield, New York, who wrote that "If you let your whiskers grow......you would look a great deal better, for your face is so thin." Lincoln and Grace later met at the train depot in Westfield on February 16, 1861, during Lincoln's trip to Washington, D.C. to be sworn in as president.

THE LINCOLN MEMORIAL

1. In 1901, the site for the Lincoln Memorial was selected. At the time the construction site was selected the land was a malarial swamp with marshy pools and limited access by bridge or road. The place where the Lincoln Memorial is located is referred to as *Foggy Bottom*.

2. On February 19, 1911, Congress created the Lincoln Memorial Commission. The chairperson for this commission was President William Taft (1909-1913).

3. In 1911, Congress authorized $2,000,000 for construction of the memorial.

4. On February 1, 1913, the memorial, designed by Henry Bacon, was approved by the Lincoln Memorial Commission.

5. On February 12, 1914, the groundbreaking ceremony for the memorial took place. On February 12, 1915, the cornerstone was dedicated.

6. Bacon was paid $150,000 for his work on the memorial.

7. Bacon used a Greek design for the structure, which was modeled after the Parthenon in Athens, Greece.

8. The memorial is on a 109.63 acre site.

9. The memorial above the foundation weighs an estimated 38,000 tons of granite and marble, and is supported by 122 solid concrete piers with steel reinforced rods driven into the bedrock to depths ranging from 44 feet to 65 feet.

10. The memorial Doric colonnade is 188 feet long by 118 feet, 6 inches wide. The word *colonnade* means a series of columns set at regular intervals. The Dorics were Greek citizens whose architecture style was basically simple.

11. The names of the 36 states in the Union at the time of Lincoln's death and the dates the states entered the Union are engraved on the frieze above the memorial's colonnade.

12. The memorial (building) is approximately 201 feet, 10 inches wide; 132 feet deep; and 79 feet, 10 inches high from the top of the foundation.

13. There are 38 marble exterior columns in the memorial: One for each of the 36 states in the Union at the time of Lincoln's death on April 15, 1865, and two at the entrance behind the colonnade.

Lincoln Memorial

14. The columns are 44 feet high and have a diameter of 7 feet, 5 inches at the base. Each column has 20 flutes (rounded grooves).

15. The exterior walls and the columns of the memorial were crafted from Colorado Yule marble.

16. The columns supporting the memorial are not fully vertical. They tilt slightly inward. This eliminates an optical illusion of having the structure appear to bulge outward. The Greeks were the first to use this technique to solve the problem of bulging.

17. The two tripods on the two buttresses flanking the steps leading up to the entrance to the memorial are each 11 feet high. Each is cut from a single block of pink Tennessee marble. The carvings on the tripods were carved by the Piccirilli Brothers.

18. The attic parapet (railing) is capped with a frieze (horizontal band) of 48 bas-relief festoons (carved or molded decoration), each representing one of the 48 states in the Union at the time the memorial was dedicated. There was an unsuccessful attempt at adding two festoons when Alaska and Hawaii became states in 1959. Instead of adding festoons to the memorial, a plaque with the names of the 49th and 50th states was attached to the memorial at the bottom of the steps leading up to the memorial.

19. The interior Ionic columns that divide the three chambers are 50 feet high. The diameter of the interior columns is 5 feet, 6 inches.

20. The central chamber containing the Lincoln statue is 60 feet wide by 74 feet deep.

21. The two side chambers containing Lincoln's speeches are 38 feet wide by 63 feet deep. The speech on the north wall is the *Gettysburg Address of November 19, 1863*, and on the south wall is Lincoln's *Second Inaugural Address of March 4, 1865*.

Lincoln's Gettysburg Address

There are five known original manuscripts of the Gettysburg Address that are believed to have been written by Lincoln, and all versions differ slightly in their wording, punctuation, and structure. It is not known which version Lincoln read from at Gettysburg, Pennsylvania, on November 19, 1863.

22. Sculptor Ernest C. Bairstow carved the interior lettering for the Gettysburg Address, the Second Inaugural Address, and the Royal Cortissoz inscription behind the Lincoln statue. He also carved the exterior details such as the states, wreathes, festoons, and eagles.

23. Sculptor Evelyn Beatrice Longman carved the decorative carvings surrounding the Gettysburg Address and the Second Inaugural Address.

24. Some of the stones used to construct the memorial weigh as much as 23 tons.

25. The interior walls and columns of the memorial were crafted from Indiana limestone. The interior floor was crafted from two-inch thick Tennessee marble.

26. The ceiling of the memorial was crafted by using bronze beams and one-inch thick Alabama marble.

27. To enhance lighting (translucency), the Alabama marble in the ceiling of the memorial was soaked in paraffin (wax) prior to assembly.

28. Jules Guerin painted the murals at the top of the north and south walls. Each mural, consisting of oil paint mixed with white wax and kerosene applied to canvas, is 60 feet long by 12 feet high, weighs 600 pounds, and depicts principle events in Lincoln's life.

29. The main theme of the mural on the south wall above the Gettysburg Address is *The Freedom of Slaves*. The mural includes the *Angel of Truth freeing a slave*. The main theme of the mural on the north wall above the Second Inaugural Address is *The Reunification of the North and South after the Civil War*.

Mural – Freedom of Slaves

30. On December 8, 1914, at age 64, Daniel Chester French was selected to sculpture the Lincoln statue. French also did such works as the 1884 *Minute Man* statue in Concord, Massachusetts.

31. Prior to French completing the final version of the Lincoln statue, he completed 3-foot by 7-foot clay models and a 6-foot plaster model of the president. The plaster model was assembled in the memorial to help determine the final size of the Lincoln statue.

32. The statue of Lincoln was sculptured from 28 blocks of White Georgia marble.

33. The pedestal and platform for the statue were crafted from Tennessee marble.

34. Starting in 1918, and under the watchful eye of French and lead by Attilio Piccirilli, the six Piccirilli Brothers of New York carved and assembled the Lincoln statue. The Piccirilli Brothers are also credited with carving the urns at the front of the memorial, the Dupont Circle fountain in Washington, D.C, and the famous lions, *Patience* and *Fortitude*, which guard the main branch of the New York Public Library on Fifth Street in New York City.

35. The statue of Lincoln is 19 feet high from his foot to the top of his head and 19 feet wide at its widest point.

36. The chair is 12 feet, 6 inches high.

37. The pedestal is 10 feet high.

38. The estimated weight of the Lincoln statue is 120 tons. A total of 175 tons with pedestal.

Statue of Abraham Lincoln

39. The figure of Lincoln is sitting for two reasons: (1) A standing figure among the columns would create too much vertical thrust; and (2) A standing figure would place the head of Lincoln too far away from the eyes of visitors.

40. The chair on which Lincoln is sitting is a formal chair from Roman antiquity. Though difficult to distinguish, the cloth draped over Lincoln's chair is a U.S. flag, and is intended to soften the hard lines of the chair.

41. Below Lincoln's hands as they rest on the chair are Roman fasces. The fasces, which appear to be sticks/rods bound together, are intended to symbolize the authority of the Republic.

42. Directly behind the Lincoln statue, the words of Royal Cortissoz are carved into the wall: "IN THIS TEMPLE AS IN THE HEARTS OF THE PEOPLE FOR WHOM HE SAVED THE UNION THE MEMORY OF ABRAHAM LINCOLN IS ENSHRINED FOREVER." Cortissoz was an art critic and lecturer who wrote inscriptions for many memorials.

43. On November 19, 1919, the Lincoln statue was completed. During December 1919, the assembly of the Lincoln statue was started in Washington, D.C.

44. On May 30, 1922, the memorial was dedicated. The construction of the memorial took eight years to complete (1914-1922).

45. The final cost of constructing the memorial totaled $2,957,000. The cost of the Lincoln statue was $88,400.

UNIQUE FACTS ABOUT THE LINCOLN MEMORIAL

1. Among the guests at the dedication was Lincoln's only surviving son, Robert. Other guests at the dedication were President Warren Harding (1921-1923), former President William Taft (1909-1913), and the principle speaker Doctor Robert Moton; President of the Tuskegee Institute from 1915 through 1935.

2. For several years escorted tours could be taken beneath the foundation of the memorial to permit visitors to see the graffiti left there by the workers who assembled the memorial. The tours have been discontinued.

3. In 1909, the 100th anniversary of Lincoln's birth, the United States one cent piece with the image of Lincoln was released. In 1914, the five dollar bill with his image was released. The Lincoln Memorial is on both the coin and paper currency.

4. One of the earlier plans proposed for a memorial to honor Lincoln called for 6 equestrian and 31 pedestrian statues that would have surrounded a statue of Lincoln.

5. Robert Lincoln's tomb is located at Arlington Cemetery, where he is buried with his wife Mary, and young son Abraham "Jack" Lincoln II, who died at age 17. The Lincoln Memorial can be seen from the site of the tomb when there are no leaves on the trees.

6. In July 2003, stone carver Andrew Del Gallo etched five lines into the steps of the Lincoln Memorial that mark the exact spot where Reverend Martin Luther King, Jr. delivered his "I Have a Dream" speech on August 28, 1963. The inscription, which is located near the top-center of the steps, cost $8,300 to complete, is 24 inches wide by 10 inches high, and consists of the following words:

"I HAVE A DREAM
MARTIN LUTHER KING, JR.
THE MARCH ON WASHINGTON
FOR JOBS AND FREEDOM
AUGUST 28, 1963"

7. Myths About the Lincoln Memorial:

- There was never an incident where anti-aircraft (AA) shells accidentally struck the memorial during World War II.

- There are no images of Lee, Grant, or anyone else on the back of Lincoln's head. It is just the way the shape of the hair was formed.

- Lincoln's hands were not formed in the shape of an A and L. French used the 1860 casts of Lincoln's hands as inspiration in forming a more relaxed shape of Lincoln's hands on the statue.

- There are no misspelled words in the Second Inaugural Address. While being carved, Bairstow initially carved a letter E in the word Future versus an F. This error was corrected, but the place where it occurred can still be identified.

- The number of steps leading up to the memorial has nothing to do with the age of Lincoln at the time of his death. Lincoln was age 56 when he died.

THE REFLECTING POOL

1. The original Reflecting pool, designed by Henry Bacon and Charles McKim, was constructed between November 1919 and December 1922. The pool cost

$600,000. Reflecting Pool as viewed from the Lincoln Memorial- circa 2010

2. The original Reflecting Pool was 2,029 feet long by 167 feet wide. It contained an estimated 6,750,000 gallons of portal water at depths of 18 inches on the sides and 30 inches in the center. (The water was drawn from the Washington, D.C. water system.)

3. From November 2010 through mid-2012, and at a cost of $30.7 million, the Reflecting Pool and the surrounding area were reconstructed. Specifics about the current pool include:

   - The pool dimensions are approximately 2,029 feet long by 167 feet wide.

   - The depth of the pool is roughly 2 ½ feet deep from the east end to the center, then rises to roughly 3 ½ feet on the west end.

   - The 2,133 pine pilings used to support the basin of the pool were driven roughly 40 feet to bedrock every 12 feet, 9 inches. The use of timber versus steel better controls settlement and reduces life-cycle cost.

   - An 8-inch-thick, 375,000 square-foot layer of concrete covers the pool. A total of 11,000 cubic yards of concrete was used.

   - The pool holds approximately 4,500,000 gallons of water. The primary source of the water is filtered water from the nearby 111-acre tidal basin.

4. Because of the need for office space during World War II, temporary multi-story office buildings were constructed around the Reflecting Pool. Ramps were constructed over the Reflecting Pool to carry workers from one side of the pool to the other. The buildings were removed between 1966 and 1971.

Photograph taken from the top of the Washington Monument facing the Lincoln Memorial (circa 1943-1944) (Source: U.S. Naval Historical Center)

FACTS ABOUT THE MEMORIAL TO THE 56 SIGNERS OF THE DECLARATION OF INDEPENDENCE

No other document symbolizes the birth of the United States more than the Declaration of Independence. And if it was not for the bravery and sacrifices of the men who drafted and signed this national treasure, the future of the nation and its citizens would have been much different than it is today. The Memorial to the 56 Signers of the Declaration of Independence honors these men, who through their support of the Declaration of Independence pledged their lives, fortunes, and sacred honor.

THE MEN WHO SIGNED THE DECLARATION OF INDEPENDENCE

1. The following are the names of the 56 signers of the Declaration of Independence and the colonies they represented. The numbers in the brackets ( ) show the number of representatives from each colony.

Delaware (3) – George Read, Thomas McKean, and Caesar Rodney; Pennsylvania (9) – George Clymer, Benjamin Franklin, Robert Morris, John Morton, Benjamin Rush, George Ross, James Smith, George Taylor, and James Wilson; Massachusetts (5) – John Adams, Samuel Adams, John Hancock, Elbridge Gerry, and Robert Treat Paine; New Hampshire (3) – Josiah Bartlett, Matthew Thornton, and William Whipple; Rhode Island (2) – Stephen Hopkins and William Ellery; New York (4) – Lewis Morris, Francis Lewis, Philip Livingston, and William Floyd; Georgia (3) – Button Gwinnett, Lyman Hall, and George Walton; North Carolina (3) – William Hooper, Joseph Hewes, and John Penn; South Carolina (4) – Thomas Lynch, Thomas Heyward, Edward Rutledge, and Arthur Middleton; New Jersey (5) – Abraham Clark, John Hart, Francis Hopkinson, Richard Stockton, and John Witherspoon; Connecticut (4) – Samuel Huntington, Roger Sherman, William Williams, and Oliver Wolcott; Maryland (4) – Charles Carroll, Samuel Chase, Thomas Stone, and William Paca; Virginia (7) - George Wythe, Richard Henry Lee, Thomas Jefferson, Benjamin Harrison, Thomas Nelson, Jr., Francis Lightfoot Lee, and Carter Braxton.

2. The number of professions represented by the signers are:

Planters (Plantation Owners) – 9; Physicians – 4; Lawyers – 19; Merchants - 10; Landowners – 2; Statesmen -1; Surveyors - 1; Politicians -2; Judges – 3; Farmers – 2; Writers – 1; Clergymen – 1; and Iron Masters -1

The above professions are listed on the granite stones of the memorial.

3. Five signers of the Declaration of Independence were later captured by the British and imprisoned. The signers were Thomas Heyward, Arthur Middleton, Edward Rutledge, Richard Stockton, and George Walton. Only Stockton was arrested as a political prisoner. The remaining four men were prisoners of war. All five men were later released from custody.

4. Some signers of the Declaration of Independence lost most, if not all, of their wealth.

5. At age 70, the oldest signer of the Declaration of Independence at the time it was signed was Benjamin Franklin from Pennsylvania.

6. At age 26, the youngest signer of the Declaration of Independence was Edward Rutledge from South Carolina.

7. John Morton was the first signer of the Declaration of Independence to die after the document was adopted. He died in April 1777, at age 53, of natural causes. One month later Button Gwinnett died at age 42 from a wound he received during a duel.

8. Thomas Jefferson, John Adams, and Charles Carroll lived the longest after the Declaration of Independence was adopted. The deaths of Jefferson, at age 83, and Adams, at age 90, on July 4, 1826, left Carroll as the last surviving signer. Carroll died in 1832 at age 96, and was the oldest and last surviving signer of the Declaration of Independence. He represented the state of Maryland.

9. Three of the signers of the Declaration of Independence later became Vice Presidents of the United States. These signers were John Adams (1st), Thomas Jefferson (2nd), and Elbridge Gerry (5th). In 1814 at age 70, Gerry died in office while vice president.

10. Two of the signers of the Declaration of Independence later became Presidents of the United States - John Adams (2nd) and Thomas Jefferson (3rd). Both men died on July 4, 1826, the 50th anniversary of the adoption of the Declaration of Independence. Jefferson died just a few hours prior to Adams.

11. At age 33, Thomas Jefferson, assisted by John Adams, Benjamin Franklin, Robert Livingston, and Roger Sherman drafted the Declaration of Independence. These draftsmen of the Declaration of Independence were referred to as the *Committee of 32Five*.

12. Robert Livingston was recalled by the colony of New York after working on drafting the Declaration of Independence, and did not sign the final version of the document. The remaining four members of the committee signed the Declaration of Independence.

13. John Hancock was President of the Continental Congress at the time the Declaration of Independence was adopted. He was born on January 23, 1737, and died on October 8, 1793, at age 56.

14. After Congress adopted the Declaration of Independence on July 4, 1776, John Hancock was the first person to sign the document, thereby authenticating it. Secretary Charles Thomson attested to the authenticity of the Declaration of Independence by affixing his signature to the document. After Hancock and Thomson signed the Declaration of Independence, it was delivered to the print shop of John Dunlap for reproduction.

15. It is believed Thomas McKean of Delaware was the last person to sign the Declaration of Independence. When Congress authorized the printing of an official copy with the names attached in January 1777, McKean's name was not included. It is believed that one of two events may have occurred: McKean signed the document in 1781 or the printer made a mistake by omitting his name.

THE MEMORIAL TO THE 56 SIGNERS OF THE DECLARATION OF INDEPENDENCE

1. The Memorial to the 56 Signers of the Declaration of Independence is located in Constitution Gardens along the Constitution Avenue side of the Mall between the World War II Memorial and the Lincoln Memorial.

2. The memorial honors the 56 signers of the Declaration of Independence.

3. A stone at the entrance to the memorial indicates that the memorial is a gift from the American Revolution Bicentennial Administration and the date 1976.

4. Joseph Brown sculptured the memorial.

5. The memorial was crafted from granite.

6. On July 2, 1984, the memorial was dedicated and opened to the public.

The Memorial to the 56 Signers of the Declaration of Independence

7. Large granite stones list the names of the men who signed the Declaration of Independence. The engravings list the name of each signer of the declaration, his occupation, the location of his home, and a reproduction of his signature.

8. The stones are grouped together by colony/state.

9. Engraved at the base of each series of large stones is the name of the colony/state the signers represented.

10. At the entrance to the memorial is a quote from the Declaration of Independence – "And for the support of this Declaration, with firm reliance on the protection of Divine Providence we mutually pledge to each other our lives, our fortunes, and our sacred honor."

FACTS ABOUT THE VIETNAM VETERANS MEMORIAL

The Vietnam War was not only the longest war ever fought by the United States, officially from 1955 to 1975, but it was also a war that divided the country more than any other conflict since the American Civil War. It pitted families and friends against each other in their support or condemnation of what many viewed as a civil war in a foreign country, while others viewed it as an invasion by one country against another.

Since the end of hostilities most Americans have come to view the Vietnam War as a conflict that went very badly. Poor leadership by a U.S. President and his advisors, a corrupt South Vietnam government, a lack of clear objectives, and the dwindling support on the home front all contributed to the withdrawal of U.S. troops from Vietnam without victory. However, time does heal wounds, and with time it became apparent by both the supporters and opponents of the war that the men and women who served in Vietnam should not be criticized and condemned for the failure of their government, but recognized for their sacrifices. This recognition came in the form of *The Wall* and the surrounding statues honoring the men and women who served in a very difficult and unpopular war.

THE VIETNAM WAR

1. Prior to the war, Vietnam was a country in Southeast Asia divided at the 17th parallel. A communist government controlled North Vietnam and a non-communist/authoritarian government, supported by the United States, controlled South Vietnam.

2. As was often the case during the Cold War, the efforts of the United States in Vietnam were intended to hold back the spread of communism.

3. In 1955, military advisors from the United States were first sent to South Vietnam. The first U.S. non-combat death in Vietnam occurred in 1956. The first combat casualty occurred in 1959.

4. In March 1965, the first large troop contingency arrived in Vietnam.

5. On April 30, 1975, North Vietnam conquered South Vietnam.

6. The president largely responsible for the U.S. commitment to Vietnam was Lyndon Johnson (1963-1969). The president responsible for the withdrawal of the military was Richard Nixon (1969-1974).

7. A total of 2,600,000 servicemen and servicewomen served in-country in Vietnam. In addition to the ground forces and air forces actually stationed in Vietnam, an additional 500,000 support forces, such as the navy off the coast of Vietnam and air forces as far away as the Philippines, Guam, and Okinawa also supported the war efforts. The U.S. military also fought in Thailand, Cambodia, and Laos.

8. The number of servicemen and servicewomen in Vietnam at any one time peaked at 543,482 in April 1969. This number dropped constantly until all of the military forces were withdrawn.

9. The average age of the infantrymen who fought in Vietnam was age 22. The average age of the nurses who served was age 23.

10. The servicemen and servicewomen who served in Vietnam served on a rotating basis, usually one-year tours.

11. Over 58,000 American deaths resulted from service in the Vietnam War. An additional 303,000 were wounded, with 153,000 requiring hospitalization because of their wounds. Over 17,000 of the dead were married. An estimated 20,000 children lost their fathers.

12. The worst year for U.S. casualties in the Vietnam War was 1968. In this year, 16,592 military personnel died in the war.

13. To provide an example of how fierce the fighting in Vietnam was, 22% of the U.S. Marines who went into battle in Vietnam were either killed or wounded: 13,091 dead and 51,392 wounded.

14. It is estimated that between 2.5 million and 3 million Vietnamese and other Asian lives were lost during the war.

15. A total of 246 servicemen were awarded Medals of Honor for their heroic actions in the Vietnam War. Of this number, 154 or 63% of the recipients sacrificed their lives.

16. On July 8, 1959, Major Dale R. Buis and Master Sergeant Chester N. Ovnand, became the first combat related casualties of the Vietnam War. In 1998, the Department of Defense recognized Air Force Technical Sergeant Richard B. Fitzgibbon Jr. as a casualty of the Vietnam War. Sergeant Fitzgibbon became a non-combat casualty on June 8, 1956, and is considered the first United States casualty of the Vietnam War.

17. When Sergeant Fitzgibbon was recognized as a casualty of the Vietnam War, he and his son, Marine Lance Corporal Richard Fitzgibbon III, killed in 1965, became one of three pairs of fathers/sons who lost their lives in Vietnam.

18. Thirty-eight sets of brothers and one set of step-brothers were killed in the Vietnam War. Sixteen chaplains also lost their lives.

19. From February 12, 1973, through April 1, 1973, 591 American POWs; 566 servicemen and 25 civilians, were liberated and returned to the United States. Army Captain Floyd J. Thompson served the longest time in captivity – 8 years, 11 months, and 19 days. Navy Lieutenant Everett Alvarez served the second longest time in captivity – 8 years, 6 months, and 8 days.

THE VIETNAM VETERANS MEMORIAL – THE WALL

THE PLANNING AND CONSTRUCTION EFFORTS – THE WALL

1. In 1979, Jan C. Scruggs started the first successful movement for the construction of the Vietnam Veterans Memorial. A native of Maryland, Corporal Scruggs served in Vietnam during 1969-1970 as a member of the 199th Light Infantry Brigade, U.S. Army.

2. Mr. Scruggs determined that the memorial must meet four criteria:

- Harmonize with its surroundings;
- Be reflective and contemplative in character;
- Show the name of every American soldier, airman, sailor, marine and member of the Coast Guard who had died as a result of service in Vietnam or was missing in action; and
- It must not make a political statement.

3. Maryland Senator Charles Mathias introduced a bill for the memorial site. On July 1, 1980, President Jimmy Carter (1977-1981) signed the bill approving the memorial site.

4. A $20,000 prize was offered for the best memorial design. The winning design was selected on May 1, 1981, from the 1,421 designs offered for consideration. The designs were displayed and evaluated in an airplane hangar at Andrews Air Force Base, Maryland, just outside Washington, D.C.

5. Maya Lin, a 21 year-old Chinese-American from Athens, Ohio, submitted the winning entry. At the time of her submission she was an architect student at Yale University. Lin's names, as well as the names of the other people involved in the project, are listed at the top of the apex of the Wall. The names can't be seen from the front of the Wall and access to the top of the Wall is restricted.

6. On March 16, 1982, work was begun on the site of the memorial, with a groundbreaking ceremony on March 26, 1982.

7. On November 13, 1982, the memorial was dedicated at a cost of $4,284,000.

THE VIETNAM VETERANS MEMORIAL –THE WALL

1. The Wall runs east to west on a 2-acre site between the Lincoln Memorial and Washington Monument. The east side of the memorial points to the Washington Monument, the west points to the Lincoln Memorial.

2. The design of the Wall is in the shape of a chevron, not a <u>V</u>. The word *chevron* is French in origin, meaning rafter or roof, which looks like two lines meeting at an angle. During the 12th century chevrons appeared on the shields and coat-of-arms of knights, barons, and kings, and were easily recognized as a symbol of honor. Chevrons have been used in the U.S. military since 1782 to denote honorable service and military rank.

3. Each of the two walls that form the chevron is 246 feet, 9 inches in length. The wall is at an angle of 125 degrees, 12 minutes.

4. The full length of the Wall is 493 feet, 6 inches. This length is based on 246.75 feet per each side of the Wall.

5. The size and weight of the Wall total 3,000 cubic feet at a weight of 175 pounds per cubic foot. Total weight of the granite without the foundation is 525,000 pounds.

6. The black granite used in the construction of the Wall was transported from mines near Bangalore, India, to Barre, Vermont, where it was cut and given its finish. Black granite was selected because of its reflecting qualities and the color allows the names to be more easily read.

Memorial Wall

7. The Wall consists of 148 panels. Each panel is 2.75 inches thick and 40 inches wide.

8. The panels on the Wall vary in height from 8 inches at the ends to 10 feet, 1.2 inches at the center of the Wall.

9. At the time of the dedication there were 70 separate inscribed panels for each side of the Wall, plus 4 panels at each end without names.

Some of the names on The Wall

10. There are from 1 to 137 lines per panel and from 5 to 6 names per line. The letters on the memorial are .53 inch high and approximately .015 inch deep.

11. The granite panels are supported by 140 concrete pilings driven approximately 35 feet into bedrock.

12. Among the inscriptions on the Wall are the following:

At the beginning of the memorial (Panel 1 East) - "IN HONOR OF THE MEN AND WOMEN OF THE ARMED FORCES OF THE UNITED STATES WHO SERVED IN THE VIETNAM WAR. THE NAMES OF THOSE WHO GAVE THEIR LIVES AND OF THOSE WHO REMAIN MISSING ARE INSCRIBED IN THE ORDER THEY WERE TAKEN FROM US."

At the end of the memorial (Panel 1 West) - "OUR NATION HONORS THE COURAGE, SACRIFICE AND DEVOTION TO DUTY AND COUNTRY OF ITS VIETNAM VETERANS. THIS MEMORIAL WAS BUILT WITH PRIVATE CONTRIBUTIONS FROM THE AMERICAN PEOPLE, NOVEMBER 11, 1982."

13. At the time the Wall was dedicated on November 13, 1982, a total of 57,939 names had been stenciled onto the Wall.

UNIQUE FACTS ABOUT THE VIETNAM VETERANS MEMORIAL –THE WALL

1. Initially, a 1973 Department of Defense directive set the date for being considered a military casualty of the Vietnam War, thus being eligible for having a name placed on the Wall, as anyone killed or declared missing on or after January 1, 1961. Then the date was changed to 1959, and in 1998 the eligibility date was again changed to November 1, 1955.

2. With the addition of five names in May 2011, the number of names on the Wall totals 58,272. This is an increase of 333 names over the number of names that had been stenciled onto the Wall since the date it was dedicated in 1982. Using a portable gritblaster, it takes approximately 10 minutes to add a name to the Wall.

3. The initial 57,939 names were grit-blasted onto the surface of the Wall in Memphis, Tennessee.

4. The names on the Wall are listed in the order the service member died, as a result of his or her service in Vietnam, or was declared missing in action. This is because there would be a great deal of confusion if the names were listed alphabetical. For example, there are fifteen Thomas Smiths on the Wall. And as prescribed by Maya Lin, the Wall's designer, "This arrangement allows those service members who died together to forever be linked." She also wanted the names to be arranged in an almost circular manner, having the first names reaching out and combing back to touch the last names of those killed or missing.

5. Available at the memorial are binders that contain the names and other personal information about the military personnel listed on the Wall. This information includes: date of birth, the date of incident – death or declared missing in action, branch of service, rank, letter O for officer or E for enlisted, hometown, state or territory, and where on the Wall the name is located. For example: Joseph Paul Antonelli was born on May 11, 1949, was killed on January 14, 1970, was an enlisted Army Specialist Four, whose hometown was Bobtown, in the state of Pennsylvania (PA), and his name is located on Panel 14W, Line 32.

6. Preceding the names on the West Wall or following the names on the East Wall symbols denote the status of the service members. A symbol of a diamond denotes that the service member's death was confirmed. A symbol of a cross denotes that the service member was missing or was in prisoner status at the end of the war, and the remains are unaccounted for. In the event a service member's remains are returned or he is otherwise accounted for, a diamond symbol is superimposed over the cross. If a man returns alive, a circle, as a symbol of life, will be inscribed around the cross.

7. If the names of the servicemen and servicewomen who died while serving their country in other parts of the world during the period of the Vietnam War were added to the Wall, an additional 20,000 names would have to be added to the Wall.

8. There are no civilian names on the Wall.

THE ADDITIONS TO THE SITE OF THE VIETNAM VETERANS MEMORIAL

THE STATUE – THREE SERVICEMEN

1. Frederick Hart sculptured the first addition to the Vietnam Memorial site. He was paid $330,000 for his work.

2. The statue is referred to as the *Three Servicemen* or the *Three Soldiers*. The lead soldier in the statue was modeled after a Marine stationed in Washington, D.C. in 1983, the soldier carrying the machine gun on his shoulder was modeled after a Cuban-American, and the African-American is a composite of several men.  Statue of Three Servicemen

3. The 7-foot high bronze statue was dedicated on November 9, 1984.

4. The 60-foot bronze flagpole next to the statue of the Three Servicemen was installed in 1983. At the base of the flag staff are the seals of the five military services: Air Force, Army, Coast Guard, Marine Corps and Navy. The flag flies 24 hours a day.

5. The following inscription is inscribed around the base of the flag:

   "THIS FLAG REPRESENTS THE SERVICE RENDERED TO OUR COUNTRY BY THE VETERANS OF THE VIETNAM WAR. THE FLAG AFFIRMS THE PRINCIPLES OF FREEDOM FOR WHICH THEY FOUGHT AND THEIR PRIDE IN HAVING SERVED UNDER DIFFICULT CIRCUMSTANCES."

6. In 2004, a carved black granite plaque, measuring 3 feet by 2 feet, was added to the site of the Three Servicemen statue. The plaque reads: "In memory of the men and women who served in the Vietnam War and later died as a result of their services. We honor and remember their sacrifice." The primary purpose of the plaque is to honor the memory of the servicemen and servicewomen whose names are not on the Wall, but their service in Vietnam may have caused physical or mental conditions that contributed to their deaths.

213

THE VIETNAM WOMEN'S MEMORIAL

1. Former Army nurse Diane Carison Evans, who served in Vietnam during 1968 and 1969, lead the 10-year effort for a memorial to honor the military and civilian women who served in Vietnam.

2. Glenna Goodacre sculptured the second addition to the memorial site, the Vietnam Women's Memorial.

3. The bronze, 2,000 pound, 6-foot, 8-inch high memorial shows three women, one of whom is aiding a wounded soldier. To symbolize that the memorial represents all women who served in Vietnam, there is no insignia of rank on the fatigues.

    The Vietnam Women's Memorial

4. To paraphrase the words of Goodacre – "Stacks of sandbags were often in photos from Vietnam...seemed natural for a nurse to be supported by sandbags....as she serves a wounded soldier...he will live. The standing woman looks up...searching for a medevac helicopter...or help from God. The kneeling figure...stares at her helmet....reflecting her despair, frustration...the horrors of war."

5. On the outside edges of the Carnelian Red granite stones are eight yellowwood trees. Each of the trees represents one of the eight military nurses who died while serving in Vietnam.

6. On Veterans Day, November 11, 1993, the memorial was dedicated. The memorial cost $4,000,000.

7. The Veterans Administration lists 7,484 servicewomen who served in the Vietnam War - 6,250 were nurses. The number of American women who served in Vietnam could be as high as 11,000.

8. The names of eight servicewomen are honored on the Vietnam Veterans Memorial - Wall. Only one of the eight women died from combat wounds. Lieutenant Sharon Ann Lane, age 25, died from shrapnel wounds when rockets hit an evacuation hospital on June 8, 1969. Of the remaining seven nurses, five died in aircraft accidents and two died from natural causes.

FACTS ABOUT THE WASHINGTON NATIONAL CATHEDRAL

Pierre L'Enfant included in his 1791 plan for the capital city a prominent place for "a great church of national purposes." The proposed site was near what is now the site of the National Portrait Gallery at 8th and F Streets. However, it was not until more than a century later that the foundation for such a place of worship was laid at Wisconsin Avenue, and nearly another century for the majestic structure to be completed.

THE CONSTRUCTION OF THE CATHEDRAL

1. On January 6, 1893, Congress granted a charter to the Protestant Episcopal Cathedral Foundation of the District of Columbia. This charter permitted the foundation to establish a cathedral and institutions of higher learning.

2. In 1896, 30 acres of land for the cathedral was secured on Mount Saint Alban, a prominent spot within Washington, D.C. A small parish church was already on the site. The current acreage totals 57 acres and is referred to as the *Cathedral Close*.

3. On September 29, 1907, a foundation stone was dedicated using the same mallet that George Washington used to set the Capitol cornerstone. This stone is a composite of two stones: A small stone, quarried from a field beside the Church of the Holy Nativity in Bethlehem, was inserted into a larger piece of American granite.

4. In 1912, the *Bethlehem Chapel* was the first part of the cathedral to be completed. It was constructed over the foundation stone that was dedicated in 1907. There are nine chapels within the cathedral.

5. In 1964, the Central Tower was completed. In 1976, the nave and the west rose window were dedicated. In 1982, the Pilgrim Observation Gallery was completed. In 1983, work on the west towers was started and was completed in 1990.

6. On September 29, 1990, the cathedral, shaped in the form of a cross, was dedicated. The cost of the cathedral totaled $65 million over an 83-year period.

7. The architectural style of the cathedral is Gothic, which is characterized by great height and pointed arches. The cathedral was constructed from easy to carve Indiana limestone.

8. The cathedral includes the following measurements and weights:

   - Outside Length: 570 feet, 8 inches
   - Inside Length: 457 feet, 8 inches
   - Width (Outside across the nave aisles): 142 feet, 6 inches
   - Width of Transepts: 289 feet, 9 inches
   - Height of West Towers: 234 feet
   - Height of Central Tower: 301 feet, 3 inches (The top of the tower is 676 feet above sea level, the highest point within Washington, D.C.)
   - Height of Nave (Inside): 102 feet, 6 inches
   - Total Weight: 150,000 tons (Largest single stone weighs 5-1/2 tons)
   - Total Area: 83,012 square feet

FACTS ABOUT THE CATHEDRAL

1. The official name of the cathedral is the Cathedral Church of Saint Peter and Saint Paul. Even though the cathedral is affiliated with the Episcopal religion, it serves the nation as a house of prayer for all people.

2. The cathedral is the sixth-largest cathedral in the world and second-largest in the United States. The largest cathedral in the United States is the St. John's Cathedral in New York.

3. The 10-foot pulpit in the cathedral, referred to as the *Canterbury Pulpit*, was crafted in England from stones from the Bell Harry Tower in the Canterbury Cathedral.

National Cathedral

4. The cathedral has three towers: St. Peter, St. Paul, and Gloria in Excelsis.

216

5. At a height of 301 feet, the Gloria Tower is the highest tower. It has within its bell chamber two sets of bronze bells, a 53-bell carillon and a set of ten English peal bells. The largest carillon bell weighs 24,000 pounds and measures 8 feet, 8 inches in diameter. There are 333 steps to the bell chamber.

6. Included in the cathedral are 231 stained glass windows, 288 angels, and 112 gargoyles. A true gargoyle is a waterspout to permit water to run off a building. The figure of Darth Vader on the cathedral is a grotesque, a decorative element, which does not function as a waterspout. The Space Window in the cathedral contains a piece of lunar rock. The rock is 2-3/8 inches long.

7. In 1938, a *Great Organ* with 8,400 pipes was installed in the cathedral. The organ was enlarged in 1963 and again between 1970 and 1975. The organ has 189 ranks and 10,647 pipes. A rank is a set of pipes.

8. There are over 220 remains interred in the cathedral, including:

    - Woodrow Wilson - The 28th President of the United States (1913-1921) and his second wife, Edith. Wilson's remains were buried in the Bethlehem Chapel of the Cathedral in 1924, then moved to the memorial bay in 1956. Wilson's Tomb
      He is the only president buried within Washington, D.C.
    - Helen Keller – Notable deaf and blind author and world-famous speaker. She wrote eleven books and spoke seven languages.
    - Anne Sullivan, born Johanna Sullivan – Best known for teaching Keller how to communicate by spelling words in her hand.

9. On March 31, 1968, at the National Cathedral, Dr. Martin Luther King, Jr. preached his last Sunday sermon before his assassination.

10. State funeral services have been held at the cathedral for the following U.S. Presidents on the given dates: Dwight Eisenhower (1953-1961) in 1969, Ronald Reagan (1981-1989) in 2004, and Gerald Ford (1974-1977) in 2006.

11. Services to celebrate the end of World War I in 1918 and World War II in 1945 were held at the cathedral.

FACTS ABOUT ARLINGTON NATIONAL CEMETERY
(BACKGROUND ABOUT THE CUSTIS AND LEE FAMILIES, THE FOUNDING OF ARLINGTON, AND ITS DESIGNATION AS A NATIONAL CEMETERY)

Very few of the over 4,000,000 international visitors who visit Arlington National Cemetery each year know much about these hallowed grounds. Seldom will visitors be familiar with how Arlington was settled, who were the first settlers to settle on the land, its pre-Civil War history, and how it became the most sacred and honored cemetery in the United States. As with any end, the history of Arlington had a beginning. This beginning has since been sculptured into what is now Arlington National Cemetery.

THE ARLINGTON HOUSE

1. Land totaling 6,000 acres was granted to Robert Howsing by the Governor of Virginia in 1669. Howsing immediately sold it to John Alexander. In 1778, 1,100 of the 6,000 acres were purchased by John Parke Custis from Gerald Alexander. In 1781, the land was inherited by John's son, George Washington Parke Custis.

2. Because John Custis' widow was unable to care for all four young children after the death of her husband, her son, George Washington Parke Custis (1781-1857), was adopted by George and Martha Washington in 1789. After Custis became an adult, and in gratitude for their care, he decided to establish a memorial to honor George and Martha on one of the many parcels of land he owned. The parcel he chose overlooks Washington, D.C. Custis owned a total of 15,000 acres of land at multiple sites.

3. Initially, the estate was to be named Mount Washington. However, when Custis concluded that several towns and estates had already been named in honor of the first president, he decided to name the estate *Arlington* after the Custis family's ancestral homestead on Virginia's eastern shore.

Arlington House

4. Designed by George Hadfield, Arlington House is a Greek revival mansion modeled after the Temple of Theseus in Athens, Greece. Due largely to the wildly fluctuating cash situation of George Custis, it took 16 years to complete the mansion.

5. Construction on the mansion began in 1802, when Custis was just age 21, and was completed in 1818 from clay bricks covered with a stucco finish of faux (fake) marble and sandstone. In 1802, the north wing was the first to be completed. The south wing was completed in 1804. Both one-story wings are 40 feet wide by 25 feet deep. After the completion of the two-story central section in 1818, which is 60 feet wide by 25 feet deep, the mansion totaled 140 feet wide from the north wing to the south wing. The mansion totals approximately 8,000 square feet; has 17 primary rooms on the two floors; additional rooms in the basement and side sections, including a winter kitchen; and closets, stairwells, and hallways.

6. The portico, the last part of the house to be completed, is 60 feet wide by 25 feet deep. The 8 Doric columns supporting the portico are 23 feet high by 5 feet, 3 inches in diameter at the base.

THE FAMILIES WHO LIVED IN THE ARLINGTON HOUSE

1. George Custis married his wife, Mary "Molly" Lee Fitzhugh, in 1804. They lived the remainder of their lives in the Arlington House. Molly died in 1853, George in 1857, and both are buried in the Custis Family plot (Section 13).

Arlington House

2. At the time of his death, George Custis owned 196 slaves. They were to be given their freedom within five years after his death.

3. Under the terms of George Custis' will, Mary Anna Randolph Custis, the wife of Robert E. Lee, was given the right to inhabit and control Arlington House for the rest of her life. At the time of her death, full title of the property would be transferred to Mary's oldest son, George Washington Custis Lee. Mary was the third of four children, but was the only child to survive through infancy.

4. Mary Anna Randolph Custis, a distant cousin of Robert E. Lee, married Lee on June 30, 1831. Robert was born in 1807, Mary in 1808.

5. Mary and Robert were married in the main hall of Arlington House and had seven children, three boys and four girls - George, William, Robert Jr., Mary, Eleanor, Anne, and Mildred. All but the first born child, George, who was born at Ft. Monroe, Virginia, were born in Arlington House. All three of their sons served in the Confederate Army. None of their daughters ever married.

6. On April 17, 1861, Virginia seceded from the Union.

7. On April 18, 1861, President Abraham Lincoln (1861-1865) offered Robert E. Lee command of the Union Army.

8. On April 20, 1861, Lee turned down command of the Union Army and left Arlington to take a commission as a brigade general in the Confederate Army. He never returned to Arlington.

9. Mary Lee left Arlington on May 15, 1861, and spent much of the Civil War on East Leigh Street in Richmond, Virginia. She returned once after the war in 1873, only to see the destruction to her estate. Robert and Mary resided at Arlington for 30 years.

10. Robert died in 1870, at age 63, and Mary died in 1873, at age 65. Both are entombed in the walls of the Lee Chapel on the grounds of the Washington and Lee University in Lexington, Virginia.

THE OCCUPATION & SALE OF ARLINGTON

1. Union soldiers occupied the Arlington estate on May 24, 1861, and built forts in its defense, including Fort Whipple in 1863. Fort Whipple was redesignated Fort Myer in 1881 and subsequently Joint Base Myer-Henderson Hall in 2009.

2. After the Army of the Potomac was created on May 27, 1861, Brig. Gen. Irvin McDowell made Arlington House his headquarters. It also served as an unofficial officers club and provided housing for officers and a venue for balls and galas.

3. In 1862, the federal government enacted legislation to collect property taxes from the insurrectionary districts, meaning land claimed by the Confederacy. The law required that the landowner be the only person permitted to pay the taxes, and the taxes had to be paid in person.

4. Since Mary Lee was the owner of Arlington, but had become an invalid confined to a wheelchair because of rheumatoid arthritis, she sent her cousin, Phillip Fendall, to pay the taxes on her property. Fendall was turned away, and the federal government confiscated the estate in 1863 for a tax default of only $92.07.

5. Due to the non-payment of the property taxes, the property, valued at $34,100, was purchased by the federal government on January 11, 1864, for $26,810 for "government use, for war, military, charitable, and educational purposes."

6. Major General Montgomery C. Meigs, the Quartermaster of the Union Army, had served with Robert E. Lee. However, because of Meigs' aversion to Lee's decision to accept a position in the Confederate Army, and the government's need to acquire land to bury the dead, Meigs convinced Secretary of War Edwin Stanton to turn 200 acres of the estate into a national cemetery.

7. On May 13, 1864, at age 21, Private William Christman, a member of the 67th Pennsylvania Infantry, became the first Union soldier to be buried at Arlington. He died of an inflammation of the abdominal wall and is buried in Section 26, Lot 19. On May 20, 1864, the first *unknown* deceased Confederate soldier was buried at Arlington. On May 30, 1864, North Carolina Private Levi Reinhardt, the first *known* deceased Confederate soldier, was buried at Arlington. He died of complications from having his leg amputated. His remains were returned to North Carolina in 1883.

8. On June 15, 1864, 200 acres of the Custis estate were designated a national cemetery. On the day the estate was declared a national cemetery, 65 Union soldiers were buried on the land. By the end of the Civil War, 16,000 fallen warriors were buried at Arlington. Arlington was one of 13 new cemeteries established for the burial of Civil War dead in and around Washington, D.C.

9. In 1873, George Washington Custis Lee (1832-1913), Robert and Mary's oldest son and heir to the estate, made a claim against the federal government for the return of or payment for the Arlington estate. The claim was rejected.

10. In 1877, Lee started a process through the Virginia court system against the federal government for trespassing on his property. The case eventually ended up before the U.S. Supreme Court, which ruled 5-4 in Lee's favor in December 1882. Accepting the fact that the property was the last resting place for many fallen soldiers, Lee never intended to have the bodies removed.

11. In March 1883, Congress appropriated $150,000 for the purchase of the Arlington estate. The sale became final in May 1883, after Lee executed the deed. The sale was approved by then Secretary of War Robert Lincoln - son of President Lincoln, and the new deed of ownership was recorded in the Alexandria County Courthouse.

12. In 1883, at the time it was purchased, Arlington National Cemetery totaled 200 acres. Future additions included 142 acres in 1889; 56 acres in 1897; 216 acres in 1966; and 10 acres in 1995 - for a total of 624 acres.

13. Arlington House served as quarters for the cemetery staff until 1925. Restoration of Arlington House was begun in 1927. Control of Arlington House was transferred to the National Park Service in 1933.

14. In 1955, an act of Congress dedicated Arlington House as a memorial to Robert E. Lee.

15. In 1966, the site of Arlington House was placed on the National Register of Historic Places.

16. In 1972, Congress officially designated the Custis-Lee Mansion as Arlington House.

17. Arlington House is managed by the National Park Service. The Department of Army manages the land around the mansion.

FACTS ABOUT ARLINGTON NATIONAL CEMETERY
(SIZE, REQUIREMENTS FOR BURIAL, CEREMONIES, NOTABLE SITES, AND EVENTS WITHIN THE CEMETERY)

The burial of President John F. Kennedy (JFK) (1961-1963) at Arlington National Cemetery turned the cemetery into one of the most sought after places to spend eternity. Requests for burials at Arlington Cemetery rose as much as 400 percent after the death of the president. This surge in requests prompted changes to the rules that governed who qualified for burial in this hallowed ground, how and where in the cemetery the remains would be honored, and what alternatives were needed to accommodate the wishes of the families.

But even without the tragedy of 1963, Arlington National Cemetery had already become the final resting place for several notable Americans. These statesmen, generals, admirals, inventors, explorers, recipients of the Medal of Honor, and the many soldiers, sailors, airmen and marines who made the ultimate sacrifice for their country, had for 100 years prior to the death of JFK been honored with ceremonies and burial at Arlington Cemetery.

WHO IS AUTHORIZED BURIAL AT ARLINGTON NATIONAL CEMETERY

1. To qualify for in-ground burial at Arlington National Cemetery, which is subject to change, a deceased must meet at least one of the following requirements:

    *   Died on active duty.

    *   Any veteran who is retired from the U.S. Armed Forces. This usually occurs after 20 years of active duty.

    *   Retired reservists who have reached age 60 prior to death, were drawing retired pay, and served a period of active duty other than for training.

- Veterans honorably discharged with at least 30 percent disability before October 1, 1949.

- Holders of the nation's highest military decorations. These decorations include one or more of the following: Medal of Honor, Distinguished Service Cross, Distinguished Service Medal, Silver Star, or Purple Heart.

- Any person who held the office of President of the United States.

- Any former member of the U.S. armed forces who served on active duty (other than for training) and who held any of the following positions: (1) An elective office of the U.S. government; (2) The office of the Chief Justice of the United States Supreme Court or of an Associated Justice; (3) Select U.S. government offices; and (4) Certain chiefs' missions.

- Former prisoners of war who died on or after November 30, 1993.

- The widow or widower of: A member of the armed forces who was lost or buried at sea or officially determined to be missing in action; a member of the armed forces who is interred in a U.S. military cemetery overseas that is maintained by the American Battle Monuments Commission; or a member of the armed forces who is interred at Arlington Cemetery as part of a group burial.

- The spouse or unmarried minor child under age 21 of any of the above, or of any person already buried at Arlington Cemetery. An unmarried dependent student qualifies up to age 23.

2. A veteran who does not qualify under the above rules may be buried in the same grave as a previously buried brother, sister, parent, or child. The veteran's spouse must waive his or her eligibility for Arlington, and the veteran can have no dependent children at the time of death.

3. In addition to in-ground burials, and as of 1980, the remains of qualified personnel may also be interred in the Arlington Cemetery's Columbarium. The columbarium consists of nine courts containing 80,000 niches.

4. The following lists some of the persons eligible for burial in the Columbarium. This list is subject to change.

    - Any member of the military who is authorized in-ground burial. And any veteran of the armed forces who served on active duty, other than for training, and whose last period of service ended honorably.

    - Certain reservists and ROTC members who die while on active duty, while performing training, or while traveling to or from training. Certain former military personnel who were being hospitalized for injuries or diseases incurred while on active duty.

    - Members of 37 civilian groups who served their country during wartime. Included in these groups are World War II veterans who were members of the Women Air Service Pilots (WASPs), U.S. Merchant Marines, civilians involved in the defense of Bataan in the Philippines, and members of the Women's Auxiliary Ferrying Squadron (WAFS).

    - Certain commissioned officers of the U.S. Coast and Geodetic Survey (National Oceanic and Atmospheric Administration) or of the U.S. Public Health Service.

    - The spouse or unmarried minor or permanently dependent child of any of the above or of any person already in the Columbarium. A student qualifies up to age 23.

    A large portion of the current services at Arlington are for cremated remains.

5. A veteran is authorized one niche in the Columbarium. The niche, which will hold two urns, is 13 inches high by 10 inches wide by 18 inches deep.

6. The President of the United States or Secretary of the Army may waive the qualifications for burial at Arlington Cemetery under special circumstances. For example, President Reagan authorized the interment of Joe "Brown Bomber" Louis in April 1981.

BURIAL AT ARLINGTON NATIONAL CEMETERY

1. Except for federal holidays, funeral services are conducted Monday through Friday from 9 a.m. through 3 p.m.

2. The burial services of veterans buried at Arlington Cemetery range from services where only a single representative of the cemetery is present at the burial to a burial with full honors requiring the services of nearly 60 military personnel.

3. Burial services for enlisted personnel consist of graveside honors by military members of the appropriate branch of the service (Army, Navy, Air Force, Coast Guard, Marines). The honors include body bearers, firing party, and a bugler. Upon request the cemetery staff will provide a military chaplain. Enlisted members of the military in the grades of Sergeant Major, Master Chief, and Chief Master Sergeant (E-9) may be transported to the gravesite on a caisson, if a caisson is available.

4. In addition to the graveside honors normally provided to personnel whose death did not result from enemy action, burial services for officers and enlisted personnel, of any rank, who are killed as a result of combat, may also include a caisson, band, and escort troops. For Army and Marine officers in the rank of full colonel and higher, the riderless horse is used. For Navy, Coast Guard, and Marine Flag Officers (admirals and generals) the Minute Guns are used to execute an honor salute to the deceased.

5. The practice of draping a U.S. flag over a coffin and presenting it to the next of kin at funerals was begun by the U.S. Army in 1918. The flag for active duty members is provided by the deceased's branch of service and by the Department of Veterans Affairs for non-active duty veterans. The flag is folded 13 times into a trim triangle, stars out. It takes one minute and fifty-four seconds to fold.

6.   The services with full honors consist of an escort officer, a flag bearer, an 18-person band, a 4-person color guard, an 18-member marching platoon, a horse-drawn caisson pulled by 6 horses, 4 Army riders, 8 body bearers, and a 7-person firing party. The firing party fires 3 volleys at the gravesite.

Uniform Layout of Military Graves/ Headstones

7.   There are two flagpoles at Arlington Cemetery. They are located near the Arlington House and Memorial Amphitheater. The flags are lowered to half-staff 30 minutes before the first burial of the day, and remain lowered until after the last burial is completed.

8.   The draping of the U.S. flag over the casket is symbolic of the services provided soldiers during the Civil War. Because caskets were seldom available for the thousands of soldiers killed in battle, the flag was often used in lieu of a casket while transporting the body to a grave. The flag was not buried with the body.

9.   The firing of three volleys of rifle fire at a gravesite is also symbolic of the Civil War. At pre-arranged times soldiers from the opposing sides agreed to a cease fire to allow for the recovery of the wounded and dead from the battlefield. The cease fire was started when soldiers from both sides showed themselves, one side fired a volley in the air to show that their rifles were empty, the other side responded in kind. After the wounded and dead had been cleared from the field, a third fired volley would signal the renewal of hostilities.

10. The playing of *taps* at a gravesite originated during the Civil War, when it was used to signal *lights out* at Union camps. Later, and because of concerns that firing a volley of shots at a gravesite might prompt an attack from the enemy, taps, consisting of 24 notes, was used to wish a fallen comrade a *good sleep* in death. Thus, taps replaced the volley near a battle site. Taps was adopted by the U.S. Army in 1874, and by the other military branches since 1900. The term *taps* originated from the fact that the call was often tapped out on a drum in the absence of a bugler.

11. The two black artillery limbers/caissons that are used to transport the veterans to their last resting place have been in service since 1918, and are also used for transporting the bodies of U.S. Presidents and other honored dead to ceremonies within the Washington D.C. area. A limber/caisson combination is 26 feet long by 5 feet, 5 inches wide, and weighs 2,400 pounds.

12. Without full authenticity, it is believed that the tradition of using a caisson to carry the body of the honored dead dates back to the reign of Henry VIII of England (1509-1547), when the bodies were transported on cannon wagons. As part of the history of the United States during time of war, both the Union and Confederate armies transported their wounded and dead on caissons during the Civil War.

13. Six horses pull the limber/caisson, with riders only on the left side of the team. This is symbolic of how the caissons were used during the Civil War: Riders on the horses on the left side and supplies being carried on the horses on the right side. The average weight of each of these strong horses is 1,800 pounds. Each team of horses is grouped into 3 pairs – the lead team in front, swing team follows, and finally the wheel team.

14. The dimensions of current grave sites are 5 feet wide by 10 feet long by 9 feet deep. If multiple caskets are buried, the first casket is placed at the 9-foot level and the second casket is placed on top of the first at the 7-foot level. Urns containing cremated remains are buried 3 feet below the surface of the ground.

15. The U.S. Veterans Administration provides the current white marble headstone for the gravesites at Arlington. The headstone, referred to as the *General type*, was approved after World War I, is formed from white marble, and measures 13 inches wide by 42 inches high by 4 inches thick. Twenty-four inches of the 230 pound white marble headstone are above ground. The headstones are crafted from Danby marble and are finished and engraved in Vermont.

16. At the end of the burial services, the *Arlington Ladies* present a letter of appreciation and thanks to the family of the deceased.

17. In 1948, the wives of active duty and retired Air Force members began to attend and participate in the funerals at Arlington. Since 1972, the *Arlington Ladies*, consisting of the wives and widows of military members from all of the military branches, attend the burials. Their attendance symbolizes the honoring of a lost family member.

18. On average, 28 funerals are conducted each day at Arlington Cemetery, totaling 6,400 each year. Due to the projected increase in the number of World War II, Korean War, and Vietnam War deceased veterans, this number is expected to peak at 30 per day. Currently, over 300,000 service members and their family members are buried in over 200,000 graves at Arlington Cemetery. Arlington is expected to be full between the years 2050 and 2060.

SOME OF THE NOTABLE PEOPLE BURIED AT ARLINGTON NATIONAL CEMETERY

1. One of ten American Revolutionary War veterans buried at Arlington Cemetery, Pierre Charles L'Enfant was born on August 2, 1754, served as an engineer during the war, and is credited with designing Washington, D.C. On June 14, 1825, L'Enfant, at age 70, died penniless and was buried on farmland in Prince George's County, Maryland. In 1909, L'Enfant's remains were reburied at a site just in front of the Arlington House.

   Burial site of Pierre Charles L'Enfant

2. On May 22, 1911, the marble monument over the gravesite of L'Enfant was dedicated.

3. Directed by George Washington, L'Enfant designed the 1782 Badge of Military Merit, a heart of purple cloth with a narrow lace or binding and the word *Merit* across the heart. It was awarded for meritorious service. The badge was used as a model by Elizabeth Will in 1932 to design the Purple Heart medal, shown to the right. The Purple Heart is awarded to members of the U.S. military or civilian nationals who sustain injuries or are killed while combating foreign forces.

229

4. Mary Randolph (1762-1828) was the first person buried on the grounds of what became Arlington Cemetery. Mary Randolph was the cousin of General Robert E. Lee's wife, Mary Lee.

5. The silver five-star insignia, shown to the right, was authorized by Congress on December 14, 1944. The six five-star admirals and generals buried at Arlington are:

- General of the Armies John J. "Black Jack" Pershing (1860-1948) - Led U.S. forces in Europe during World War I. Pershing was promoted to this rank on September 3, 1919. Authorized to wear the insignia as a result of his position as General of the Armies during World War I. He wore four gold stars at this rank.

- General of the Army George C. Marshall (1880-1959) – Army Chief of Staff for the duration of World War II. After World War II, Marshall was appointed ambassador to China and later as Secretary of State. Credited with the success of the Marshall Plan, an economic plan that was instrumental in rebuilding the countries of Western Europe after World War II. Served as President of the Red Cross and was awarded the Nobel Peace Prize for the Marshall Plan. Promoted on December 16, 1944.

- Admiral of the Fleet William "Bull" Halsey (1882-1959) - Instrumental in several victories against Japanese forces in the Pacific theater of World War II. Promoted on December 21, 1945.

- General of the Army, then General of the Air Force, Henry "Hap" Arnold (1886-1950) - Commanded the United States Army Air Forces during World War II. He was also the first Air Force Chief of Staff in 1947. Promoted on December 21, 1944.

- Admiral of the Fleet William D. Leahy (1875-1959) - Performed duties as Chief of Staff for presidents Roosevelt (1933-1945) and Truman (1945-1953). Promoted on December 15, 1944.

- General of the Army Omar Bradley (1893-1981) - Commander of the U.S. 1st Army during the invasion of Normandy, an Army Chief of Staff, and the first Chairman of the Joint Chief of Staff. Promoted on September 20, 1950, and has been the last five-star U.S. general or admiral.

Bradley's Headstone

6. Joe Louis Barrow (1914-1981), known as the Brown Bomber - Twice heavy-weight boxing champion of the world. He was awarded the Legion of Merit for his services in the U.S. Army during World War II. Louis donated over $100,000 to the Army and Navy relief efforts during World War II. The actor Lee Marvin (1924-1987) is buried next to Mr. Barrow.

7. Audie Leon Murphy (1924-1971) – Murphy was born in Texas and was the 6th of 12 children. At just 5 feet, 7 inches tall and weighing approximately 145 pounds, Murphy became the most decorated World War II combat soldier in the United States Army by the time he was age 21. Receiving over 30 medals and citations, the medals include: Medal of Honor, Distinguished Services Cross (second highest award for valor), two Silver Stars, Legion of Merit, two Bronze Stars, and three Purple Hearts. Murphy died at age 46 on May 28, 1971, Memorial Day weekend, in the crash of a small plane near Roanoke, Virginia. Murphy's gravesite is near the Amphitheater on the opposite side of the Tomb of the Unknowns. The site can be identified by a gray stone walkway and a chain barrier.

Headstone of Murphy

8. President William Taft (1857-1930) – Born in Ohio, Taft's accomplishments include: Graduated from Yale in 1878 and Cincinnati Law School in 1880; Civil Governor-General of the Philippines (1901-1903); Secretary of War (1904-1908); Supervised the initial construction of the Panama Canal (1907); 27th President of the United States (1909-1913); and 10th Chief Justice of the United States Supreme Court (1921-1930).

Headstone of Taft

9. General Abner Doubleday (1819-1893) – A Union general during the Civil War. He has been credited with developing some of the rules for the game of baseball. Headstone of Doubleday is photographed to the right.

10. General James "Jimmy" Doolittle (1896-1993) - Led U.S. bombers on the first mission over Japan during World War II. He was awarded the Medal of Honor for his actions.

11. John Lincoln Clem (1851-1937) – Entered the Union Army during the Civil War at age 9; promoted to the rank of sergeant at age 13, youngest soldier ever to hold this rank in the U.S. Army; known as Drummer Boy of Chickamauga, wounded twice in combat during Civil War; appointed second lieutenant by President Grant in 1871; saw action during Spanish-American War; and retired in 1916 after 53 years of active military service at the rank of major general.

Headstone of Clem

12. Three memorial stones near the Amphitheater pay tribute to three teams of astronauts who were killed performing their duties. These teams are the Apollo 1 astronauts (1967) and the crews of the Challenger (1986) and Columbia shuttles (2003).

13. Robert Todd Lincoln (1843-1926) - The son of President Abraham Lincoln (1861-1865). In his own behalf, he was a successful lawyer and businessman, Secretary of War (1881-1885), and U. S. Minister to Great Britain (1889-1893).

Tomb of Robert Lincoln, his wife Mary, and son Abraham -Nicknamed Jack

14. Lieutenant Thomas E. Selfridge (1882-1908) - First military air casualty. Killed when a plane flown by Orville Wright crashed at Fort Myer, Virginia, on September 17, 1908.

15. General Jonathan M. Wainwright (1883-1953) - Commanded American and Filipino forces in the Philippines after General MacArthur was directed to leave the Philippines during World War II. He surrendered these forces to the Japanese in 1942. At the rank of lieutenant general, Wainwright was the highest ranking U.S. officer held as a prisoner of war (POW) during World War II. He was a POW from May 1942 through August 1945. Awarded the Medal of Honor for his actions in the Philippines.

UNIQUE HEADSTONES AND MONUMENTS

1. Between 1885 and 1895, twenty-six men who served as generals during the Civil War were buried in Section 1 at Arlington Cemetery. Many Civil War veterans had unique markers placed at the head of or over their final resting places.

2. Colonel Joseph Cates has a huge cannonball formed from polished black marble over his gravesite.

3. The remains of Major General Wallace Fitz Randolph (1841-1910) are buried under actual Civil War-era cannon. He told his wife that "he had spent his entire life behind an artillery piece and wouldn't mind spending eternity under one."  Randolph Cannon

4. At age 22, Major John Meigs (1841-1864), the son of General Montgomery Meigs, was killed in action near Harrisonburg, Virginia, in 1864. After his death and burial in Section 1, Meigs' gravesite was marked with a metal sculpture that shows the young man lying dead in his uniform, his pistol near his boot, and the hoof-prints from horses around his body. Major General Montgomery C. Meigs (1816-1892), and his wife Louisa (1816-1879), are buried near their son.  Meigs' Gravesite

5. In April 1866, General Meigs had the remains of unknown soldiers removed from the battlefields within a 25 mile radius of Washington, D.C. and brought to Arlington to be sealed in a vault in September 1866. The tomb was later designated as the *Tomb of the Unknown Dead of the Civil War*. The subterranean concrete vault is in the shape of a wagon wheel with spokes, and the remains within the vault are broken down by the type of bones - skulls in one section, legs in another, arms in a third, etc. The vault is capped with a granite sarcophagus that reads "Beneath this stone repose the bones of 2,111 unknown soldiers."  Tomb of the Unknown Dead of the Civil War

6. Some of the recipients of the Medal of Honor have their medals identified on their headstones through just the words "Medal of Honor." Others have the words and the medal engraved on their headstones. The headstone, photographed to the right, shows the words and medal on Army Sergeant Allen L. Eggers' (1895-1968) headstone. Eggers was a veteran of World War I.

7. The mast of the USS *Maine*, photographed to the right, is a memorial to the men who were killed on the battleship in 1898. The remains of 266 sailors are buried at the site. This tragedy ignited hostilities between Spain and the United States - The Spanish-American War (1898).

8. One of the most notable memorials at Arlington Cemetery is the *Confederate Memorial*. This memorial, which is located in Section 16 near the entrance to Fort Myer, is dedicated to the Confederate soldiers who served in the Civil War. Facts about the memorial include:

- In 1900, Congress authorized that a section of Arlington Cemetery be set aside for the burial of Confederate dead.

- On March 4, 1906, a request for a Confederate Memorial was granted by then Secretary of War William Howard Taft.

- The Daughters of the Confederacy funded the construction of the Confederate Memorial.

  Confederate Memorial

- Former Confederate soldier Moses Ezekiel (1844-1917), a VMI cadet who fought in the Battle of New Market, Virginia, created the Confederate Memorial. He is buried at the base of the memorial.

- On November 12, 1912, the cornerstone was laid.

- On June 4, 1914, the memorial was dedicated on the 106th anniversary of Jefferson Davis' birth. The dedication was before 3,000 Union and Confederate veterans.

- President Woodrow Wilson (1913-1921) presided over the dedication.

- The memorial is 32 feet high.

- The figure of a woman at the top of the memorial is symbolic of Peace. She faces south and is crowned with olive leaves. In her left hand extends a laurel wreath toward the South, acknowledging the sacrifice of her fallen sons. Her right hand holds a pruning hook resting on a plow stock, which symbolizes the biblical passage "And they shall beat their swords into plows shares and their spears into pruning hooks."

- The plinth on which she stands is embossed with four urns, symbolizing the four years of the Civil War. Supporting the plinth are 14 inclined shields on the frieze, which depict the coat-of-arms for each of the 13 Confederate states and Maryland, which supported the South during the war.

- Another frieze is of life-sized figures depicting 32 Southern soldiers going off to war. It also includes six vignettes illustrating the effect of the war on Southerners of all races.

- The remains of 482 Southerners are buried around the Confederate Memorial, including 397 Confederate soldiers. Unlike the rounded headstones for the Union dead, the Confederate headstones are pointed. Congress authorized the shape of the headstones in 1906. With doubtful authenticity, it has been said that a common joke between Southerners was that the headstones were pointed so "No damn Yankees could sit on the headstones during their visits to Arlington."

OTHER FACTS ABOUT ARLINGTON NATIONAL CEMETERY

1. John Metzler Sr. (1909-1990), was a sergeant in the U.S. Army during World War II and the cemetery's superintendent for 21 years (1951-1972). His son, John Metzler Jr., a Vietnam War veteran, served as the cemetery superintendent for nearly 19 years (1991-2010).

2. To date, a total of 63 foreign nationals have been buried at Arlington Cemetery. They include 24 British military personnel, 13 French military personnel, and 3 prisoners of war (POW) from World War II: 1 German and 2 Italians. The latest foreign national buried at Arlington has been an Iraqi, buried in 2005.

235

3. During the late 1880s and early 1900s, there were several unique entrance gates to Arlington Cemetery. One of the gates honored Union Generals Edward Ord and Godfrey Weitzel (non-arched), and a second honored Union General Philip Sheridan (arched). The only remaining gate from this period, in its original style, honors the memory of Union General George B. McClellan, Commander of the Army of the Potomac. It was constructed in 1879, and stands at the original site of the cemetery's main entrance.

McClellan Arch

4. Initially, the government used wooden headboards to mark the gravesites. The wooden headboards cost $1.23 each and had to be replaced every five years. In 1873, Congress approved a Civil War type headstone for known dead. It is an upright slab design of marble or durable stone 4 inches thick, 10 inches wide and 12 inches in height extending above the ground. In 1903, a stone 39 inches high by 12 inches wide by 4 inches thick was adopted.

Last Cast Iron Marker at Arlington - Union Captain Daniel Keys, West Virginia Rangers in Section 13, Lot 13615, Died in 1883

5. Approximately 1,500 headstones in Sections 23 and 27 have headstones marked U.S.C.T. These headstones cover the graves of the United States Colored Troops who served in the Civil War. Roughly 179,000 black soldiers and 19,000 black sailors served during the Civil War. Of this number, 80 were commissioned officers and sixteen received the Medal of Honor.

6. After President Lincoln issued his Emancipation Proclamation, thousands of refugee slaves from the South streamed north into Washington, D.C. To house the refugees in a safe location, the Union Army dedicated a *Freedman's Village* near Arlington Cemetery on December 4, 1863. Freedman's Village consisted of over 100 buildings, including a hospital, a school, churches, and shops. The community existed until the 1890s. At its peak, Freedman's Village stretched from near what is now the Tomb of the Unknowns to near the Pentagon.

7. In 1929, James "Uncle Jim" Parks died at the age of 93. Parks was a former slave who was born and died at Arlington. A father of 22 children, he helped dig the graves for the first soldiers buried at Arlington during the Civil War and the grave of General Montgomery Meigs in 1892. Buried in Section 15, Lot 2.

8. More than 3,800 inhabitants of Freedman's Village are buried in the Jim Crow section of the cemetery, Section 27. Their headstones are marked "Civilian" or "Citizen."

Headstone marked "Citizen"

9. Lieutenant Colonel of Volunteers Alexander T. Augusta (1825-1890), was the first black commissioned surgeon in the Union Army. Even though he was a surgeon and commissioned officer, he was paid the wages of a black enlisted soldier. Augusta was the first black officer buried at Arlington - Section 1, Lot 124.

10. Until 1948, the men and women buried at Arlington were separated by race, color, religion and national origin.

11. In 1961, Arlington became the first national cemetery to abolish the traditional practice of side-by-side burials. The caskets of family members eligible to be buried at Arlington are buried over each other in a single grave.

12. On May 30, 1868, Arlington Cemetery was the site where the first Decoration Day, now Memorial Day, was commemorated. The term Decoration refers to the act of decorating the graves of the deceased with flowers and other items for remembrance.

13. There are approximately 8,000 trees planted at Arlington.

14. Servicemen and servicewomen entitled to a headstone at a national cemetery even though they are not buried there are for those remains that are not recoverable (referred to as Cenotaph headstones); are buried at a cemetery not managed by the Veterans Administration; or are buried overseas in a military cemetery. The words "In Memory Of" are inscribed above the name on the headstone.

237

FACTS ABOUT THE KENNEDY GRAVESITES AT ARLINGTON NATIONAL CEMETERY

Almost from the day John F. Kennedy was elected to the Presidency of the United States in November 1960, he and his immediate family were considered the primary figures in an American version of *Camelot*. Young, full of energy, handsome, and beautiful, they were perceived as what was right with the world, and it would be through their efforts the world would be made safer and better for generations to come. However, this dream for the future was shattered on November 22, 1963, when a madman with a gun extinguished a glowing star in the form of John F. Kennedy. A second horrible tragedy occurred on June 5, 1968, when Robert F. Kennedy; the president's brother, former U.S. Attorney General, and U.S. Senator, was killed by a terrorist who chose to be remembered through one act of cowardliness versus a lifetime of good.

Gone, but not forgotten, John Kennedy, Jacqueline Kennedy, Robert Kennedy, and Edward "Ted" Kennedy rest with other distinguished Americans and fallen heroes at Arlington National Cemetery.

THE LIFE AND BURIAL OF JOHN F. KENNEDY

1. On May 29, 1916, John Fitzgerald Kennedy was born in Brookline, Massachusetts. He was the second of nine children.

2. Prior to being elected to the presidency, Kennedy graduated from Harvard University in 1940 and served in the U.S. Navy between 1941 and 1945, which included service during World War II. He was awarded the Navy and Marine Corps Medal for saving the lives of his men when their Patrol Boat 109 was rammed by a Japanese destroyer on August 2, 1943; wrote the Pulitzer prize-winning book *Profiles of Courage* in 1955, which describes acts of bravery and integrity by eight United States Senators from throughout the Senate's history; and served as a member of the House of Representatives from 1947 through 1953 and a U.S. Senator from Massachusetts from 1953 through 1961.

3. In November 1960, at age 43, Kennedy became the youngest man and first Catholic to be elected to the presidency. On January 20, 1961, Kennedy was sworn in as the 35th President of the United States.

4. During his presidency, Kennedy was known for his fight against organized crime, support of civil rights, the failed Bay of Pigs invasion of Cuba, pushing for space explorations, and successfully resolving the 1962 crisis between the United States and the Soviet Union over the removal of Soviet made missiles from Cuba.

5. The events of President Kennedy's Death and Burial:

- On November 22, 1963 (Friday) at 12:30 p.m. (Eastern Standard Time), in Dallas, Texas, Kennedy was shot by an assassin using a high-powered rifle. The first shot struck him in the throat, the second in the head. A third shot may have been fired, but missed hitting Kennedy.

- On November 22nd, at 1 p.m. (Eastern Standard Time), Kennedy was pronounced dead. He was age 46 and had served just 2 years, 10 months, and 2 days as President of the United States.

- On November 22nd, Kennedy's body was returned to Washington, D.C. on the presidential plane Air Force One. The flight took 2 hours and 18 minutes.

- From late afternoon on November 23rd through early afternoon on November 24th, Kennedy's body lay in repose in the East Room of the White House.

- From the afternoon of November 24th through late morning on November 25th, Kennedy's body lay in state in the Rotunda of the United States Capitol Building. Between 200,000 and 250,000 people viewed the closed casket containing his body.

- On November 25th, services for Kennedy were conducted at St. Matthew's Cathedral in Washington, D.C.

- After the funeral services on November 25th, Kennedy's body was carried on a caisson to Arlington National Cemetery.

- After Kennedy's body arrived at the cemetery, fifty fighter jets, each one representing a state in the Union, flew directly over the gravesite, followed by Air Force One. A total of 5,473 military personnel participated in the funeral services for Kennedy.

- On November 25, 1963, at 3:13 p.m. (Monday), Mrs. Kennedy, with the aid of President Kennedy's younger brother Robert, lit the eternal flame at Kennedy's gravesite.

6. On December 3, 1963, at age 27, Captain Michael Groves, the officer responsible for the military arrangements for the president, e.g. body-bearers, death-watch, caisson escort, etc. died from a heart attack less than two weeks after the president's burial.

7. There were three possible gravesites considered for the burial of President Kennedy at Arlington Cemetery. The 1st was near the mast of the USS *Maine*, the 2nd was on Dewey Circle, and the 3rd was below the Arlington House. Robert Kennedy chose the site below the Arlington House, which was later approved by Mrs. Kennedy.

8. Mrs. Kennedy requested that President Kennedy's burial be modeled after the ceremonies rendered to President Abraham Lincoln in 1865. She also requested that a contingency of Irish Guards be present at the president's burial.

9. President Kennedy was buried in a casket crafted from hand-rubbed 500 year old African mahogany. It took eight men to carry the casket versus the normal six men.

10. The 800 pound bronze casket that was used to transport President Kennedy's body from Dallas, Texas, to Washington, D.C. sustained a broken handle and deep scratches. In February 1966, to eliminate the possibility of the casket becoming a morbid piece of displayed history; it was flown to a spot off the Maryland-Delaware coast and dropped into 9,000 feet of water.

11. Twenty-three other burials were performed at Arlington Cemetery on the day President Kennedy was buried.

12. The items buried with President Kennedy consist of three letters, a pair of cufflinks, a piece of scrimshaw (decorative work) engraved with the Presidential Seal, a silver rosary, and a PT-109 tie clasp. The symbol PT-109 was the number of the patrol torpedo boat Kennedy commanded when it was rammed and sunk by a Japanese destroyer during World War II.

13. Construction of President Kennedy's permanent gravesite began in 1965 and was completed on July 20, 1967.

14. Two of the Kennedy children were buried near their father on December 4, 1963. Patrick, who was born on August 7, 1963, and died on August 9, 1963, was moved from Brookline, Massachusetts; and an unnamed daughter who was stillborn on August 23, 1956, was moved from Newport, Rhode Island.

15. The current 3.2-acre burial site is located just below where President Kennedy was first laid to rest. The initial burial plot totaled 20 feet by 30 feet and was surrounded by a white picket fence.

16. During the night of March 14, 1967, the remains of President Kennedy and his two children were moved to their permanent graves.

Kennedy Grave Site

17. The stones covering the immediate Kennedy gravesite consist of several individual Cape Cod granite stones selected by the Kennedy family and quarried from a site near the president's home in Massachusetts. Even though the stones extend several feet underground, weigh as much as 500 pounds each, and are anchored to one another, attempts have been made to steal the stones.

18. The sedum and fescue plants between the stones are intended to give the appearance of stones lying naturally in a Massachusetts field. The Kennedy family paid $632,364 for the construction of the area immediately surrounding the graves. The government paid approximately $1,800,000 for the remainder of the site.

19. It is believed Mrs. Kennedy got the idea for the eternal flame when she recalled the eternal *Flame of Remembrance* at the Tomb of the Unknown Soldier of World War I at the Arc de Triomphe in Paris, France, during a visit to the city. The idea of an eternal flame could have also been influenced by her visit to the site of the eternal flame in Gettysburg, Pennsylvania during March 1963.

20. On the wall below the Kennedy gravesite are seven inscriptions from President Kennedy's January 20, 1961, inaugural address.

21. Created by the Institute of Gas Technology of Chicago in Illinois, the flame burns from the center of a five-foot circular flat-granite stone at the head of the grave. To ensure the flame, fueled by natural gas, is not snuffed out by wind, rain, or snow, an electric spark at the tip of the nozzle constantly ignites the gas. The device also blows a continuous flow of air at the flame, keeping it a uniform color. The flame has been extinguished for maintenance on several occasions and then relit.

22. While living at Arlington, Robert E. Lee and his family often enjoyed picnics on the site that is now the Kennedy gravesite.

23. President Kennedy was shot and killed in Dallas, Texas, while campaigning for re-election. A federal investigation committee determined Lee Harvey Oswald was the sole killer of the president. Jack Ruby, a Dallas strip-tease-club owner, killed Oswald on November 24, 1963, while Oswald was in the custody of the Dallas Police. In 1967, Ruby died in prison from cancer.

24. There are several thoughts about whether Oswald was the sole perpetrator of President Kennedy's murder. Some people believe the Soviets or Cubans were responsible for the killing; others believe the Central Intelligence Agency was involved; a third group believe organized crime (Mafia) wanted Kennedy dead; and a fourth group felt Oswald was just a nut who wanted to be remembered in history for his infamous crime.

25. Lifetime Secret Service protection for former U. S. Presidents was started after President Kennedy's assassination. However, all former presidents after William Clinton (1993-2001) are protected for only the first 10 years after the president leaves office, unless special considerations are applied.

26. Evelyn Maurine Norton Lincoln (1909-1995), President Kennedy's secretary from 1953 to 1963, is buried at Arlington National Cemetery. Her ashes are enclosed with her husband's, a World War II veteran, in a niche in the columbarium.

THE LIFE AND BURIAL OF ROBERT F. KENNEDY

1. On November 20, 1925, Robert Francis Kennedy was born in Brookline, Massachusetts. He was the seventh of nine children.

2. Robert graduated from Harvard University in 1948 and the University of Virginia School of Law in 1951.

3. Robert was instrumental in the successful election campaigns of his brother, John F. Kennedy, served as the U.S. Attorney General from 1961-1964, and served as a U.S. Senator from New York from 1965 until his death in 1968.

4. On June 5, 1968, at age 42, Robert was shot while campaigning for the presidency of the United States in Los Angeles, California. He died the next day.

5. Robert left a widow and 11 children.

6. Robert had qualified for burial at Arlington Cemetery because he had served in the U.S. Navy during World War II and had been an elected official - U.S. Senator.

Gravesite of Robert F. Kennedy

7. Burial ceremonies were conducted at Arlington Cemetery after the funeral motorcade arrived at the cemetery at 10:30 p.m., June 8, 1968. Over 1,500 candles were distributed to the mourners.

8. Robert's burial has been the only known nighttime burial conducted at Arlington Cemetery.

9. The folded flag of the United States was presented to Robert's wife, Ethel, by former astronaut and U.S. Senator John Glenn.

10. The white Christian crosses at the heads of Robert and Ted's gravesites are the only wooden grave markers authorized at Arlington Cemetery. Robert's original marker was crafted from pine and installed in 1968; the 2nd was crafted from redwood and installed there in 1970 and stolen in 1981; and was replaced with the original cross.

11. In 1971, Robert's formal gravesite was completed.

12. Two of Robert's most notable addresses are inscribed on the wall below his gravesite. The quote **"Some men see things as they are and ask 'Why?', I dream of things that never were and ask, 'Why not'."** was used in his campaign speeches in 1968, and is a variation from the writings of George Bernard Shaw. The other **"It is from numberless diverse acts of courage and belief that human history is shaped each time a man stands up for an ideal or acts ...."** is quoted from his *Day of Affirmation* address at the University of Capetown, South Africa on June 6, 1966.

THE LIFE AND BURIAL OF JACQUELINE L. KENNEDY

1. On July 28, 1929, Jacqueline Lee Bouvier was born in South Hampton, New York.

2. In 1951, the 5-foot, 8-inch tall Jacqueline Bouvier, with brown hair and brown eyes, graduated from George Washington University with a degree in French literature.

3. On September 12, 1953, Jacqueline "Jackie" Bouvier married Senator John F. Kennedy. She was age 24, he was age 37.

4. On January 20, 1961, Jacqueline became first lady at age 31. On November 22, 1963, Jacqueline was widowed as a result of the assassination of President Kennedy.

5. In 1968, Jacqueline married Aristotle Onassis. Though separated during most of their marriage, they remained married until his death in 1975. She never remarried after the death of Onassis.

6. On May 19, 1994, Jacqueline Bouvier Kennedy Onassis died from the effects of non-Hodgkin's lymphoma cancer at age 64. This type of cancer attacks the immune system of the body.

7. On May 23, 1994, Jacqueline was buried next to her first husband, John Kennedy.

8. On October 6, 1994, Jacqueline's grave marker was installed.

9. On July 16, 1999, at age 38, John and Jackie's son, John F. Kennedy Jr., was killed in a plane crash with his wife, Carolyn Bessette Kennedy, age 33, and sister-in-law Lauren Bessette, age 34. On July 22, 1999, their cremated remains were scattered at sea off the coast of Massachusetts near Martha's Vineyard.

10. John and Jackie's only surviving child, a daughter, Caroline Bouvier Kennedy, was born on November 27, 1957.

THE LIFE AND BURIAL OF EDWARD "TED" KENNEDY

1. On February 22, 1929, Edward Moore "Ted" Kennedy was born in the Boston suburb of Brookline, Massachusetts, on the 200th anniversary of George Washington's birth. The name *Ted* is used as a nickname for persons named *Edward* in the Irish culture.

2. In June 1951, Ted enlisted in the U.S. Army as a private and was honorably discharged in March 1953 as a private first class.

3. In 1956, Ted graduated from Harvard University with a degree in history and government. In 1959, he graduated from the University of Virginia School of Law.

4. Ted won the 1962 U.S. Senate seat through a special election in Massachusetts for the Senate seat vacated by his brother, John, when John was elected President of the United States.

5. Ted served 46 years as a Democrat U.S. Senator - November 7, 1962 through August 25, 2009.

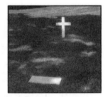

6. Ted was married from 1958 through 1982 to Joan Bennett Kennedy and from 1992 to his death to Victoria Reggie Kennedy. He fathered three children by his first wife.

Gravesite of Ted Kennedy

7. Ted died from a brain tumor on August 25, 2009, in Hyannis Port, Massachusetts, at age 77, and was buried at Arlington National Cemetery on August 29, 2009, near his brothers Robert and John. Ted qualified for burial at Arlington because he had held an elected office and was honorably discharged from the U.S. Army.

8. There were many tragedies in Ted's life. These include the death of his brother, Joseph, during a World War II mission (1944), and whose body was never found; the failed 1941 lobotomy of his sister, Rosemary, and her death in 2005; the death of his sister, Kathleen Agnes, in a plane crash in 1948; the assassinations of his brothers, John and Robert, in 1963 and 1968; and the deaths of his sisters, Patricia in 2006 and Eunice in 2009. The remaining sibling at the time of his death was Jean Kennedy Smith. He also endured a 1964 plane crash that broke his back and the 1969 Chappaquiddick incident that resulted in the death of Mary Jo Kopechne. An event that may have cost him the presidency.

COINCIDENCES BETWEEN PRESIDENTS LINCOLN AND KENNEDY

After John Kennedy's death, it was determined that there were several coincidences between the lives and deaths of presidents Lincoln and Kennedy. The coincidences include:

*Lincoln was elected president in 1860, Kennedy in 1960. *Both were shot from behind and in the head. *Their successors, both named Johnson, were southern Democrats (Andrew from Kentucky, Lyndon from Texas), and both were former U.S. Senators. *Andrew Johnson was born in 1808, and Lyndon Johnson was born in 1908. *John Wilkes Booth was born in 1839, and Lee Harvey Oswald was born in 1939. *The names John Wilkes Booth and Lee Harvey Oswald each contain fifteen letters. *Both presidents lost children through death while in the White House. *John Wilkes Booth shot Lincoln in a theater and ran to a warehouse. *Lee Harvey Oswald shot Kennedy from a warehouse and ran to a theater. *The names Lincoln and Kennedy each contain seven letters. *The names Andrew Johnson and Lyndon Johnson each contain thirteen letters. *Both assassins were killed before being brought to trial. *Both Johnsons were opposed for re-election by men whose names start with the letter G, Grant and Goldwater. (Grant won the election, Goldwater lost.) *Both were married while in their 30s to women in their 20s. *Lincoln won a seat in the House of Representatives in 1846. Kennedy won a seat to the House in 1946. *Lincoln tried and failed to get his party's nomination for vice president in 1856, and Kennedy failed in 1956. *Stephen A. Douglas, who was born in 1813, was defeated by Lincoln for the presidency in 1860. *Richard Nixon, who was born in 1913, was defeated by Kennedy in 1960. *Lincoln and Kennedy were both shot on a Friday as they sat next to their wives. *Lincoln and Kennedy were both buried in mahogany caskets.

FACTS ABOUT THE PRESIDENTIAL PLANE AND THE AUTOMOBILE USED BY PRESIDENT KENNEDY

1. Facts About the Presidential Plane:

    - Any Air Force aircraft that transports the President of the United States is designated *Air Force One* when the president is onboard. It is designated *Air Force Two* when it transports the vice president. The same applies to the aircraft of the other military branches, e.g. *Army One, Marine One*, etc.

    - Completed in 1962 at a cost of $8,000,000, the first jet specifically built for use by a U.S. President was a Boeing 707, designated Special Air Mission (SAM) 26000. The first president to use the jet was John Kennedy.

    Photo – Courtesy of the National Museum of the United States Air Force

    - Technical notes about (SAM) 26000 include:
        - Maximum speed: 604 miles per hour (mph)
        - Ceiling: Above 43,000 feet
        - Range: 6,000+ miles
        - Engines: Four Pratt & Whitney TF33 (JT3D-3B) turbofans of 18,000 pounds (lbs.) thrust each
        - Load: 40 passengers or 26,200 lbs. of cargo
        - Crew: 7 or 8

    - SAM 26000 was used to transport Kennedy's body from Dallas, Texas, to Washington, D.C. after his assassination on November 22, 1963, and was later used to transport Lyndon Johnson's body to Texas after his state funeral on January 24, 1973, in Washington, D.C. Johnson was sworn in as the 36th U.S. President on the plane after Kennedy's assassination.

    - In March 1998, and after 36 years of serving eight presidents and flying over 5,000,000 air-miles, SAM 26000 was retired from service. It is currently on display at the National Museum of the Air Force at Wright-Patterson Air Force Base, near Dayton, Ohio.

2. Facts About the Presidential Automobile:

- The automobile transporting President Kennedy when he was shot was a modified 1961 four-door Lincoln Continental with a 1962 grill. It was built in Wixom, Michigan and leased by the government from the Ford Motor  Co. on June 14, 1961, for $500 a year. The above photo was taken prior to the assassination and shows the removable glass roof.

- The Secret Service assigned code word *X100* to the presidential limousine used by Kennedy. The license plate number of the limousine at the time it was being used by Kennedy was GG-300, which was issued by the government of Washington, D.C. The license plate numbers are changed periodically and are still issued by the government of Washington, D.C.

- The dark blue Lincoln Continental originally cost $7,347, but was modified at a cost of nearly $200,000 by professional auto-body builders Hess and Eisenhardt in Cincinnati, Ohio. The modifications extended the vehicle's length to 21 feet, 8 inches, or 3.5 feet longer than it originally was; increased the weight to 7,800 pounds; and increased its width to 6 feet, 7 inches. The vehicle was powered by a 300 horse power V-8 engine.

- After Kennedy's assassination, the Lincoln Continental was extensively modified at a cost of $500,000 prior to its use by presidents Johnson through Carter. The color of the vehicle was changed to black and the roof was made permanent.

- In 1977, and after 16 years of service, the Lincoln Continental was retired and returned to the Ford Motor Company. In 1978, it was donated to the Ford Museum  in Dearborn, Michigan, where it is on display. Lincoln Continental

- Due to security reasons, all presidential limousines after the one used by President Ronald Reagan (1981-1989) are destroyed through tests by the Secret Service. These tests are intended to test the safety systems installed in the limousines.

248

FACTS ABOUT THE TOMB OF THE UNKNOWNS AT ARLINGTON NATIONAL CEMETERY

The participation of the United States in World War I was short when compared to the fighting endured by the European countries of Great Britain, France, Germany, Austria, and Italy. Hostilities in Europe began in 1914, but it wasn't until 1917 that the United States declared war against the Axis powers, particularly Germany and Austria-Hungry. But even with its delayed entry into the conflict, the United States suffered over 116,000 dead and missing during the war.

After this Great War, as World War I (1914-1918) became known, the Allied powers of Great Britain, France, Italy, and the United States took steps to honor their dead and missing warriors. On November 11, 1920, the unknown soldier for Great Britain was entombed in the floor of Westminster Abby in London. France honored its unknown soldier on January 21, 1921, with ceremonies at the Arc de Triomphe in Paris. Italy was the next to honor its unknown patriot with ceremonies in Rome on November 4, 1921. And finally on November 11, 1921, which was initially referred to as *Armistice Day* and later *Veterans Day*, the United States honored its unknown soldier of World War I through ceremonies at Arlington National Cemetery. These ceremonies were for the first of four burials at Arlington to honor the unknown soldiers who sacrificed their lives in the service of their country.

THE TOMB OF THE UNKNOWN OF WORLD WAR I

1. Of the 4,355,000 servicemen and servicewomen who served in the military during World War I, a total of 116,516 lost their lives while serving their country. Of the total deaths, 53,513 were combat deaths.

2. At the end of World War I, there were 1,237 graves of Americans at cemeteries in the United States and overseas that were marked "Unknown." Meaning they could not be identified. The remains of several other soldiers have never been recovered.

3. In 1921, Congress approved a resolution providing for the burial of an unknown American soldier at Arlington Cemetery to represent all the unknown soldiers of World War I.

4. On March 4, 1921, the last day of his presidency, President Woodrow Wilson (1913-1921) signed a bill authorizing the selection and burial of an American unknown soldier of World War I at Arlington Cemetery.

5. In 1921, the remains of four unknown soldiers were exhumed from cemeteries in France, placed in identical caskets, and taken to Charlons-sur-Marne, France.

6. In a formal ceremony, Sergeant Edward F. Younger, a highly decorated combat infantryman of World War I, selected the soldier who would be returned to the United States and entombed in a crypt at Arlington Cemetery. After his death in 1942 at age 44, Sergeant Younger was buried in Section 18, Lot 1918-B.

7. Sergeant Younger selected the soldier by placing a spray of white and pink roses on one of the four caskets.

8. The unselected soldiers were reburied at the Romagne Cemetery in France.

9. The remains of the soldier, selected as the American unknown soldier of World War I, were returned to the United States onboard the USS *Olympia*, a cruiser and the former flagship of Admiral Dewey. The *Olympia* was decommissioned after carrying the remains of the unknown soldier to the United States.

10. On November 9, 1921, after arriving at the U.S. Navy Yard in Washington, D.C., the unknown soldier was transported to the Capitol Rotunda to lie in state for two days.

11. The unknown soldier was placed on the same catafalque that was used to support the casket of President Abraham Lincoln in 1865.

12. On November 11, 1921, President Warren G. Harding (1921-1923), former President William Taft (1909-1913), and General John "Black Jack" Pershing, Commander of the United States Forces in Europe during World War I, were among those who accompanied the casket to Arlington Cemetery.

13. Former President Woodrow Wilson (1913-1921) attempted to attend the ceremony, but due to ill health, was unable to travel any farther than the White House.

14. The traffic around Arlington Cemetery on the day of the ceremony was so congested that President Harding had to get off the road and travel through Potomac Park on the grass. He was late for the ceremony.

15. To accommodate the over 100,000 people who attended the funeral ceremony, large loud speakers were installed at the ceremony site at Arlington Cemetery.

16. The American unknown soldier of World War I was awarded a Medal of Honor and a Distinguished Service Cross. Plus several other medals awarded by other countries.

17. During the ceremony Chief Plenty Coups, a Crow Indian, placed his war bonnet and coup stick at the tomb in tribute to the unknown soldier of World War I. The items are on display in the Trophy Room of the Amphitheater.

18. After the ceremony, the casket containing the unknown soldier was lowered into a vault layered with 2 inches of French soil.

19. Architect Lorimer Rich designed the Tomb of the Unknown, which was selected from 74 submitted designs.

20. Thomas Hudson Jones sculptured the Tomb of the Unknown.

21. The Tomb of the Unknown was crafted from white Yule marble quarried in Colorado and dressed/finished in Vermont.

22. The Tomb of the Unknown, without the crypt, weighs 79 tons.

23. The Tomb of the Unknown consists of seven individual pieces assembled into four primary sections. These primary sections consist of:

- A one piece, 16-ton Base
- A four piece, 15-ton Sub-base
- A one piece, 36-ton Die (Also referred to as Dye)
- A one piece, 12-ton Cap

24. The dimensions of the Tomb of the Unknown are:

- At its highest point, the Tomb is 10 feet, 3/4 inches high.

- The width at the base of the Tomb is 8 feet, and 6 feet 8 inches at the top.

- The length at the base of the Tomb is 13 feet, 11 inches, and 12 feet, 7 inches at the top.

Tombs of the Unknown

25. The three figures on the shrine represent Peace, Victory, and Valor. Peace is holding a dove, Victory is holding a palm branch, and Valor is holding a sword – Peace through Victory by Valor.

26. Located on each of the north and south faces of the Tomb are three wreaths. Each wreath represents one of the six major campaigns American servicemen fought in during World War I. These campaigns consist of Chateau-Thierry, Ardennes, Oise-Aisne, Meuse-Argonne, Belleau Wood, and the Somme. The inverted wreaths represent mourning.

Wreaths on the Tomb of the Unknown of WWI

27. No one knows who authored the phrase "Here Rests in Honored Glory An American Soldier Known but to God" that is engraved on the west side of the Tomb of the Unknown of World War I.

28. On December 28, 1931, the cap to the Tomb of the Unknown was set in place.

29. The carving of the figures and wreaths on the die block was completed after the marble had been set in place at Arlington Cemetery.

30. On April 9, 1932, the Tomb of the Unknown was opened to the public without any official dedication ceremony.

31. The construction cost of the Tomb of the Unknown for World War I totaled $48,000.

32. Frank W. Buckles, the last U.S. veteran of World War I, died in 2011, at age 110, and is buried in Lot 34-581 at Arlington.

THE TOMBS OF THE UNKNOWNS OF WORLD WAR II AND THE KOREAN WAR

1. After World War II, it was decided to bury the remains of a World War II unknown soldier in a tomb similar to the one used for the unknown of World War I and to locate the tomb just below the one for World War I. However, construction of the tomb was delayed because the United States was fighting in the Korean War at the time the tomb for World War II was being considered.

2. During World War II (1941-1945), there were 87,976 American servicemen, excluding merchant marines, whose remains could not be identified or recovered.

3. During the Korean War (1950-1953), there were 9,037 servicemen whose remains could not be identified or recovered.

4. After the end of the Korean War, it was decided to honor the unknown soldiers of both World War II and the Korean War on the same date - Memorial Day, May 30, 1958.

5. The procedures for selecting the unknown soldiers of World War II and the Korean War were:

   • On May 12, 1958, at the Epinal American Military Cemetery in France, 13 unidentified American remains from Europe and North Africa were brought together for selection.

- On May 12, 1958, Major General Edward O'Neil placed a wreath before one of the caskets. This act designated the remains as a candidate for the Tomb of the Unknown Soldier from the European theater of World War II.

- On May 15, 1958, Master Sergeant Ned Lyle selected the Korean War Unknown on the island of Oahu, Hawaii. The wreath of blue and white carnations represented the Korean War Service Medal.

- On May 16, 1958, six remains from the Pacific theater of World War II were brought to Hickam Air Force Base, Hawaii.

- On May 16, 1958, Colonel Glenn Eagleston placed a lei on the selected candidate from the Pacific theater of World War II.

- On May 26, 1958, the remains of the World War II and Korean War Unknowns were placed in new bronze caskets and arranged on the deck of the USS *Canberra* off the coast of Cape Henry, Virginia. The *Canberra* was a heavy cruiser named in honor of the Australian cruiser HMAS *Canberra*, which was severely damaged by gunfire and torpedoes from Japanese warships and subsequently sunk by U.S. Navy warships at the Battle of Savo Island in the Pacific in 1942.

- The casket containing the remains of the Korean War Unknown was placed between the two unknowns from World War II.

- Seaman First Class William R. Charette, the Navy's only remaining active duty Medal of Honor recipient, placed a floral wreath in front of the casket containing the remains of the soldier selected as the World War II Unknown.

6. The remains of the unselected serviceman from World War II were wrapped in the traditional white sailcloth shroud and buried at sea eight miles off the coast of Cape Henry, Virginia. This distance from the shore is a prerequisite for deep sea burials.

7. The remains of the honored unknowns of World War II and the Korean War were returned to the United States onboard the USS *Blandy*. The USS *Blandy* was a destroyer named for Admiral William H. P. Blandy, who is known for overseeing some of the atomic bomb tests at Bikini Island in the Pacific Ocean from 1946 to 1958.

8. On May 27, 1958, the honored unknowns arrived at the U.S. Navy Yard in Washington, D.C.

9. On May 28, 1958, the honored unknowns were transported to the Capitol Rotunda to lie in state.

10. On May 30, 1958, the unknowns were buried at Arlington Cemetery after a ceremony that was attended by 216 surviving Medal of Honor recipients. A total of 464 Medals of Honor were awarded for services during World War II and 133 for services during the Korean War.

11. Both unknown servicemen were presented a Medal of Honor by President Dwight D. Eisenhower (1953-1961).

THE TOMB OF THE UNKNOWN OF THE VIETNAM WAR

1. The latest unknown serviceman represented the dead and missing of the Vietnam War (1958 - 1975).

2. Over 58,000 servicemen and servicewomen sacrificed their lives or were declared missing in action while participating in this very unpopular war.

3. Over 1,800 servicemen remain missing.

4. Of all the remains recovered from the battlefields of North Vietnam, South Vietnam, Laos, and Thailand, only one set of recovered remains was unidentifiable at the time the Unknown of the Vietnam War was laid to rest at Arlington Cemetery.

5. Even though there was only one set of unknown remains, tradition called for a dockside ceremony in Pearl Harbor, Hawaii, where Marine Crops Sergeant Major Allan Kellogg selected the remains of the Unknown of the Vietnam War. Sgt. Kellogg was awarded a Medal of Honor for throwing himself on a live hand grenade in 1970 in order to save his comrades during the Vietnam War.

6. The remains of the Unknown of the Vietnam War were transported from Hawaii aboard the USS *Brewton* to Alameda Naval Base, California. On May 25, 1984, the remains were flown to Andrews Air Force Base, Maryland, then transported via motorcade to the Capitol Building in Washington, D.C., where they laid in state in the Rotunda for three days.

7. On May 28, 1984, the remains of the Unknown of the Vietnam War were transported on a caisson to Arlington Cemetery.

8. President Ronald Reagan (1981-1989) presented the Unknown of the Vietnam War with the Medal of Honor during the ceremonies.

9. On May 14, 1998, the remains of the Unknown of the Vietnam War were disinterred for genealogical Deoxyribonucleic Acid (DNA) testing to determine if the remains could be identified.

10. On June 30, 1998, it was announced that the remains had been identified as those of Air Force Lieutenant Michael J. Blassie. The 24-year-old flyer had been shot down near An Loc, South Vietnam, on May 11, 1972, and was later reburied at the Jefferson Barracks National Cemetery near St. Louis, Missouri.

11. A request from Lieutenant Blassie's family for the Medal of Honor that was awarded to him when he represented the Unknowns of the Vietnam War was denied. The medal will remain displayed next to the other medals awarded to the Unknowns of World War I, World War II, and Korean War in the amphitheater, and will represent the other unknowns of the Vietnam War.

12. The Department of Defense decided in 2000 that no remains from the Vietnam War would be placed in the crypt at the Tomb of the Unknowns unless it is proven that they will never be identified.

13. An inscription has been placed on the crypt cover of the Vietnam War Unknown that reads "Honoring and Keeping Faith with America's Missing Servicemen, 1958-1975."

UNIQUE FACTS ABOUT THE TOMB OF THE UNKNOWNS

1. Unlike the Tomb of the Unknown of World War I, a large exterior marble cap does not cover the Unknowns of World War II, the Korean War, and the Vietnam War. However, the remains of these honored dead are very well protected. On top of each tomb is a four-ton piece of marble inscribed with the name of the war in which the Unknown made the ultimate sacrifice for his country. Below the marble, eight tons of concrete add even more protection. And finally, a one-inch steel plate covers the steel vault containing the casket of the Unknown. The marble covering each crypt is 42 inches wide by 98 1/4 inches long by 10 inches thick.

2. When the remains of the Unknowns were buried, a U.S. President or Vice President represented the next of kin. President Warren Harding (1921-1923) represented the Unknown of World War I, President Dwight Eisenhower (1953-1961) represented the Unknown of World War II, Vice-President Richard Nixon (1953-1961) represented the Unknown of the Korean War, and President Ronald Reagan (1981-1989) represented the Unknown of the Vietnam War.

3. On June 2, 1958, the crypts for the Unknowns of World War II and Korean War were filled with concrete slabs and topped with white marble. The marble tops bore only dates: 1941-1945 for the World War II Unknown and 1950-1953 for the Korean War Unknown. At this time the dates 1917-1918 were carved into the pavement in front of the Tomb of the Unknown for World War I.

4. The Medals of Honor awarded to the honored unknowns are not buried with their remains. After the ceremonies the medals are secured in the Trophy Room of the Amphitheater.

THE HISTORY OF THE 3rd INFANTRY - OLD GUARD

1. The origin of the American version of the Old Guard was the First American Regiment, which was organized after the Revolutionary War on June 3, 1784.

2. General George Washington chose the color blue for the uniform of the First American Regiment.

3. During 1846-1848, the 3rd Infantry Regiment fought in Mexico, and was first referred to as the *Old Guard of the Army* by General Winfield Scott as a testimony to the 3rd Infantry's service during the war with Mexico.

4. The 3rd Infantry fought in many major battles during the American Civil War. Over 90% of the soldiers who served in the 3rd Infantry became casualties, wounded or dead, during the conflict.

5. The black-and-tan buff strap worn on the left shoulder by each member of the 3rd Infantry is a replica of the knapsack strap used by their 19th century unit predecessors to display their distinctive colors and to distinguish them from other U.S. Army units.

6. In November 1946, as a result of budget cuts and the restructuring of the U.S. military, the 3rd Infantry was deactivated.

7. In April 1948, as a result of its notable history, the 3rd Infantry was reactivated to provide security for Washington, D.C. and to participate in ceremonies.

8. Since 1948, the 3rd Infantry has been headquartered at Fort Myer, Virginia, an army installation adjacent to Arlington Cemetery.

9. The strength of the Old Guard number between 1,200 and 2,000 personnel.

10. The 3rd Infantry is the official ceremonial unit for the U.S. Army.

11. The 3rd Infantry is the oldest active infantry unit of the U.S. Army. It was activated on June 3, 1784.

12. Officially sanctioned by the War Department in 1922, the Old Guard is the only unit in the U.S. Army that is permitted to march with fixed bayonets.

13. The 3rd Infantry is the only U.S. military unit that has a Fife and Drum Corps. This is the Corps that performs in Colonial red uniforms so it can be "better seen through the smoke of battle."

14. It is the 3rd Infantry that places the flags in front of each headstone just before Memorial Day. Since 1948, this tribute, which takes from three to four hours to complete, is known as *Flags-in*, and calls for a small United States flag to be placed one foot from and centered in front of each headstone. A flag is also placed before each columbarium niche and each crypt at the Tomb of the Unknowns.

15. Until 1994, and because the Old Guard is a combat unit, women were not assigned to the unit.

THE HONOR GUARD AT THE TOMB OF THE UNKNOWNS

1. From November 11, 1921 to 1925, no watchmen or Honor Guards were assigned to protect the Tomb of the Unknown. This lack of security allowed people to walk over the crypt of the honored dead, many actually enjoyed picnics on the plaza.

2. From 1925 to March 1926, civilian watchmen were responsible for protecting the Tomb of the Unknown. At this time only the remains of a soldier killed in World War I were buried at the site.

Changing of the Guard at the Tomb of the Unknowns

3. From March 1926 through July 1937, military guards were posted at the Tomb of the Unknown during daylight hours only.

4. On July 2, 1937, the twenty-four-hour military Honor Guard at the Tomb of the Unknown was established.

5. On April 6, 1948, the 3rd United States Infantry Regiment assumed the sole responsibility for guarding the Tomb of the Unknown.

6. The Honor Guards are assigned to Company E of the 3rd United States Infantry Regiment. Both men and women may be selected to perform duties as an Honor Guard. Only one out of every five soldiers who apply for duties as an Honor Guard is selected.

7. The Honor Guards perform their duties at the Tomb of the Unknowns for an average period of between 12 and 18 months. Tradition calls for a departing Honor Guard to leave a rose at the base of each of the three crypts and the marble tomb at the Tomb of the Unknowns at the end of his/her final shift (walk).

8. All male soldiers who are selected for Honor Guard duties at the Tomb of the Unknowns must be between 5 feet, 10 inches and 6 feet, 4 inches tall. All females must be between 5, feet, 8 inches and 6 feet, 2 inches tall. Depending on their height, each soldier is assigned to a shift that is referred to as a *Relief*. The height of the members assigned to each Relief consists of the following:

    *   1st Relief – 6 feet, 2 inches to 6 feet, 4 inches
    *   2nd Relief – 6 feet to 6 feet, 2 inches
    *   3rd Relief – 5 feet, 8 inches to 6 feet

9. Each Relief consists of a Relief Commander and as many as six sentinels. The number of sentinels is dependent on the number of proficient sentinels available.

10. A Relief of Honor Guards is commanded by Non-commissioned Officers (NCOs). There are five levels of responsibilities at the Tomb of the Unknowns. These levels consist of the following:

    *   Sentinel - Is the soldier who stands watch at the Tomb and usually holds the rank of Private First Class through Specialist. Average age is 22.

    *   Assistant Relief Commander (ARC) - Serves in the rank of Corporal or Sergeant and is the Relief Commander's chief assistant. Average age is 24.

- Relief Commander (RC) - Serves in the rank of Staff Sergeant and is responsible for conducing the Changing of the Guard, and the welfare and morale of the Relief as a whole. Average age is 27.

- Assistant Sergeant of the Guard (ASOG) - Typically serves in the rank of a senior Staff Sergeant in the platoon and is primarily responsible for conducting the daily administrative duties associated with the Relief, including the initial training of the new sentinels. Average age is 28-29.

- Sergeant of the Guard (SOG) - Serves in the rank of Sergeant First Class and is responsible for the conduct and actions of the platoon. The Sergeant of the Guard is the soldier who aids the President of the United States during the Presidential Wreath Ceremonies at the tombs. Average age is 30.

11. An Honor Guard trainee, who is referred to as the *New Man* or *New Soldier*, is trained by experienced members of the Honor Guard. The trainee only performs duties as an Honor Guard at the Tombs of the Unknown during the hours the cemetery is closed, and the shifts are usually two hours in length.

12. Periodically throughout the training process the New Soldier's knowledge of the cemetery and the history of the military is evaluated. A score of at least 95% must be obtained. After approximately 9 months the final evaluation of the New Soldier's knowledge dress, walk, and how he presents himself is made.

13. The Tomb Guard Badge was first authorized on September 9, 1957, and was created in February 1958.

14. The Tomb Guard Badge is a metal badge, silver in color, 2 inches in width by 1-15/32 inches in height, consisting of an inverted open laurel wreath surmounted by a representation of the front elevation of the Tomb of the Unknown Soldier. The upper section includes the three figures of Peace, Victory, and Valor, and the base bears in two lines the words HONOR GUARD.

Tomb Guard Badge

15. If the New Soldier is deemed proficient, he is entitled to wear the Tomb Guard Badge on a temporary basis, and must serve honorably for nine months before he is authorized to wear the badge permanently.

16. If a soldier is awarded the Tomb Guard Badge and he fails to conduct himself at the level required of an Honor Guard, even if he leaves the U.S. Army, the authorization to wear and even possess the badge may be revoked. Each badge awarded is assigned a number and the number is hung on the office wall of the Honor Guards. If the wearing of the badge is revoked, then the round metal tag that has the number of the badge is removed, and is replaced by one that has the word *Revoked* imprinted on it.

17. The first soldier to be awarded the Tomb Guard Badge was William Daniel. He served as a tomb sentinel and sergeant of the guard at the Tomb of the Unknown Soldiers from February 1957 through June 1960. A former POW during World War II, Daniel retired in 1965 after 22 years of U.S. Army service. He was buried in Section 35 at Arlington Cemetery in 2009.

18. The first female soldier to be awarded the Tomb Guard Badge was Sergeant Heather Lynn Johnsen. The 5 feet, 11 inches tall former military policewoman was awarded the Tomb Guard Identification Badge on March 25, 1996. The license plate on her car during the time she served as an Honor Guard read TOMB GRL.

19. Because wool is the only fabric that will adequately hold a crease in hot weather, it is the only fabric used for the blouse (tunic) worn by the Honor Guard.

20. The Honor Guards may wear an overcoat when the temperature falls below 45 degrees and a raincoat during inclement weather.

21. During the hours Arlington Cemetery is open to the public, all uniforms are Dress Army Blues, reminiscent of the uniforms worn by the Continental Army during the American Revolution and the Union soldiers during the Civil War. The style currently worn by the Honor Guards is similar to the style worn by army personnel in the late part of the 1800s.

22. The shoes worn by the Honor Guard are leather shined to a mirror finish. The soles of the shoes have extra layers of leather and rubber to force the Honor Guard to lean back so that the yellow strip down the side of the pant leg is vertical and to protect the soldier's feet from heat and cold. The shine to the shoes is obtained by using 800 through 2000 grid sand paper to sand the pores and then using polish and water for the finish. This use of polish and water is referred to as a *spit shine* by military personnel who often use polish and their own spit to generate the shine.

23. During the hours Arlington Cemetery is closed to the public, the Honor Guards wear what is referred to as *BDU*s, Basic Drab Uniform. This uniform consists of camouflaged fatigues and combat boots. Subdued cloth Honor Guard badges are authorized on the BDUs. The cloth badge consists of an olive green base cloth with the badge in black and olive green embroidery.

24. The Honor Guard sentinels carry an M14 rifle that weighs 9.5 pounds and has been used by the Honor Guards since 1960. It replaced the M1 Garand rifle, which weighs 11.2 pounds and was used by the Honor Guards from 1948 to 1960.

25. The M14 rifle is basically a product improved M1 Garand. The M14 has an effective range of 500 yards and uses a 7.62 cartridge in a 20-round magazine.

26. The bayonet on the M14 is an M6 bayonet with a total length of 11.5 inches (6.75 inch blade). It has been carried by the Honor Guards since 1960.

27. To provide a better grip on the custom-made, wood-handled, M14 rifle, some of the Honor Guard sentinels have been known to dampen their cotton gloves with water prior to assuming their duties at the Tomb of the Unknowns.

28. As the Honor Guard paces at Post #1, which is referred to as *The Walk*, the rifle is always on the shoulder away from the Tomb. The rifle is on the left shoulder when the guard paces north and on the right shoulder when the guard paces south. This right and left shoulder arms symbolizes the act of protecting the Tomb.

29. The Honor Guard paces in front of the Tomb at a pace of 90 steps per minute. A rubber *fat man* belt under the uniform helps support the back and provide the look of an hourglass torso. There is no official limit on the belt size, e.g. 29/30 inches as believed.

30. The handgun carried by the Sergeant of the Guard is an M9 9mm Baretta.

31. The duties of the Tomb Guard are staffed on a rotating system. Each relief has the following schedule: An initial shift of 24 hours on, then 24 hours off, another 24 hours on, 24 hours off, a third 24 hour shift, then 96 hours off. Then their schedule is repeated.

32. During the daylight hours of winter; October 1 through March 31, the Changing of the Guard ceremony occurs on the hour.

33. During the daylight hours of summer; April 1 through September 30, the Changing of the Guard ceremony occurs every 30 minutes. The ceremony takes approximately seven minutes.

34. When the cemetery is closed, whatever the season, the Honor Guard is on duty for a two-hour shift. The shifts are performed through less formal roving guard duties.

35. The black mat on the plaza in front of the crypt is 63 feet long. It is replaced for each Memorial Day and Veterans Day weekend.

36. The Honor Guard takes 21 steps across the mat, faces the Tomb for 21 seconds, and then turns for the return 21 steps. The number 21 is considered the highest level of honor bestowed on the subject receiving the honor. The New Soldier is tested for the correct and consistent number of steps and seconds. The Honor Guard paces north to south and then retraces his steps.

37. A shelter, which is referred to as *The Box*, is located to the left of the Tomb as visitors look from the Memorial Amphitheater steps. The shelter is used by the sentinels to retreat to while flowers are being presented to the honored unknown soldiers, taps is being played, and during inclement weather. There is also a phone in the shelter for emergencies.

FACTS ABOUT THE MEMORIAL AMPHITHEATER AT ARLINGTON NATIONAL CEMETERY

Initially, the Memorial Amphitheater was a site where homage was paid to the servicemen and servicewomen who died in conflicts fought by the United States prior to World War I. The conflicts include the Revolutionary War, War of 1812, Mexican-American War, Civil War, and Spanish-American War. Since the Tomb of the Unknown Soldier was dedicated in 1921, the Amphitheater has played a significant part in the ceremonies rendered to the servicemen who rest in the Tomb of the Unknowns, and to all American servicemen and servicewomen who have made the ultimate sacrifice for their country.

THE MEMORIAL AMPHITHEATER

1. The new Amphitheater replaces the old white Amphitheater located near the Arlington House. The old Amphitheater, which still stands, was dedicated in 1868 and held up to 1,500 seats.

Old Amphitheater

2. Congress authorized the new Memorial Amphitheater on March 4, 1913, with the ground breaking performed on March 1, 1915.

3. President Woodrow Wilson (1913-1921) dedicated the cornerstone to the Amphitheater on October 15, 1915. He is credited with establishing the precedent for presidential visits to the Amphitheater.

4. A United States flag with a field of 36 stars, was flown on a special flagpole until the cornerstone was installed. The flag signified the 36 states in the Union at the end of the Civil War.

New Amphitheater and Tomb of the Unknowns

5. Once the cornerstone was installed, the Civil War era flag was replaced with one consisting of a field of 48 stars, one star for each state in the Union in 1915.

6. The dedication ceremony for *America's Temple of Patriotism* was conducted on May 15, 1920.

Interior of the Amphitheater

7. Designed by Fredrick D. Owens, the Amphitheater was modeled after Greek and Roman amphitheaters and was mainly crafted from Imperial Danby marble from Vermont.

8. The Amphitheater is in the shape of a 152-foot by 200-foot ellipse, has 42 special seating boxes and entrances at the 4 axes, and was designed to hold up to 5,000 people for annual services on Easter, Memorial Day, Veterans Day, and other special events. There is also a small chapel beneath the Amphitheater stage.

9. The names of 44 U.S. involved battles from the American Revolution War through the Spanish-American War are inscribed around the frieze above the colonnade. In addition, the names of 14 U.S. Army generals and 14 Navy admirals from periods of history prior to World War I are inscribed on the sides of the Amphitheater's stage.

10. Inside the apse, which is the vaulted part of the Amphitheater, is a quote from a 1775 letter from General Washington that reads "When we assumed the soldier we did not lay aside the citizen." Over the stage is President Abraham Lincoln's Gettysburg Address. Above the west entrance is the Latin quote "DULCE ET DECORUM EST PRO PATRIA MORI" from Horace's *Ode III,* which means "It is sweet and fitting to die for one's country."

11. The Amphitheater was originally constructed with 48 crypts under the colonnade in the catacombs of the structure to accommodate the remains of citizens from the 48 states. The crypts were never used for this purpose and were replaced by offices, restrooms, and space for the Honor Guards. The United States flags that were used to cover the caskets of the unknown soldiers and the medals awarded them are displayed in the Trophy Room of the Amphitheater.

FACTS ABOUT THE WOMEN IN MILITARY SERVICE FOR AMERICA MEMORIAL AT THE GATEWAY TO ARLINGTON NATIONAL CEMETERY

History has recorded a multitude of acts of valor by women who have served their country during times of war and national crisis. From the days of the Revolutionary War, when Mary Ludwig Hays, the legendary Molly Pitcher, replaced her husband as a cannoneer during the Battle of Monmouth in New Jersey, to the women in the cockpits of jets during the conflicts in the Middle East, American women have been quick to answer the call to duty. The Women In Military Service For America Memorial was a long overdue tribute to the service, bravery, and professionalism of the officers and enlisted women who have made unlimited contributions to the protection of the United States. To quote Vice President Gore at the memorial's dedication ceremonies, "At long last, here in our nation's capital, we can unveil a memorial that says to every servicewoman, past and present, thank you for what you have done."

THE ARLINGTON CEMETERY HEMICYCLE

1. One of the highlights of the Women In Military Service For America Memorial is the Arlington Cemetery Hemicycle. The hemicycle is a 30-foot-high, neoclassical retaining wall that was designed by McKim, Mead, and White in 1927 and dedicated in 1932 by President Herbert Hoover (1929-1933).

2. The Arlington Cemetery Hemicycle was initially intended to be a gateway to Arlington Cemetery and was part of the construction plan that included the Memorial Bridge.  Hemicycle -Women In Military Service For America Memorial

3. Due to the economic depression of the late 1920s and 1930s, construction was halted on the Hemicycle and was not completed until the construction of The Women In Military Service For America Memorial.

4. The basic building material of the Hemicycle is reinforced concrete, faced with Mount Airy Granite from a quarry in Virginia.

5. The Hemicycle is 226 feet long by 30 feet high.

6. The thickness of the front wall of the Hemicycle ranges from 2 feet, 6 inches to 3 feet, 6 inches.

7. The decorative elements of the Hemicycle wall include the symbolic laurel and oak leaf wreaths used to honor valor and sacrifice, Greek key patterns, rosettes, tridents, faces, and Roman sacrificial urns.

8. The wall of the Hemicycle includes 10 niches with pilasters on each side. The outer, center, and middle niches on each side are semicircular and 3 feet, 6 inches deep. The two other niches on each side are rectangular and 2 feet deep. All niches are 19 feet high by 9 feet across. There is an oak leaf wreath within the rectangular niches. At the center of the circular wall is a large semicircular niche, the *Great Niche*, which is 20 feet across by 30 feet high, and contains accent panels and coffers of red Texas granite. Forming the keystone of the Great Niche is the Great Seal of the United States of America. On each side of the Great Niche and slightly lower than the Great Seal of the United States are large Seals of the Department of Army (south side) and the Department of the Navy (north side). At its base is a fountain.

9. On the sides of the Hemicycle are two large ornate wrought iron gates. The one on the north side is the Schley Gate, named after Admiral Winfield Scott Schley, hero of the Battle of Santiago, Cuba, during the 1898 Spanish-American War. The one on the south side is named in honor of President Theodore Roosevelt (1901-1909). Iron Gate

10. The iron gates were refurbished by the Women In Military Service For America Memorial Foundation as part of the restoration of the Hemicycle and construction of the memorial. They were presented as a gift by the memorial foundation to the American public.

11. The seals for the U.S. Marine Corps and the U.S. Army are on the Roosevelt Gate. The seals of the U.S. Navy and U.S. Coast Guard are on the Schley Gate. The U.S. Air Force was not established as a separate branch of the military until 1947, several years after the gates were installed in 1932.

THE WOMEN IN THE MILITARY SERVICE FOR AMERICA MEMORIAL

1. The Women In Military Service For America Memorial is the only major national memorial dedicated to the over 2.5 million American women who have served in the nation's defense since the American

Revolution. The Women in Military Services for America Memorial Entrance

2. On November 6, 1986, President Ronald Reagan (1981-1989) signed into law legislation authorizing the construction of the memorial in Washington, D.C. or in a district around the city.

3. In 1989, the Weiss-Manfredi design for the memorial was chosen.

4. Michael Manfredi and Marion Gail Weiss, a husband and wife architectural team from New York, submitted the winning plan for a 33,000-square-foot memorial. Manfredi's mother served as an Army nurse for 11 years, part of which was during World War II and the Korean War.

5. In 1995, President William Clinton (1993-2001) attended the groundbreaking for the memorial.

6. On October 18, 1997, the memorial was dedicated.

7. It took 13 years from concept to dedication for the memorial to be constructed.

269

8. Vice President Albert Gore represented President William Clinton at the dedication ceremonies, which had over 40,000 attendees.

9. Retired Air Force Brigadier General Wilma L. Vaught was instrumental in guiding the construction of the memorial.

10. The oldest military member present at the ceremonies was Frieda Mae Hardin, who at age 101, recalled her experiences as a World War I veteran while she served in the U.S. Navy during 1918. Frieda died in 2000, just before her 104th birthday anniversary. She is buried at Arlington Cemetery.

11. The cost of the memorial totaled about $22,500,000. The federal government contributed $9,500,000 toward the restoration and preservation of the original structures on the site.

12. The memorial is on a 4.2-acre site.

13. The hemicycle forms one side of a semicircular sky-lit exhibition gallery.

14. A marble-paneled wall lines the opposite side of the below-grade exhibition gallery.

15. More than 3,500 truckloads of dirt were hauled away from behind the hemicycle.

16. The roof of the memorial is a 250-foot long terrace with an arc that has 138 glass panels. The glass panels are tilted upward at an angle of about 20 degrees and are arranged around the balustraded-top of the hemicycle. Each of the rectangular panels is 1-inch thick and was built to sustain an 800-pound load. **CAUTION!!! Don't stand on panels**.

17. Scattered among the glass panels are 108 panels suitable for inscription. Some of the panels have been inscribed with quotes from politicians, notable citizens, and members of the military.

Panels on the Roof of the Memorial

18. Some of the 400-pound tablets also contain tributes to the service and sacrifices of the women. One of the tables is a 1961 tribute by President John F. Kennedy (1961-1963).

19. The memorial houses a 33,000 square-foot education center, which houses the exhibit gallery and provides access to the gift shop, theater, Register, Hall of Honor, offices and other public spaces. Some of which are underground and excavated into the hillside.

20. The memorial has a 196-seat theater, in which are shown films about military women and their history and roles. The theater is also used for conferences, lectures, speeches, and musical and theatrical productions.

21. A computerized interactive database registry of names and stories of women who have served is available to visitors.

22. The *Hall of Honor* is dedicated to the women who died while serving their country, were prisoners of war, or received the nation's highest awards.

23. Displayed in the Hall of Honor is a block of Colorado Yule marble, the companion piece to the one used for the Tomb of the Unknowns.

24. The memorial gallery includes 16 alcoves, which house special and permanent exhibits chronicling the history of women's service. The exhibits include unique artifacts and memorabilia, photographs, and audio-visual displays relating to women's service from the American Revolution to the present.

Some of the 16 Alcoves

25. The memorial's reflecting pool is 80 feet in diameter and is covered with black granite from a quarry in Culpeper, Virginia. The reflecting pool holds 60,000 gallons of water.

26. The reflecting pool sits at the center of the *Court of Valor*, the grand plaza fronting the memorial.

27. The sound of the 200 jets of water coming from the fountain on the Court of Valor represents the individual voices of women blending in a collective harmony of purpose, coming to rest in the reflecting pool.

28. Another symbolic example of the challenges that have confronted women in the military is the four stairways penetrating through archways in the wall created by opening up four of the wall's original ten blank, statuary niches. The glass-enclosed stairways through the interior concourse create a passage from the old wall to the terrace above, symbolizing women breaking through the barriers.

UNIQUE FACTS AND MILESTONES ABOUT WOMEN IN THE MILITARY (1775-PRESENT)

1. The following are statistics about women who served their country in the military as of September 2008 (sources DOD and U.S. Coast Guard):

Women in Military Conflicts		Women Prisoners of War	
Spanish-American War	1,500	Civil War	1
World War I	35,000	World War II	90
World War II (Era)	400,000	Desert Storm	2
Korea (In Theater)	1,000	Operation Iraqi Freedom	3
Vietnam (In Theater)	7,500		
Grenada (Deployed)	170	Includes 1 American Red Cross and 3 Army civilians	
Panama (Deployed)	770		
Desert Storm (In Theater)	41,000		

2. During the American Revolution of 1775-1783, women served on the battlefields as nurses, water bearers, cooks, laundresses, and saboteurs.

3. In 1776, Margaret Corbin manned her husband's cannon when he was killed during the battle of Fort Washington, New York.

4. In 1778, Deborah Samson of Plympton, Massachusetts, disguised herself as a young man and served for the whole term of the Revolutionary War as Robert Shirtliffe.

5. During the War of 1812 women served as nurses aboard the ship *United States*.

6. During the Mexican-American War (1846-1848) women disguised themselves as men and served in the infantry.

7. During the Civil War (1861-1865) women provided casualty care and nursing to Union and Confederate troops at field hospitals and aboard the Union Hospital Ship *Red Rover*. They also disguised themselves as men in order to serve.

8. On November 11, 1865, Doctor Mary Walker (1832-1919) was awarded the Medal of Honor for her service during the Civil War. She is the only woman to date to be awarded this medal.

9. During the Spanish-American War (1898) the Army assigned 1,500 civilian contract nurses to Army hospitals in the United States, Hawaii, Cuba, Puerto Rico, Guam and the Philippines, as well as on the Hospital Ship *Relief*. Twenty nurses died during the term of their service.

10. In 1901, the Army Nurse Corps was established, in part due to the extraordinary performance of the contract nurses during the Spanish-American War. In 1908, the Navy Nurse Corps was established. The nurses served without rank or benefits.

11. Over 35,000 female service members served within the United States and overseas during World War I (1917-1918). The Navy enlisted 11,880 women as Yeoman (F), the first women to serve in the United States military in an official capacity, other than nurses. In addition, the Marine Corps enlisted 305 women and the U.S. Coast Guard, 2 women. All were discharged following the war.

12. In 1920, military nurses were granted relative ranks from 2nd lieutenant to major, but without full rights and privileges.

13. During World War II (1941-1945), each of the services established women's components and some 400,000 women served within the United States and overseas in nearly all non-combat jobs. However, many women did serve in combat areas.

14. First Lieutenant Annie G. Fox was the first woman to be awarded a Purple Heart medal for wounds. The medal was awarded for wounds she sustained while serving at Hickam Field during the December 7, 1941, Japanese attack on Pearl Harbor, Hawaii.

15. In 1947, Army and Navy nurses were awarded permanent commissioned officer status. Lieutenant Colonel Florence Blanchfield, Chief of the Army Nurse Corps, was the first woman to hold a permanent commission in the U.S. Army or any other military branch.

16. In 1948, the Women's Armed Services Integration Act granted women permanent status in the Regular and Reserve forces of the Army, Navy, Marine Corps, and Air Force up to the grades of lieutenant colonel/lieutenant commander (O-5).

17. During the Korean War (1950-1953), approximately 3,000 female service members served on the ground, aboard hospital ships, and on evacuation aircraft. Approximately 1,000 were nurses.

18. In 1976, women were admitted to the service academies.

19. In 1978, the Coast Guard opened all assignments to women, including ships and aircraft. In the same year, the Navy opened non-combat ships to the assignment of women.

20. The first women to attain the rank of general or admiral in their respective branches of the military are:

   - Army Nurse Corps - Brigadier General Anna M. Hayes in 1970
   - Army - Brigadier General Elizabeth P. Hoisington in 1970
   - Air Force - Brigadier General Jeanne M. Holm in 1971
   - Navy Nurse Corps - Rear Admiral Alene B. Duerk in 1972
   - Air Force Nurse Corps - Brigadier General E. Ann Hoefly in 1972
   - Navy - Rear Admiral Fran McKee in 1976
   - Marines - Brigadier General Margaret A. Brewer in 1978
   - Coast Guard – Rear Admiral Vivien S. Crea in 2000

21. The first woman to attain the rank of <u>full</u> general or admiral was Army General Ann E. Dunwoody. She was promoted in 2008.

22. The first women to attain the highest enlisted rank – E-9 in their respective branches of the military are:

- Navy (WAVES) – Master Chief Anna Der-Vartanian in 1959
- Army (WAC) – Sergeant Major Carolyn H. James in 1960
- Marines (USMC) – Master Gunnery Sergeant Geraldine M. Moran in 1960
- Air Force (WAF) – Chief Master Sergeant Grace A. Peterson in 1960
- Coast Guard (SPARS) - Master Chief Yeoman Pearl E. Faurie in 1964

23. In 1986, World War II veteran Rear Admiral Grace Murray Hopper retired from the Navy at age 80. She was a mathematician and a pioneer in data processing and computer science. Admiral Hopper developed a computer programmer language, which lead to the development of COBOL, and coined the term "bug in the system" when she actually discovered a moth in a malfunctioning mainframe computer. She died in 1992 at age 85.

24. In 1991, the 1948 legislation prohibiting women from serving aboard combat aircraft was repealed.

25. In 1993, the legislation banning women from serving aboard combat ships was repealed.

26. In 1995, Air Force Colonel Eileen Collins became the first woman pilot astronaut when she piloted *STS-63 Discovery.*

27. In 2005, Sergeant Leigh Anne Hester became the first woman to be awarded a Silver Star as a combat soldier. Sergeant Hester was deployed to Iraq as part of Operation Iraqi Freedom. The first woman to be awarded a Silver Star for gallantry was U.S. Army Nurse 1st Lt Mary Roberts Wilson during World War II. She died in 2001 at age 87.

28. As of 2010, women comprised approximately 14% of the active-duty military force and 17% of the Guard and Reserves.

FACTS ABOUT THE UNITED STATES MARINE CORPS MEMORIAL
(IWO JIMA STATUE)

Since being established on November 10, 1775, the United States Marine Corps has served throughout the world. And whether it was confronting the Barbary pirates on the coast of Africa, assaulting the Pacific islands of Tarawa and Okinawa during World War II, going head-to-head with the Viet Cong in the jungles of Vietnam, or destroying the Taliban in the deserts of the Middle East, the Marines are often the "First to Fight."

The United States Marine Corps Memorial honors the thousands of Marines who have sacrificed in the defense of the United States. *"Semper Fidelis* – Always Faithful."

THE ISLAND OF IWO JIMA & THE BATTLE

1. At approximately 5 miles long by 2-1/2 miles at its widest point, the Pacific island of Iwo Jima is located 760 miles southeast of Tokyo, Japan. Its importance to the Allies during World War II was to provide airfields in support of bombing raids on mainland Japan and to eliminate the threat of enemy fighters shooting down American bombers.

2. The name *Iwo Jima* or *Iītō* means "sulfur island." The Marines described the terrain as a *Jungle of Stone.*

3. The Japanese had constructed on Iwo Jima an elaborate seven-layer defensive system that included 16 miles of tunnels connecting 1,500 man-made caverns. Above ground, Japanese defenses included 750 blockhouses and pillboxes. One underground hospital could treat 400 injured men.

4. The highest peak on Iwo Jima is Mount Suribachi, a 550-foot volcanic peak on the southern tip of the island. Seizing Mount Suribachi cost the U.S. 28th Marine Regiment 500 casualties out of the approximate 1,000 Marines who attacked the fortifications.

5. On February 19, 1945, after 74 days of almost constant bombing and shelling, Iwo Jima was invaded by 70,647 Marines and 570 Army assault troops. The 15th Fighter Group, U.S. Army Air Force, arrived on Iwo Jima on March 6, 1945, and the U.S. Army's 147th Infantry Regiment arrived on March 20, 1945.

6. On March 25, 1945, the battle for Iwo Jima ended. The victory over the Japanese resulted in 26,000 American casualties, including 6,825 deaths. These casualties included 17,372 Marines, including 5,931 deaths. Of the nearly 22,000 Japanese defenders, only 1,083 survived the 36-day battle. The Marines suffered 20% of their World War II combat casualties on Iwo Jima. On April 18, 1945, the Marine invasion force left Iwo Jima. The last two Japanese soldiers hiding on Iwo Jima surrendered in 1949.

7. The sacrifices of the American military on Iwo Jima is credited with saving the lives of an estimated 28,000 airmen who would have crashed due to damage or malfunctions to their aircrafts on their missions to and from Japan.

8. Twenty-two Marines and five Navy personnel who served in the battle for Iwo Jima were awarded the Medal of Honor for valor. Four of the five Navy personnel awarded the medal were medics.

THE MEN WHO RAISED THE FLAG ON IWO JIMA

1. Six men were immortalized in the photograph taken by Joe Rosenthal as they raised the second United States flag atop Mount Suribachi.

2. The five Marines credited with raising the historical U.S. flag on Mount Suribachi are: Michael Strank, Harlon H. Block, Franklin R. Sousley, Rene Gagnon, and Ira Hayes. All of the Marines were assigned to Easy Company, 2nd Battalion, 28th Regiment, 5th Division. The sixth man, John H. Bradley, was assigned to the company as a Navy Pharmacist Mate (medic).

3. Strank, Sousley, and Block were later killed on Iwo Jima.

4. Strank, Hayes, and Gagnon are buried at Arlington Cemetery.

5. On November 10, 1919, Mychal Strenk was born in Jarabenia, Czechoslovakia. In 1922, he migrated to Franklin Borough, Pennsylvania, where he changed his name to Michael Strank. In 1939, at age 19, Strank enlisted in the Marines and was assigned duties as a rifleman. In February 1942, he was promoted to sergeant and served as a Marine Raider on the Pacific island of Bougainville in 1943. Strank was the first of the six men to die. On March 1, 1945, at age 25, Strank was killed when a shell exploded near him on Iwo Jima. In 1947, Strank was buried at Arlington Cemetery after his remains were returned from Iwo Jima.

The Men – The Marine Corps Memorial

6. On November 6, 1924, Harlon Block was born on a small farm in Rio Grande Valley, Texas. In early 1943, at age 18, he enlisted in the Marines and graduated from paratrooper school in May 1943. Block participated in the battle for Bougainville in 1943. On March 1, 1945, at age 20, Brock was killed by an exploding shell just a few hours after the death of Sergeant Strank. In 1947, Block was buried in Weslaco, Texas, after his remains were returned from Iwo Jima.

7. On January 12, 1923, Ira Hayes was born on the Gila River Indian Reservation for the Pima Indian tribe in Arizona. Pima means River People. In 1942, at age 19, he enlisted in the Marines and graduated from paratrooper school in November 1942. Hayes participated in the battles for Bougainville in 1943 and Iwo Jima in 1945. After his discharge from the Marines, Hayes was unable to adjust to life after the war. As an alcoholic, he died on January 24, 1955, from exposure to freezing cold on the Gila River Indian Reservation. At age 32, Private Hayes was buried at Arlington Cemetery.

Note: When Hayes died, an unauthorized face mask was cast to be used to make a bust of Hayes. The bust was never completed and in 2009 the mask was returned to the Hayes' family, where it was destroyed and buried next to the graves of his parents on the Gila River Indian Reservation.

8. On September 19, 1925, Franklin Sousley was born outside the small town of Hilltop, Kentucky. In 1944, at age 18, he enlisted in the Marines and was assigned duties as a rifleman. Iwo Jima was the first and last battle for Private Sousley. On March 21, 1945, at age 19, Sousely was killed by a bullet to the back. In 1947, Sousley was buried in Elizaville, Kentucky, after his remains were returned from Iwo Jima.

9. On March 7, 1925, Rene Gagnon was born in Manchester, New Hampshire. In 1943, at age 17, he enlisted in the Marines and was assigned duties as a rifleman. Iwo Jima was the first and only time Private Gagnon saw combat. After the war, Gagnon was assigned to China and was discharged in 1946. After returning home, he worked in the mills in Manchester. On October 12, 1979, at age 53, Gagnon died from a heart attack and was buried in Manchester. He was reburied at Arlington Cemetery in 1981.

10. On July 10, 1923, John Bradley was born in Antigo, Wisconsin. In 1943, at age 19, he enlisted in the Navy, and was assigned duties as a Navy Pharmacist's Mate Second Class (medic). He was awarded the Navy Cross for his efforts in saving Marine lives on Iwo Jima and a purple heart for the serious wounds to his legs during the battle. After the war, Bradley married, fathered eight children, and owned a funeral home in Antigo. Of the six men, PM2/C Bradley was the last to pass away. He died on January 11, 1994, at age 70, and is buried in Antigo, Wisconsin.

THE UNITED STATES MARINE CORPS MEMORIAL

1. The United States Marine Corps Memorial shows a United States flag being raised over Mount Suribachi during the World War II battle of Iwo Jima. It honors all Marines who have died or otherwise sacrificed while serving their country.

2. On February 23, 1945, a 40-man combat patrol reached the top of Mount Suribachi and raised a small 54 inches by 28 inches U.S. flag secured to a length of pipe weighing over 100 pounds. This flag was obtained from the attack transport ship USS *Missoula*. A larger flag measuring 96 inches by 56 inches later replaced this smaller flag.

3. The replacement flag is photographed in the below photograph. Mabel Sauvageau, whose employee #320 is on the flag, is credited with sewing the flag at the Mare Island Naval Shipyard in Vallejo, California. It was obtained from the tank landing ship LST-779 and flew for three weeks before it was chewed up by strong winds and was removed. Both flags were returned to the United States on May 9, 1945, to be used as propaganda for the 7th War Bond Drive. Marines raised the flags at each stop of the 33-city tour.

4. On February 23, 1945, the fifth day of the battle, photographer Joe Rosenthal, a 5 feet, 3 inch tall, 32 year old Associated Press photographer with very poor eyesight, took the 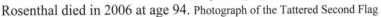 photograph of the second flag being raised on Mount Suribachi. It took just 1/400th of a second to take this historic photograph. Rosenthal died in 2006 at age 94. Photograph of the Tattered Second Flag

5. Marine Sergeant William "Bill" Genaust (1907-1945) is credited with using a 16 millimeter color motion picture camera to film the raising of the second flag on Mount Suribachi. On March 4, 1945, Genaust was killed in an unknown cave on Hill 362A on Iwo Jima. His remains remain entombed in the cave.

6. The memorial was designed by Horace W. Peaslee. He died in 1959 at age 74.

7. Felix de Weldon, an Austrian immigrant who served as a Navy Petty Officer during World War II sculptured the Marine Corps Memorial. De Weldon died in 2003 at age 97.

Marine Corps Memorial

8. The men depicted in the memorial, starting at the bottom of the flagpole and working upward are: Corporal Harlon H. Block, Private First Class Rene Gagnon (whose down turned head is near Block's left elbow on the opposite side of the pole), PM2/C John H. Bradley (facing forward behind Block), Sergeant Michael Strank (leaning over Gagnon's back), Private First Class Franklin Sousley (immediately behind Bradley) and Private First Class Ira Hayes (the rear figure whose outstretched hands are not quite touching the flagpole).

9. In 1945, the planning of the memorial began.

10. The three survivors of the battle; Gagnon, Hayes, and Bradley, volunteered to act as models for the memorial.

11. Photographs and physical data were used to build the models of the three deceased Marines – Strank, Sousley, and Block.

12. A steel frame resembling the bone structure of a human body was assembled to support the huge figures under construction.

13. The figures were initially molded unclothed so the men's muscular strain would be evident after the clothing was added.

14. The marines and sailors on Iwo Jima wore cotton sage green herringbone twill uniforms, known as HBTs; standard leather boots known as boondockers; and an M1 steel helmet. These uniform items are accurately recreated in the memorial sculpture.

15. The memorial figures were initially finished in plaster. It took three years for the figures to be cast in bronze at a foundry in Brooklyn, New York.

16. The memorial was assembled from 12 major pieces of casting, with the largest piece weighing more than 20 tons. The 12 major pieces were formed from 108 smaller plaster molds.

17. The figures of the men stand 32 feet high, which is six times larger than life-size.

18. The figures, placed on a rock slope, rise about 6 feet from a 10-foot base, making the memorial 78 feet high overall.

19. The flagpole is 60 feet long.

20. The memorial weighs approximately 100 tons, rests on a 700 ton concrete base, and is covered by 389 tons of polished Swedish black granite. Total weight – 1,189 tons. The statue is the largest bronze statue in the world.

21. One of the inscriptions on the memorial reads "In honor and in memory of the men of the United States Marine Corps who have given their lives to their country since November 10, 1775." Another inscription is a tribute rendered the marines on Iwo Jima by Fleet Admiral Chester W. Nimitz "Uncommon Valor was a Common Virtue." In addition, the principal Marine Corps engagements since the founding of the Marine Corps are inscribed on the base of the memorial.

22. In September 1954, work on assembling the memorial was begun.

23. On November 10, 1954, President Dwight D. Eisenhower (1953-1961) dedicated the memorial on a 7.5 acre site. The date marked the 179th anniversary of the Marine Corps.

24. The construction cost of the memorial, donated by active and retired Marine and Navy personnel, totaled $850,000.

25. The M1 Grand rifle is 16 feet in length and the M1 carbines are 12 feet in length. The combat knives are 5-1/2 feet long, and the helmets are 3-1/2 feet in diameter.

26. The canteen, if filled, would hold up to 8 gallons of water.

27. A June 12, 1961 Presidential Proclamation signed by President Kennedy authorized the flag over the memorial to fly 24 hours a day.

28. The original first and second flags raised over Mount Suribachi on February 23, 1945, are displayed on a rotating basis at the Marine Corps Museum near the Quantico Marine Corps Base, in Triangle, Virginia.

Note: Iwo Jima was traditionally called Iwōtō (modern term Iōtō). When Japanese naval officers arrived to fortify the island before the American invasion they mistakenly called it Iwo Jima. This mispronunciation became mainstream and was the one used by American forces who arrived during World War II. In 2007, the pronunciation of the island's name was everted to the pre-war Iōtō. The island was returned to Japan in 1968.

FACTS ABOUT THE PENTAGON

In 1939, the leadership of the United States foresaw the eventual entrance of the United States into World War II. As a result, they decided that by consolidating the War Department, the United States would be better prepared for war if war did occur. Their efforts and those of thousands of laborers resulted in the construction of a large concrete structure on wasteland known as *Hell's Bottom*. However, not even the planners, who witnessed the construction of a tall, five-sided building in Virginia, could have imagined the significance of how the Pentagon would influence the history of the United States.

THE CONSTRUCTION OF THE PENTAGON

1. The military officers largely responsible for supervising the construction of the Pentagon were Brigadier General Brehon B. Somervell and Colonel Leslie R. Groves.

2. The chief architect was George E. Bergstrom, and the prime contractor was the John T. McShain Company of Philadelphia.

3. A pentagon is a plane figure with five angles and five sides. Thus the name of the structure – *The Pentagon*.

4. The Pentagon appears to be in the shape of a fort, symbolic of an era in which forts were used widely to protect the citizens and interests of a nation.

The Pentagon   (View from Arlington National Cemetery)

5. The term *The Pentagon* was first used as a reference to the building in December 1941, when the U.S. Postal Services delivered mail to the site addressed to the *Pentagonal* or *Pentagon building*.

6. The basic plans and architectural perspectives for the Pentagon were completed in 4 days and the initial designs and drafting were completed in 34 days.

7. Located in Virginia, the original shape of the Pentagon was dictated by how the planned site on Arlington Farms was fronted on Arlington Ridge Road and the Arlington Memorial Bridge approach and how it intersected at an angle of approximately 108 degrees. On August 26, 1941, President Roosevelt ordered that the site of the building be moved to its current location because he didn't want it to obstruct the view of Washington, D.C. from Arlington Cemetery. The replacement design called for the building to retain its pentagonal shape because a major redesign would have been costly in time and money. This relocation also freed the designer from the constraints of the asymmetric Arlington Farms site, thus permitting a regular pentagon.

8. On September 11, 1941, construction on the Pentagon was started. On April 29, 1942, the first occupants moved into the Pentagon. Less than nine months after construction was started.

9. At its peak, over 15,000 workers labored on the Pentagon on round-the-clock shifts. The hourly wage for unskilled laborers was 85-90 cents and $1.62 for skilled labors, such as carpenters.

10. On January 15, 1943, construction on the Pentagon was completed, just one year and four months after construction was started. This move permitted the consolidation of personnel from 17 buildings under the War Department. The Army occupied the Pentagon in 1942; the Navy in 1948; the newly established Air Force in 1947; and the Marines in 1996.

11. The Pentagon was constructed primarily from reinforced concrete and Indiana limestone. By using reinforced concrete the builders saved over 38,000 tons of steel, enough to build a battleship.

12. Construction of the Pentagon required the addition of 5.5 million cubic yards of earth, the installation of 41,492 concrete piles placed every 28 feet, and the use of 680,000 tons of sand and gravel processed into 435,000 cubic yards of concrete.

13. Each of the five outer walls of the Pentagon is 921 feet long. This is longer than the length of three football fields.

14. The walls of the Pentagon consist of 6 inches of Indiana limestone (outer layer), 8 inches of brick (middle layer), and 10 inches of concrete (inner layer). A total thickness of 24 inches.

15. The height of the Pentagon is 77 feet, 3.5 inches.

16. There are five rings to the Pentagon. The most inner ring is A ring and the most outer ring is E ring.

17. The Pentagon consists of five floors, plus the mezzanine and basement. The decision to add a fifth floor to the Pentagon was not made until after work on the roof over the fourth floor had already begun. Today, there are still no windows on the exterior of the Pentagon's fifth floor due to the late change.

18. The initial cost of the Pentagon building was $49,600,000.

19. The center court of the Pentagon covers 5 acres. The snack bar in the middle of the court is referred to as *Ground Zero*.

20. The cost of the land totaled $2,245,000. The cost of the land, building, parking, etc. totaled $82,000,000 versus the initial estimate of $35,000,000.

21. There are 17.5 miles of corridors in the Pentagon. Each level of the Pentagon has 10 corridors leading from the exterior wall to the offices near the interior wall facing the central courtyard.

22. There are three corridors circling the Pentagon. These corridors are set up in a way that permits a person to walk between almost any two points in the Pentagon within seven minutes.

23. The Pentagon was initially intended to provide working space for 40,000 civilian and military personnel. Space was dramatically reduced with the installation of elevators, escalators, etc.

THE PRESENT DAY PENTAGON

1. The gross floor space of the Pentagon is 6,636,360 square feet, with the office space totaling 3,705,793 square feet. When it was built, the office space of the Pentagon totaled 1.7 million square feet of space. The Pentagon is the largest working office in the world.

2. A lattice of copper strands has been installed under each floor of the Pentagon to filter out noise from external sources and to cause signal interference if there are attempts to use listening devices from the floors above or below.

3. Between 1997 and 2011, a $4.5 billion renovation of the Pentagon was completed. With the exception of the concrete, the exterior limestone façade, and a 1,600-square-foot interior section for historical preservation, very little of the original World War II-era building remains. Some of the renovations include:

   - Blast-Resistant Windows – Each window cost $10,000, including installation. Each window and steel frame weighs about 2,500 pounds. The glass is nearly two inches thick.

   - Steel Beams – Structural steel beams were added throughout all five floors to strengthen the walls.

   - Inner Wall Coverings – Interior wall coverings are made from a blast-resistant cloth similar to Kevlar, which is used to make bulletproof vests. The fabric was stretched between the steel beams to prevent debris from becoming shrapnel in the event of an external explosion.

4. Over 30 miles of access roads have been constructed around the Pentagon. Near the Pentagon are 67 acres of parking space for 8,700 vehicles in 16 parking lots.

5. The Army Library in the Pentagon resulted from a 1944 consolidation of 28 government libraries in the Washington, D.C. area. The library is a direct descendant of the old War Department Library, established in 1800, and is the second oldest U.S. government library in existence. The oldest is the Library of Congress. The Army Library currently stores approximately 300,000 publications and 1,700 periodicals in various languages.

6. The primary sources of heat for the Pentagon are oil and natural gas.

7. The Pentagon also consists of:

    -131 Stairways   -19 Escalators   -13 Elevators
    -284 Restrooms   -691 Water Fountains   -4,200 Clocks
    -7,754 Windows   -10,000 miles of telephone cable
    -16,250 Light Fixtures (Approx. 250 light bulbs are replaced daily)

8. The Pentagon has twice as many bathrooms as is necessary. When it was built the state of Virginia still had segregation laws requiring separate toilet facilities for blacks and whites.

9. There are currently between 23,000 and 26,000 civilian (defense and non-defense) and military personnel working in the Pentagon.

THE PENTAGON MEMORIAL

1. On September 11, 2001, a hijacked Boeing 757, Flight #77, traveling at an estimated speed of 345 miles per hour, struck the Pentagon. The impact caused the death of 59 innocent people on the plane; 53 passengers and 6 crew members, and 125 people in the Pentagon; 55 military personnel and 70 civilians, when it struck rings E through C. A block of limestone with the date *September 11, 2001*, marks the site of the plane's impact.

2. The damaged section of the Pentagon was reoccupied just 11 months after the September 11, 2001 crash.

3. *The Pentagon Memorial* was designed by Julie Beckman and Keith Kaseman and was dedicated on September 11, 2008. It is located in a 1.93 acre park next to the Pentagon in the southwest corner of the military reservation site.

Pentagon Memorial

4. Engraved in the stone at the entrance to the memorial is the date and time the airplane crashed into the Pentagon – September 11, 2001, 9:37 a.m.

287

5. There are 184 wing-shaped, cantilevered arched benches; one for each victim of the terrorist attack. The benches are crafted from steel and aluminum inlaid with panels of gravel. **Each week from 3 to 5 benches were formed under 3,000 degree temperatures at the MetalTek International Foundry in Pevely, Missouri, prior to being shipped to the Bucthel Metal Finishing Corporation in Elk Grove Village, Illinois for nearly 100 hours of grinding, welding, and polishing. Each bench cost more than $100,000 to produce and is expected to last more than 150 years.**

6. The memorial benches are 14 feet long and weigh approximately 1,100 pounds. The name of each victim is inscribed on the end of the bench. **If the name is facing the Pentagon, the victim died as the result of injuries sustained in the building. If the name is facing away, the victim died aboard the plane.**

7. The benches are arranged in rows according to the victim's year of birth. **The youngest victim was Dana Falkenberg, age 3. The oldest victim was John Yamnicky, age 71. The last two benches produced were for Dana and her sister, Zoe, age 8. The other children killed in the crash of Flight #77, all age 11, were Bernard Brown, Asia Cottom, and Rodney Dickens.**

8. The western edge of the memorial site is defined with the AGE WALL – a wall that grows in height one inch per year relative to the age lines that organize the site at large. As visitors move deeper into the site, the wall gets higher – it grows from 3 inches <u>above the perimeter of the first bench</u> to 71 inches <u>above the perimeter of the last bench</u>. This symbolizes the ages of the victims. Rising from 3 inches, the age of Dana, to 71 inches, the age of John.

9. Birth years, used to locate the age lines, are inlaid stainless steel numbers set flush with the finished horizontal surface of the perimeter benches. The birth years are flanked by the stainless steel age lines that permeate the whole site.

10. *The Air Force Memorial*, which is intended to "evoke flight and flying spirit", can be seen from the Pentagon Memorial. Dedicated on October 14, 2006, three stainless steel spires are central to the design of the Air Force Memorial, the highest reaching 270 feet above the 3-acre site.

Air Force Memorial

FACTS ABOUT MOUNT VERNON
(HOME OF GEORGE AND MARTHA WASHINGTON)

No other man contributed more to the birth and infancy of the United States than George Washington. As a soldier he led a small and poorly equipped army to victory against the British Empire, as a statesman he was deeply involved in developing the guidelines that led to the formation of a federal government and the approval of the Constitution of the United States, and as a president he did much to ensure a democratic government was formed that would serve its citizens.

In taking note of Washington's many accomplishments, it should be remembered that Washington was also a prosperous farmer and plantation owner. Skilled in crop rotation and the day-to-day management of his lands, Washington enlarged his holdings nearly four-fold during his lifetime. By touring Mount Vernon, visitors will not only view the beauty of a plantation on the banks of the Potomac River, but will walk in the footsteps of the first president, his family, and the workers who made the plantation a success.

THE MEMBERS OF THE WASHINGTON FAMILY

1. In 1674, George Washington's grandfather, John Washington, was the first to settle on the land that became *Mount Vernon*. At the time, it was referred to as *Little Hunting Creek Plantation*.

2. In 1726, Washington's father, Augustine Washington, acquired Little Hunting Creek.

3. Mary Washington gave birth to George Washington on February 11, 1732, on the Pope's Creek Plantation in Virginia. George was the 5th of nine children – having two half-brothers, two half-sisters, three brothers, and one sister. Three siblings died in childhood.

4. Washington's birth date was changed to February 22nd when England adopted the Gregorian calendar in 1752, replacing the Julian calendar. The site of Washington's birth is near the site of Robert E. Lee's birth.

5. George Washington had no middle name.

6. As an adult, Washington was 6 feet, 2 inches tall and weighed approximately 175 pounds during his younger years and between 195 and 220 pounds during his older years. He had reddish brown hair and blue eyes. He did not wear a wig.

7. In 1735, when Washington was three-years-old, Augustine Washington moved his family to Little Hunting Creek.

8. In 1738, Augustine moved his family to the Ferry Farm near Fredericksburg, Virginia.

9. In 1743, Washington's brother, Lawrence, inherited the Little Hunting Creek Plantation when their father died at age 49.

10. In 1743, Washington was only 11 years old when his father died. He inherited ten slaves and 500 acres of land.

11. Lawrence changed the name of the plantation from Little Hunting Creek to Mount Vernon in honor of British Admiral Edward Vernon.   Lawrence served under Admiral Vernon in the Caribbean, while serving in the Royal Navy.

12. In 1751, George, at age 19, accompanied Lawrence to Barbados in the Caribbean for the unsuccessful treatment of Lawrence's tuberculosis. George also contracted and recovered from smallpox during the trip.   In 1752, Lawrence, at age 34, died at Mount Vernon. (This was George's only trip outside his own country.)

13. In 1754, George, at age 23, moved to the Mount Vernon estate from his boyhood farm – Ferry Farm, and rented the estate from his sister-in-law, Anne, widow of his brother Lawrence. Under the terms of Lawrence's will, George was declared the residuary heir to Mount Vernon until the death of Anne, at which time George would inherit the estate.

14. In 1761, after the death of Anne Washington at age 33, George inherited Mount Vernon.

15. From 1754 to 1799, Washington increased the size of his land holdings to approximately 51,000 acres in what are now the states of Virginia, Pennsylvania, Maryland, West Virginia, Kentucky, and Ohio. These acres included the 8,000 acres on five farms (Mansion House, Dogue Run, Union, Muddy Hole, and River) that formed the Mount Vernon estate. At its peak, approximately 340 members of Washington's family, his slaves, and paid workers lived and worked on these five farms. Washington also bought property in various towns, including six lots in Squares 634 and 637 in what is now Washington, D.C. (The Mount Vernon Ladies Association owns approximately 500 acres of the Mansion House farm from Washington's estate.)

16. From 1754 to 1759, Washington was away from Mount Vernon for long periods of time as he served as commander of the Virginia militia.

17. On January 6, 1759, Washington married Martha "Patsy" Dandridge Custis. Martha was a wealthy widow with two children - John (b1754-d1781) and Martha (b1755-d1773). After John's death, George and Martha adopted two of John's children – George (b1781-d1857) and Eleanor (b1779-d1852).

18. When Washington acquired Mount Vernon, the mansion had six rooms. When he married Martha the mansion had eleven rooms.

19. From 1775 through 1783, Washington was absent from Mount Vernon while he performed duties as Commander-in-Chief of the Continental armies, and from 1789 through 1797while serving as the first President of the United States. During these years Washington visited Mount Vernon just 17 times. (Washington's brother, John Augustine, and cousin, Lund Washington, managed Mount Vernon much of the time Washington was away.)

20. On December 14, 1799, Washington died at age 67 from what is believed to have been a streptococcal infection, an infection of the throat. Some historians believe Washington would have lived longer if he had not been bled four times. The medical procedure of bleeding is when a patient is intentionally cut to allow the sickness to flow from the body.

21. Constructed in 1758, the third floor of the mansion contains Washington's study and little parlor. After Washington's death, Martha spent much of her time in a small bedchamber on this floor. Because of the narrow stairwell leading to the room and the small size of the room, access is limited to special occasions, for example, during the annual Christmas tours.

THE DISPOSITION OF MOUNT VERNON AFTER GEORGE AND MARTHA WASHINGTON'S DEATHS

1. In 1802, the Washington estate was divided after Martha Washington's death. The majority of the estate, including the mansion and 4,000 acres, was willed to Washington's nephew, Rushrod Washington, the son of John Augustine Washington, George's brother.

2. In 1829, Rushrod Washington, an Associate Justice of the U.S. Supreme Court, left the mansion to his nephew, John Augustine Washington.

3. In 1850, John Augustine Washington's widow deeded the property to her son, John Augustine Washington, Jr.

4. In 1850, John Augustine Washington, Jr. unsuccessfully attempted to sell Mount Vernon to the federal government.

5. Between the years of 1829 to 1853, Mount Vernon had fallen from a productive and self-sustaining plantation to a poorly run and dilapidated farm. The roof of the mansion had to be propped up with the masts from old ships to keep it from collapsing.

6. Established in 1854, the Mount Vernon Ladies' Association launched a campaign to save and restore the estate of Mount Vernon.

7. Ann Pamela Cunningham served as the first Regent (Chair-person) of the Mount Vernon Ladies' Association. She and twelve female vice-regents were the charter members who worked toward restoring and maintaining Mount Vernon.

8. In 1858, with the support of a $69,000 contribution from Edward Everett of Massachusetts, the Mount Vernon Ladies' Association (MVLA) contracted to purchase Mount Vernon and 200 surrounding acres from George Washington's great-grandnephew, John Augustine Washington, Jr., for $200,000.

9. The Mount Vernon Ladies' Association made the last payment for Mount Vernon on December 9, 1859. Two years ahead of schedule. In 1860, Mount Vernon was opened to the public. It had been restored to its 1799 appearance, the final year of Washington's life.

THE BUILDINGS AND SITES ON THE MOUNT VERNON ESTATE

1. In 1735, Augustine Washington constructed the central part of the mansion, a one-and-a-half-story structure.

2. In 1757, George Washington enlarged the central part of the mansion to two-and-a-half-stories.

Mount Vernon Mansion

3. The basic footprint of the mansion shows its dimensions to be 93 feet by 32 feet. This does not include the piazza or front porch of the mansion, which runs the length of the mansion and is 14 feet, 3 inches wide. The 21-room mansion totals approximately 8,000 square feet, excluding the basement, piazza (large covered porch) and cupola (small dome on the roof). It is also 59 feet high from the ground to the top of the *Dove of Peace* weathervane.

4. The pine exterior of the mansion has been rusticated. This is a process involving the use of varnish, paint, and sand to create the appearance of stone.

5. At the very top of the mansion, Washington added a cupola, which served as both a decorative rooftop element and a practical device. With windows open, the cupola helped to cool the mansion on sultry summer days.

6. In 1787, a Dove of Peace weathervane was placed atop the cupola. The original weathervane is in the museum at Mount Vernon.

7. When Washington inherited the Mount Vernon estate in 1761, the mansion consisted of four rooms and a central passage on the first floor and three bedrooms on the second floor.

8. In 1774, the south wing was added to the mansion. In 1776, the north wing was also added. Between 1778 and 1780, the covered walks leading from both sides of the mansion were constructed.

9. Because good ventilation was enabled by having the two end doors to the hall opened, the center hall of the mansion was often used as a parlor in warm weather.

10. A key to the Bastille, in Paris, France, is displayed on the wall between the downstairs bedroom and dining room. The key was presented to George Washington by General Marquis de Lafayette in 1790.

11. The dining room is the largest room and last room added to the mansion. Completed in 1788, it was in the dining room that Washington received notice of his election to the presidency of the United States on April 14, 1789.

12. The decorative molding and plasterwork around the dining room reflect Washington's nationalism and his role as a leading agriculturist. The motifs include farming tools; oak leaves, symbolizing national strength; olive branches for peace; grapevines for the harvest; and compotes signifying the abundance of the earth.

13. The original 14th century version of the Washington family coat-of-arms consists of three red stars over two red stripes on a shield. George Washington modified the crest over the mantel in the mansion by adding a mythical griffin (animal having the head, foreparts, and wings of an eagle and the body and hind legs, and tail of a lion) emerging from a ducal coronet. He also added the words "Exitus Acta Probat" which translates to the "Results Prove the Deed" beneath the shield on his book (identification) plate.

The two red stripes and three stars from Washington's Coat-of-Arms is the design for the city flag of Washington, D.C. and is part of the design for the Purple Heart medal.

14. The music room or Little Parlor contains a harpsichord - a musical instrument assembled in London in 1793. Washington purchased it for his granddaughter, Nelly Custis. It was the first piece of original furniture to be returned to Mount Vernon after the Mount Vernon Ladies' Association assumed ownership.

15. Washington's study is also on the first floor. In this room, Washington shaved and dressed each morning between 4:00 and 5:00 a.m. The contents of his study include:

- A ceiling high bookcase filled with 884 books.
- A Hepplewhite secretary-bookcase that was designed and assembled by John Aitken in Philadelphia around 1797.
- A leather-covered revolving desk chair crafted in New York around 1790. Washington used this chair during his eight-year-presidency.

16. On the second floor of the mansion are six additional bedrooms, including the master bedroom where Washington died in 1799. Martha also used the room for her office.

17. Washington designed and installed the piazza, large covered porch/veranda, onto the mansion. The piazza, which faces the Potomac River, was constructed from English flagstone in 1777.

Piazza on Mount Vernon

18. The view from the piazza is much the same today as it was when Washington lived at Mount Vernon. In 1954, and in order to protect the view from Mount Vernon, 485 acres of land on the Maryland side of the Potomac were purchased. Today, much of the view includes the 5,000-acre National Piscataway Park. The park was established in 1961 and stretches for six miles from Piscataway Creek to Marshall Hall, Maryland, on the bank of the Potomac River.

19. The small dwellings surrounding the mansion include a kitchen, the butler's house, gardener's house, storehouse, smokehouse, washhouse, coach house, stables, spinning house, icehouse, greenhouse, and slaves' quarters.

20. Washington planned the upper garden as a pleasure garden. The lower garden was used as a source of fresh vegetables.

21. It is estimated that between 50 and 100 slaves are buried in the Slave's Burial Ground. In 1929, a memorial marker was placed at the site. In 1983, a larger marker was placed at the site.

22. At the time of George Washington's death, he and Martha owned 316 slaves. Through his will, Washington directed that his slaves be freed after Martha's death. However, Martha granted freedom to all of the Washington owned slaves by 1801.

THE BURIAL SITE OF GEORGE AND MARTHA WASHINGTON

1. On December 18, 1799, four days after his death, Washington was placed in a burial vault in an area on Mount Vernon that is referred to as the *Vineyard Enclosure*. Martha did not attend the burial, which was a common practice at the time, and was laid to rest beside Washington after her death on May 22, 1802.

2. In 1831, the bodies of George and Martha Washington were removed from the old family burial vault to a vault inside a brick tomb just a few hundred feet from the original burial site.

3. George Washington selected the site for the new burial tomb prior to his death.

Vault containing the remains of George and Martha Washington

4. In 1837, the bodies of George and Martha Washington were moved from the vault to two marble sarcophagi inside the brick tomb. (There are 25 family members buried in the vault behind the tomb where George and Martha Washington lie.)

5. On a stone tablet over the entrance to the vault is inscribed the brief legend, "Within this Enclosure Rest the Remains of Gen. George Washington."

6. On the sarcophagus that contains George Washington's remains and under the Coat-of-Arms of the United States is inscribed the word "WASHINGTON."

7. On the sarcophagus that contains Martha Washington's remains is inscribed the words "Martha, Consort of Washington." On the foot is inscribed, "Died May 22, 1802, aged 70 years."

8. On the back wall of the open vault above the iron door of the inner vault an insert stone bears the following passage, "I am the resurrection and the life, saith the Lord, he that believeth in me, though he were dead, yet shall he live; and whosoever liveth and believeth in me shall never die". Book of John, chapter 11, verses 25 & 26.

9. In 1816 & 1832, Congress considered moving the remains of George and Martha Washington to a tomb within the U.S. Capitol Building, but the move was opposed by the Washington family.

LITTLE KNOWN FACTS ABOUT GEORGE AND MARTHA

1. Even though Washington took very good care of his teeth, he lost his first tooth in 1756 at age 24 and his last tooth in 1796 at age 64. A 2005 laser scanning of George Washington's false teeth revealed that they consisted of gold, lead, ivory, and human and animal teeth – no wood. Some of the teeth were actually formed from hippopotamus ivory.

2. Washington was the first President of the United States under the Constitution; was the only president to be unanimously elected; had no political party affiliation; ran unopposed both terms; and encouraged the use of the title "Mr. President."

3. Martha was only 8 months, 20 days older than Washington. He was age 26 and she age 27 at the time they were wed. She was born on June 2, 1731 and he was born on February 22, 1732.

To order *Just The Facts About Washington, D.C.* directly from the author, please visit our website at www.home.earthlink.net/~abekennedy or write to A & N Books, LLC, P.O. Box 1094, La Plata, MD 20646-1094.

<u>NOTES</u>

NOTES

NOTES

NOTES

NOTES

To Johanna,
A big thankyou for all of your help through the sales success program. It has been a joy and privilege to work with you.
Warmly
[signature]
Aug 2022

The Art and Science of
Building Customer Trust

How to fast-track trust and
earn new, repeat and referral business.

David Penglase
B.Bus(HRD), MBA, MProfEthics, MScAPP
Best-selling author of INTENTIONOMICS

Published by: Busybird Publishing

National Library of Australia Cataloguing-in-Publication data: Penglase, David, author.

Title: The Art and Science of Building Customer Trust / David Penglase

ISBN:
978-1-925692-39-6 (paperback)
978-1-925692-40-2 (ebook)

Subjects: Business. Leadership. Marketing. Selling. Customer Service. Success in business.

Busybird Publishing
2/118 Para Road
Montmorency, Victoria
Australia 3094
www.busybird.com.au